OTHER TITLES BY E. J. DIONNE, JR.

Why Americans Hate Politics

They Only Look *Dead:*
  Why Progressives Will Dominate the Next Political Era

Community Works:
  The Revival of Civil Society in America
  (editor)

What's God Got to Do with the American Experiment?
  (editor with John J. Dilulio, Jr.)

Bush v. Gore:
  The Court Cases and the Commentary
  (editor with William Kristol)

Sacred Places, Civic Purposes:
  Should Government Help Faith-Based Charity?
  (editor with Ming Hsu Chen)

United We Serve:
  National Service and the Future of Citizenship
  (editor with Kayla Meltzer Drogosz and Robert E. Litan)

Stand Up

Republican Toughs,
Democratic Wimps,
and the Politics of Revenge

Fight
Back

E. J.
DIONNE, JR.

SIMON & SCHUSTER   New York   London   Toronto   Sydney

SIMON & SCHUSTER
Rockefeller Center
1230 Avenue of the Americas
New York, NY 10020

For information regarding special discounts for bulk purchases,
please contact Simon & Schuster Special Sales at 1-800-456-6798
or business@simonandschuster.com

Designed by Jeanette Olender
Manufactured in the United States of America

1   2   3   4   5   6   7   8   9   10

Library of Congress Cataloging-in-Publication Data
Dionne, E. J.
Stand up fight back : Republican toughs, Democratic wimps, and the politics
of revenge / E. J. Dionne, Jr.
p.   cm.
Includes bibliographical references (p.) and index.
ISBN 0-7432-5858-4
1. United States—Politics and government—2001– 2. United States—Politics and
government—1993-2001. 3. Political culture—United States. 4. Revenge—Political
Aspects—United States. 5. Political parties—United States. 6. Democratic Party (U.S.)
I. Title.

E902.D56 2004
306.2'0973'090511—dc22   2004045155

For James, Julia, and Margot

With All My Love

For if the trumpet give an uncertain sound,

who shall prepare himself to the battle?

I Corinthians 14: 8

Contents

Introduction   1
Divided Against Ourselves: A Letter to Some Friends

1. Put on a Compassionate Face   21
How an Idea Got Bush Elected and Got Him into Trouble

2. "He's Ours. He's All We've Got"   47
How 9/11 United Us—and Divided Us Again

3. What's Wrong with the Democrats?   87

4. Talking the Other Guy's Talk   103
Why Democrats Are Afraid of Their Own Principles

5. We're All in This Together   137
How the Right Won with the Media, the Think Tanks, and the Loudmouths

6. A Fair Fight   177
Why Democrats and Liberals Should Stop Being Afraid

Notes   209

Acknowledgments   225

Index   231

Introduction

Divided Against Ourselves: A Letter to Some Friends

Think of this book as a letter to three friends: one a liberal, one a moderate, one a conservative. It is a letter that tries to explain the strange and very disturbing turn American politics have taken over the last four years.

At times, it's an angry letter. It reflects irritation and disappointment with both President Bush and the Democratic Party. At other times, it is, or at least tries to be, a reflective letter. It's an attempt to understand what has happened to us. In particular, why are American politics now so bitterly polarized? Why did Bush refuse to take full advantage of the opportunity he had to unite the country? Why have Democrats, too often, been such a feeble opposition? And why has revenge become such a consuming force in our political life?

Since letters to friends should never be wholly negative, this one also tries to offer some hope that there are ways out of the mess in which we find ourselves.

My three friends might well take different things from what I write. The liberal friend will certainly share my frustrations with Bush. For many liberals—and a great many who are moderate—the sense of alienation, estrangement, and anger inspired by this president is unlike anything they have experienced in their political lifetimes. Okay, perhaps some still hold Richard Nixon in lower esteem—although personally, I think you can make a case for Nixon in this context. I've run into the most dedicated Nixon haters who now find themselves even more apoplectic about George W.

The line that may have captured this liberal alienation best came from my staunchly progressive friend Harold Meyerson in *The American Prospect*. He began an article on Bush with this sentence: "I miss Ronald Reagan." That is not a sentence Harold, or anyone of his views, ever expected to write. I understand what he was saying.

But I'd also want my liberal friend to join with me in reflecting on how things came to this point and, in particular, on how those on our side of the fence have failed. I won't dwell on this too much here because the Democrats' flaws are the subject of the third chapter of this book, and a recurring theme. Democrats and many on the left seem to be in a state of perpetual identity crisis. Nothing seems to thrill Democrats more than interminable conversations over who they are and what their party is. By contrast, the Bush administration and the Republican Party always seem to know where they stand. At the very least, they usually present themselves that way. The irony is that because Republicans are so certain about whom and what they represent, they are better able to compromise when necessary—or, as is more often the case, to spruce up their public image with such flourishes as "compassionate conservatism."

Democrats, on the other hand, suffer in two ways from their chronically unresolved arguments over whether to "move to the left" or "move to the center." The endless public repetition of such tactical arguments makes Democrats look like opportunists. If they were principled, why would they worry so much about positioning? But—talk about the worst of both worlds—by creating this sense of opportunism, of being a party that is never quite sure what it stands for, Democrats actually limit their capacity to seize opportunities. Their identity crisis creates among their core supporters a sense that the party can't be counted on. Republicans are sure of their "base" and can thus maneuver to reach out to the broader electorate as voting day draws closer. Democrats have to reassure their own base—over and over and over. The result is that Democrats always seem to be trying to nail down one special interest group or another. Secure in their base, Republicans can play their interest group politics quietly, out of public view.

The question I would pose to my liberal friend is: If Bush is as dumb as so many of his opponents claim, exactly what does that make us? Addressing what's dysfunctional among Democrats and liberals is one of the central purposes of this book. Why did it take the Democrats so long to stand up and fight back?

My moderate friend is, I'm sure, deeply frustrated with the polarization of American politics and the plain nastiness of what left and right, Republicans and Democrats, regularly say about each other. As a newspaper columnist, I am blessed by hearing often from my readers, especially in e-mail. Many readers are very kind and say warm things—sometimes even when they disagree with me. But my moderate friend's fears are confirmed by the fact that three of the most common forms of e-mail I have received over the last couple of years are: (1) sharp attacks on any criticisms of the president as unpatriotic, liberal, anti-American "spew," to pick the interesting word used by one of my correspondents; (2) enthusiastic praise for the very same columns from readers who consider Bush vile, opportunistic, right-wing, etc.; and (3) modest praise mixed with criticism from those who think I should hit Bush even *harder* for being a liar, a cheat, an election thief, a militarist—and worse. Yes, e-mailers to columnists tend to hold stronger views than most people. Still, the e-mail is getting angrier—on both sides.

How, this moderate friend might ask, has a fundamentally middle-of-the-road country gotten a politics characterized by so much meanness and division? Why do so many in politics have so little ability to understand or even hear each other across partisan lines? And why is sensible compromise now so devalued in politics, especially in Congress? I try to get at these questions here.

My moderate friend might also fairly ask me: Why have *you* gotten so angry? He might point out that back in 1991, in a book called *Why Americans Hate Politics,* I argued against polarization, and in favor of political civility and a new political center. Yes, indeed, I did write that "liberalism and conservatism are framing political issues as a series of false choices." I insisted: "On issue after issue, there is a consensus on where the country should move or at least on what we should be talking about; liberalism and conservatism make it impossible for that consensus to express itself."

He might point out that for a little over a decade, I have been arguing that a majority of Americans were seeking a politics that was moderate in spirit and progressive in its aspirations. That theme linked *Why Americans Hate Politics* with a later book, *They Only Look Dead: Why Progressives Will Dominate the Next Political Era.*

It is the natural tendency of human beings to insist that they are being consistent with their earlier selves, and I am no exception. I still believe that Americans *are,* on the whole, moderate. They do not assign mythic status to either government or the economic market. They want the government to look out for their interests and to protect them from the market's excesses. But they aspire to the wealth that the market can create. They are neither blue-nosed moralists nor indifferent to moral values. The prevailing American view was described well by the political philosopher William Galston, who says that many, perhaps most of us, are "tolerant traditionalists." In our pragmatic, sometimes inconsistent, but generally moral way, we Americans try to square our affection for tradition with an understanding that we are a diverse country and that changes in styles and moral codes are not always threatening. Tradition survives, after all, through a paradoxical process that combines a reverence for the old ways with an acceptance—sometimes qualified—of the new.

In the 1990s, the country was on a course to recognize that it was possible, even necessary, to achieve the sort of reconciliation I described in those earlier books. A market economy did seem to thrive alongside a rather active government. The rich could pay their fair share of taxes— and still get richer. The poor could be lifted from poverty if government did the right things and if unemployment dropped. The government could do things for citizens that the market would not do on its own in areas such as education, child care, after-school care, the environment, and worker safety.

Bill Clinton's project was about achieving this balance, and in large part it worked. Unfortunately, Clinton had other well-known problems that played into the hands of his enemies and helped reignite the very sort of political polarization he was committed to ending.

I have some tough things to say here about Clinton and the ways in which he set back some of the hopes he inspired. But I also think that the roots of the polarization I describe can be traced in part to the ferocity of the campaign against Clinton and the ease with which Republicans challenged our basic institutions by seeking to settle their differences with Clinton through impeachment.

Even after Clinton was long gone, his opponents couldn't let go, at least judging from the Web sites and talk radio shows and cable television. Their goal has been to discredit not just Clinton's personal moral habits (wasn't that done long ago?) but also his policy legacy, which is about more than Clinton himself. The hope is to bury the successes of the Clinton years beneath sex scandals and a pile of bad pardons and turn his time in office into a totally unusable past. This might be seen as the explicit purpose of yet another anti-Clinton work—conservative writers never seemed to tire of producing them—published in the fall of 2003 and entitled, appropriately, *Legacy.* Here is how its author, Rich Lowry, the editor of *National Review*, summarized Clinton's political achievement: "By the end, Clinton had forged a kind of amoral majority, consisting of Hollywood and the entertainment industry, pro-abortion feminists, urban secularists, and a swath of straying husbands and wives with a personal interest in moral non-judgmentalism." Now there's an astonishing take on a country that elected Clinton twice. It misses entirely the moderate, mainstream coalition that Clinton, in fact, built.

Clinton's ideological opponents did all they could to shift attention away from those Clinton policy successes that were a rebuke to their own agenda. They could not tolerate the fact that he raised taxes on the wealthy, and that all Americans—including the wealthy—then prospered. They couldn't accept that moderation replaced Reaganism as the nation's reigning political philosophy. They were still furious that Americans did not fall into line behind their impeachment drive. And so they committed themselves to a reeducation campaign that would continue until the last Clinton supporter died.

Ah, but revisiting anything about Clinton is so tiresome, my moderate friend would say, and my friend would be right. But the Clinton impeachment was only one example of the right's willingness to use radical means to achieve allegedly conservative ends. The 2003 recall campaign against Gray Davis and the midterm redrawing of district lines in Texas to expand the Republican majority in the House were both exceptionally immoderate approaches to governance. And, yes, it is hard for many of us to forget the U.S. Supreme Court's novel interpretation of the Constitution that abruptly halted recounts in Florida and put Bush into the White House in 2000.

My moderate friend may or may not agree with all of this. But these pages try to make the case that George W. Bush's greatest failure was his refusal to take advantage of the broad national support that rallied around him on and after September 11, 2001. For a brief moment, the old partisanship disappeared. There was reconciliation in the face of a grave national challenge. I am convinced that had Bush adjusted to the new circumstances, he could have created a broad and sustainable Republican majority. Doing so required him to moderate his ideological proclivities—especially where large tax cuts for the wealthy were concerned—and reach out to the many Americans who, in the months immediately after 9/11, were ready to respond to his leadership. He had the opportunity to unite his own political base with the forces that had rallied to Senator John McCain in 2000, inspired by a spirit of patriotism and reform. Instead, Bush used 9/11 to win a congressional election, to push through more of his ideological agenda, and to wage war on Iraq. I would insist to my moderate friend that President Bush reaped the bitterness he sowed and that genuine moderation will only be possible if this latest version of aggressive conservatism is defeated.

And so to my conservative friend, who no doubt is already groaning. Many conservatives are genuinely mystified as to why Bush has inspired such antipathy among Democrats and on the left. They honestly believe that liberals have gone nuts. So my friend David Brooks wrote in the June 30, 2003, issue of *The Weekly Standard* in an article entitled: "Democrats Go Off the Cliff."

"Across the country," Brooks wrote, "Republicans and conservatives are asking each other the same basic question: Has the other side gone crazy? Have the Democrats totally flipped their lids? Because every day some Democrat seems to make a manic or totally over-the-top statement about George Bush, the Republican party, and the state of the nation today.

"The Democrats," Brooks continued, "indeed look like they're turning into a domestic version of the Palestinians—a group so enraged at their perceived oppressors, and so caught up in their own victimization, that they behave in ways that are patently not in their self-interest, and that are almost guaranteed to perpetuate their suffering."

Democrats, he insisted, "are unhappy, tone deaf, and over the top." His therapeutic conclusion was that "if you probe into the Democratic mind at the current moment, you sense that the rage, the passion, the fighting spirit are all fueled not only by opposition to Bush policies, but also by powerlessness."

Another conservative friend, Peter Berkowitz, a brilliant professor at George Mason University, argued that liberals and Democrats had Bush entirely wrong, that Bush was in fact far more moderate and pragmatic than any of his opponents could ever admit. Berkowitz offered his views in an essay that appeared in *The Boston Globe* on August 10, 2003—the summer of 2003 seems to be when conservatives in large numbers began worrying about the sanity of liberals. He argued: "By maintaining high levels of domestic federal spending, intervening cautiously in the country's continuing cultural conflicts, and waging a war to remove the threat posed by Saddam Hussein that was also consistent with the imperatives of 'humanitarian intervention,' Bush has governed in a manner that should not leave progressives foaming with rage.

"Bush's conservatism," Berkowitz continued, "is certainly less rigid and doctrinaire than that of Newt Gingrich and his minions, who swept to power in 1994 and, in a most unconservative spirit, sought to remake the federal government by drastically reducing its size. Bush seems to have more or less made his peace with a New Deal–style welfare state."

Parts of this book are aimed at relieving the concern of smart conservatives such as Brooks and Berkowitz over the state of the liberal mind. I think they should at least be able to understand that there are good reasons for liberal and Democratic alienation and anger. Indeed, if conservatives as intelligent and open-minded as Brooks and Berkowitz cannot fathom why liberals are so angry, that itself is evidence of the collapse of communication across political lines.

In passing, Brooks acknowledges that some conservative may have gone just a bit nuts over Bill Clinton. "Now it is true," he writes, "that you can find conservatives and Republicans who went berserk during the Clinton years, accusing the Clintons of multiple murders and obsessing over how Vince Foster's body may or may not have been moved. And it is true that Michael Savage and Ann Coulter are still out there accusing the liberals of treason." Note how Brooks, writing in a magazine that passionately advocated Clinton's impeachment, tries to turn Clinton hatred into a marginal tendency by ascribing it to the conservative fringe.

Fortunately, Brooks goes on, conservatives found a sunny leader to put an end to all of this. "The Republicans had their own little bout of self-destructive, self-pitying powerlessness in the late 1990s," Brooks wrote, "and were only rescued from it when George W. Bush emerged from Texas radiating equanimity."

But of course no one took better advantage of Clinton hatred than Bush with his promises to "restore honor and dignity to the White House." He did not have to say whom he was talking about. The Bush White House kept up the barrage on Clinton, even accusing Clinton employees—falsely, as it turned out—of utterly wrecking the White House in January 2001, before the Bushies arrived.

And one of the most striking facts of post-9/11 America was the double standard that conservatives tried to impose. Whereas any attack on Bill Clinton was morally justified, any attack on George W. Bush was a sign of lunacy, a lack of patriotism, or the probability that the attacker was secretly French.

The Republicans' effort to create a double standard concerning what can be acceptably criticized in a presidency—depending on whether the president is a Republican or a Democrat—is documented throughout this book. But consider, first, that attacks on Clinton during his presidency were not confined to marginal figures, as Brooks implies. It was James A. Baker III who said that Clinton "squandered American credibility and undermined our preeminence around the world." It was Dick Cheney who called Clinton's handling of Haiti an "abject national embarrassment." It was Henry Kissinger who said Clinton's administration "has not been able to distinguish between professorial concepts and foreign policy." It was the current House majority leader Tom DeLay who insisted that "the president does not have the divine right of a king"—he was talking about Clinton—and accused the administration of providing the public with "the spin, the whole spin, and nothing but the spin." And Senator Orrin Hatch of Utah simply called Clinton "a jerk."

It is astonishing that Republicans should now be shocked that Democrats might finally decide to use comparably tough words to criticize a Republican president. Bush's defenders do not even pause to notice that these attacks came only after many months during which Bush's critics held their tongues and supported him in a crisis.

As for Berkowitz, he is certainly correct that Bush was careful to avoid Gingrichian language about government, a point explored in some detail in these pages. Bush, in fact, is as shrewd a politician as Clinton was. Like Clinton, Bush is acutely aware of the potential of divisive social issues to divide his coalition. That is why he speaks exactly as carefully on these questions as Berkowitz says he does.

But Berkowitz leaves out the other possibility: that Bush has launched the same assault on government as Gingrich did, but without Gingrich's honesty or directness. Bush hopes that his policy of reducing government revenues and creating large deficits through tax cuts will achieve the same result Gingrich wanted, but over a longer period and indirectly. Bush learned from Gingrich that a direct assault would not work. But he wants to get to the same place Gingrich did.

My conservative friend might reply, paralleling David Brooks's argument, that liberals are mad at Bush because he is effective. That's true—and incomplete. They are angry at Bush because he is disguising his real intentions behind soothing rhetoric; because he says the war on terrorism is the highest priority of his administration—but not so high that he is willing to abandon some of his tax cuts to pay for it; because he calls for "sacrifice," but not from his favored constituencies. They are angry because Bush used the national unity inspired by the attacks of 9/11 on behalf of exactly the same ideological agenda he was pushing before the attacks happened and to gain partisan advantage in an election. They are angry because Bush wanted to go to war against Saddam Hussein but didn't emphasize up front his real reasons for fighting and never admitted the potentially large costs of the enterprise.

My conservative friend will, I fear, be persuaded by very little of this. But I am assuming that my friend cares about the national interest and knows that political polarization can have highly unconservative results. So I am hoping that, in a quiet moment, this friend would consider whether the future of conservatism is best served by a strategy of indirection. Is it truly conservative to pursue budget policies that lock in deficits for future generations, requiring those who come after us to pay the bill for current political gains? Is it conservative to pursue big government policies abroad and small government tax policies at home? Is it conservative to exacerbate political tensions that undercut national resolve in the face of threats from abroad? Is it conservative to push political institutions to their limits through impeachments, recalls, the abrupt redrawing of political boundaries, and attempts to give a strong political tilt to the nation's judiciary?

And having asked these questions, I'd invite my conservative friend to consider whether that most essential of conservative tasks—preserving the values, the institutions, and the security of our nation—is best carried out through the increasingly manipulative politics that now pass for conservatism.

II

Since I am asking politicians to place all their cards on the table, I should do the same. To begin with a question of tone: Temperamentally I'm moderate. I prefer a political world characterized more by hope than by anger. Civility and openness are virtues. I spend a lot of time with conservative friends who teach me a great deal, and a lot of what I've written about conservatism in the past has been respectful, occasionally even admiring. Even in this much more critical book, I argue that the recent successes of the Republican right are in significant part the result of smart and serious work over many years. A question that recurs over and over is: Where were we liberals and progressives? Why did it take us so long to understand what was happening? The sharper tone of this book is the result of a sense of crisis, an impatience with Bush's use of security as a political weapon, and a reaction to the politics of revenge that began to take hold in the mid-1990s. This book began as an expression of frustration not with Bush but with the Democrats. It was astounding that Democrats had allowed so much of the initiative in politics to flow to the right and to the Republicans. Democrats seemed helpless, especially in the fall of 2002, before the brilliant if often shameless moves of Bush, Karl Rove, and their allies. Worse still, Democrats could not decide which fights to pick—and could not offer the country a clear direction.

But it was also true that Democrats were forced to deal with the radically new political circumstances created by 9/11. Democrats may have dealt with a difficult political situation badly, but it *was* a difficult political situation. As I argue in chapter 1, it was Bush, not the Democrats, who seemed to be floundering in the summer of 2001. Bush's ideological overreaching was hurting him, as it would come to hurt him again later. Everything did change after the attacks on the World Trade Center and the Pentagon. Democrats were astonished at the ways in which Bush used 9/11 for his own purposes, which is part of the reason why they floundered. Because our current politics cannot be understood apart from the terrorist moment, I spend some time describing how terrorism has altered the rhythms of American political life.

As I was writing, the logic of the political circumstances continued to play itself out. Bush's use of terrorism for his own political ends created a backlash in the Democratic Party that, in retrospect, can be seen as inevitable. Howard Dean's presidential candidacy took off in 2003 because he captured the frustration of his party over its failures to challenge Bush and its intense desire to fight back. He understood the dynamic earlier than his rivals did—though with time, the rest of the Democratic presidential field became ever more critical. Dean rose because he gave the

Democratic Party the backbone transplant so many in its ranks felt it needed. He fell and was displaced by John Kerry because Democrats, eager to defeat Bush, decided that Kerry was better placed to win. Democrats in Congress who had suffered personally from the activities of the Bush electoral machine also came to be convinced that capitulation to Bush brought no rewards—though this did not stop those Democrats who helped give Bush his victory on the Medicare prescription drug bill in late 2003. And what had seemed obvious only to some—that the administration had offered shifting and not always candid rationales for going to war with Iraq—slowly became conventional wisdom in the country. The postwar period went far worse than Bush and his advisers had predicted. The weapons of mass destruction did not turn up. And while Saddam's capture temporarily strengthened Bush's hand—who could not applaud the apprehension of a genuinely evil thug?—it did not wipe away doubts about the administration's prewar claims or postwar strategy. Indeed, not long after Saddam's capture, David Kay, the U.S. weapons inspector, declared flatly that the prewar intelligence on the alleged threat from Saddam's weapons had been wrong.

The result was the political polarization that is another theme of this book. I speak of a new politics of revenge fully aware that revenge is an old theme in public life. Coming from Massachusetts, where settling grudges sometimes seems one of the more honorable motives in politics, I know about payback. And revenge has played itself out before on the larger American stage. In the Jacksonian period, Democrats played the revenge card for years against the supposedly "corrupt bargain" with Henry Clay that put John Quincy Adams—one of our most underrated historical figures, by the way—into the White House. The cycle of revenge was at work in politics after the Civil War when "waving the bloody shirt" was for decades a highly successful Republican tactic. We saw it again in the McCarthy era when some on the Republican right used charges of Communist sympathy against liberals to express their rage at the two-decade-long dominance of American politics by New Dealers.

Now the cycle of revenge engulfs us again. It creates a politics in which each side depends for victory more on mobilizing its loyalists than on persuading the uncommitted. The military metaphor, "rallying the troops," is appropriate to a moment when the rules of war seem to have supplanted the more restrictive (and, one might say, more civilized) habits of a less polarized political time. So divided are we along party and ideological lines that there is even disagreement as to when this cycle of war started. Conservatives often trace it back to the battle over the confirmation of Clarence Thomas to the Supreme Court or, in the case of diehards, to the Democrats' use of the Watergate scandal to drive Richard Nixon from the White House. Democrats point back to the Clinton Wars, to Nixon's own brutal form of politics, or even to McCarthy, as the starting point.

What can be agreed upon is that there has been no peace—except in that brief interlude after 9/11—since Bill Clinton was inaugurated as president in January 1993. A significant portion of the Republican Party never accepted Clinton's 43 percent victory margin as granting him legitimacy. These Republicans insisted that Clinton had simply pulled the wool over the public's eyes as to who he really was and what he really stood for. They made it their business to discredit him through investigations and one highly personal charge after another. They sent the country into the crisis created by impeachment, even though the voters in 1998 rebuked the Republicans and signaled their distaste for the whole enterprise. The angriest voices were amplified through their access to conservative foundation money and through the rise of new conservative and right-wing media outlets—talk radio, first of all, and later cable television, especially the Fox News network, which in turn influenced the other cable news stations.

To every action there is an equal and opposite reaction. Democratic counter-rage began to build during the Clinton impeachment, but it could never reach full force because so many Democrats were themselves embarrassed by the Lewinsky scandal. It was far easier to attack Clinton's critics than to defend the president's behavior. Many Democrats—

including perhaps *especially* those who had placed the most hope in Clinton—were furious that he threw away an opportunity to transform politics and the nation on a relationship with a White House intern.

Still, Democrats were primarily angry at Republicans, and their rage was purified in the battle over Florida in 2000. Here, no sex scandal muffled their fury over Republican efforts to block recounts after an election in which so many in the core Democratic constituencies—notably African-Americans and the elderly—had seen their votes cast aside because of irregularities. Even if the Republicans had not caused the irregularities (though many Democrats were suspicious), surely Democrats were owed a fair count of their own vote. But with a ruthlessness that stunned even partisan Democrats, Republicans tried to stop all hand-recounts. And after saying that voters, not lawyers, should decide the elections, the Bush campaign went to court over and over. It was the perfect denouement that a 5-to-4 ideological majority on the U.S. Supreme Court handed the election to Bush. Many of the most important skirmishes in the politics of revenge had been organized around battles over the judiciary. The decision of independent counsel Kenneth Starr to expand his probe into Clinton's sex life seemed, to Democrats at least, a misuse of the judicial process for partisan purposes. Now, all the decent drapery was ripped off, all the illusions were shattered. Five Supreme Court justices behaved not as remote, fair-minded jurists but like political bosses plunking shamelessly for their party's guy—a president who, in turn, would pack the courts with people just like them. So, at least, it seemed to many Democrats.

Yet if the country was polarized, it was a peculiar kind of polarization. The campaigns of Bush and Gore in 2000 both paid tribute to the moderate tenor of American politics. Bush tried to blur any differences with the Democrats on such popular issues as prescription drug benefits under Medicare and a patient's bill of rights. He insisted that his tax cuts would keep the surplus intact. Al Gore used populist themes, but they were carefully chosen. His targets were oil companies, drug companies, polluters, and HMOs—roughly speaking, the least popular corporate entities in the United States. Gore's was a carefully calibrated populism beneath which lay a theme of continuity: why should any voter want to disturb the prosperity of the Clinton-Gore years? Yet Gore's own anger over the Clinton scandal and how it affected his candidacy made it impossible for Gore to take full advantage of the administration's successes.

In retrospect, it is probably foolish to be surprised that the brief moment of harmony after 9/11 was only a moment. The forces of revenge were too deeply embedded in politics. Still, it is odd to have a moderate country polarized so starkly. If Clinton lost his opportunity to end the polarization by unleashing the political furies with his affair, Bush consciously abandoned his opportunity in pursuit of a more narrowly based Republican majority.

That is why I believe moderates will ultimately draw back from the tactics of polarization that Bush and his allies pursued so successfully until problems in Iraq and in the economy caught them up short. Indeed, my hunch is that Republicans will ultimately be forced to try a different kind of politics. But for Bush, it is too late to chart a new course.

This book is an expression of frustration but also a gamble on hope. I believe now, as I did before the 2000 elections, that America's progressive tradition is more relevant to the current moment than conservatism. The economic changes of the last two decades—the rise of the postindustrial economy, the implications of globalization and outsourcing, the development of a more competitive form of capitalism—require not deregulation, but a new and better set of rules. The recent financial scandals were to our time what the rise of the trusts represented for the era of Theodore Roosevelt and Woodrow Wilson. Today's progressives, like their forebears, don't seek to destroy capitalism but to reform it. They have not abandoned their belief in the value of a competitive economy. But they insist that a capitalist economy can only work if a limited but effective government looks out for the common good—and especially for those left behind in the competition and those who lose out when they play by the rules while other don't.

Once upon a time, the progressive tradition was strong in both of our political parties. But the political realignment that began in the 1960s, moved forward in the 1980s, and reached its completion in this decade has, for the moment, turned the Republican Party into a bastion of conservatism. The Democrats have become not only the party of the New Deal but also the party of liberal Republicanism—the Republican tradition that includes the first Roosevelt and such distinguished figures as Jacob Javits, Nelson Rockefeller, Charles Mathias, John Chafee, Dan Evans, Clifford Case, and, in many ways, Dwight D. Eisenhower. In the current moment, the Democratic Party carries the banner not only of the left but also of the center. The need to represent both the center and the left is a problem for the Democrats, as will be made clear here. But it is also an obligation and an opportunity. Democrats will succeed if they manage this task. They will fail if they don't.

III

Because September 11, 2001, will always be the most important moment in George W. Bush's presidency, the first two chapters of this book focus on the time immediately before and after that terrible day. Chapter 1 draws attention to what is now easily forgotten: that Bush was in enormous political trouble on September 10, 2001. Although he had won his big tax cut—which pleased his political base, displeased his enemies, and was greeted with a yawn by the rest of the country—Bush was losing control of the political agenda. His popularity ratings were falling. Democrats felt they could take the initiative, not a trivial fact for a party so often given to timidity.

I pay particular attention to Bush's call for a "compassionate conservatism" because it is a great mistake for Bush's political opponents to underestimate the shrewdness that lies at the heart of Bush's political project. Compassionate conservatism was a brilliant construction—even if it was, as Bush speechwriter David Frum has suggested, primarily a marketing tool. It was Bush's way of creating the appearance of moderation without alienating his political base. It was also a way of making conservatism more attractive by insisting that conservatives cared about the poor in our midst.

Yet the very act of creating the appearance of moderation without its substance was bound to cause Bush trouble. The defection of Vermont Senator Jim Jeffords from the Republican Party was the most important political event of Bush's pre-9/11 presidency. By leaving the Republican Party, Jeffords sent a signal to moderate and moderately progressive Americans that there were deep inconsistencies between Bush's warm words toward the poor and his administration's policies. There was also a large gap between Bush's rhetoric about the poor and his administration's open and exceptional generosity toward the wealthy, reflected in his tax policies. It is often said that Democrats and liberals came to loathe Bush because of the Iraq War. But that is not true. The gap between the president's rhetoric and his actions in the domestic sphere began the estrangement. Later, events simply confirmed what so many already believed.

Everything seemed to change on 9/11. The second chapter traces the remarkable rallying around Bush that followed the terrorist attacks—and the way that Bush's political use of the attacks during the 2002 election campaign only aggravated the divisions that had temporarily disappeared. Speaking personally, I am still astonished that Bush did not seize the moment to transform the country and its politics. Never has a president seen so many of his critics (this one included) rooting so hard for his success. Rarely has the country rallied with such near unanimity to the colors—and I use that word literally, given the proliferation of flags (including one my son put on the bumper of our car) in the fall of 2001. This was a moment when many of the deepest divisions in the country, some of them going back to the Vietnam War, might have been healed. It was also a moment when even Americans who had been highly critical of the use of American power in the past rallied to military retaliation against Al Qaeda and the Taliban in Afghanistan.

To put it plainly, many of Bush's critics who rallied to him in crisis felt ripped off and exploited when he carried on with politics as usual as the 2002 elections approached. Bush's cynical use of the prospect of war in Iraq and the homeland security issue to win an election demeaned what had been a special moment in our history. National unity, love of the flag, the rebirth of patriotism—these were genuine responses to a vicious attack on our country. That 9/11 was used to win an election and to push for yet more tax cuts could only be seen by Bush's critics as a violation of solidarity. It was a solidarity that existed not because Bush was president but because the country was willing to rally to *any* president leading us at such a time. That Bush did not appreciate this will always be the blackest mark on his presidency, whether or not he wins reelection.

The Democratic Party was traumatized by 9/11. It rallied to Bush, only to see its support repulsed. It took months for Democrats to find the will to oppose Bush—and even Democrats who had doubts about his policies were reluctant to take the fight to him, so fearful were they of being accused of being seen as "soft" or unpatriotic.

But there are deeper problems in the Democratic Party, and these are discussed in chapter 3. The Clinton years seemed in many ways to be a time of triumph for Democrats—even if they lost control of both houses of Congress and a majority of the nation's governorships. The country, after all, opposed Clinton's impeachment and gave a plurality of its votes to Al Gore in the election of 2000.

Yet as I argue in chapter 3, the party that once galvanized a nation by declaring that there is nothing to fear but fear itself became afraid— afraid of being too liberal, of being weak on defense, of being culturally permissive, of being seen as apologizing for big government. They became so obsessed with telling people who they were not that no one knew who they were. Democrats began to understand in the 2004 primaries that the country desperately needed a confident and forward-looking opposition. But for too long, Democrats seemed to embody neither strength nor hope.

In chapter 4, I focus specifically on the ways in which Democrats and progressives have adopted the language of their political opponents. It is impossible to understand the defensiveness of Democrats without understanding that they have, more than they realize, given up their own tongue in favor of the rhetoric of their opposition. I am particularly critical of the way in which Democrats and progressives have ceded moral language to the right, fearing that to speak too much of morality would make them seem either judgmental or impractical.

In chapter 5, I trace the forces that have led us both to the politics of revenge and to the weakness of the Democratic and progressive opposition. Bitterness among conservatives created new institutions and a style of attack politics not seen since the McCarthy era. The Clinton era left a terribly mixed legacy. And Democratic political consultants, responding to the facts handed them, often chose the path of accommodation.

The final chapter proposes remedies to the mess. For Democrats and progressives, it suggests arguments they should stop having—and arguments they should start making. For the country as a whole, it suggests a new politics of patriotism that takes seriously what happened on September 11, 2001. A progressive patriotism, the sort that united the country during World War II and the earliest days of the Cold War, would insist upon both individual rights and mutual obligations. It would take an optimistic view of America's role in the world and reject a pessimism that claims the United States must act alone because the rest of the world is a hostile place. It would have enough faith in the American Experiment to believe that much of the world would join us if we made our case and battled not for what so many see as empire but for democracy.

It became obvious during the 2004 presidential primaries that the times were changing. Democrats, independents, and progressive Republicans were emboldened: They began standing up for a new direction in politics and fighting back against efforts to still their voices. This book is offered in tribute to their determination and to argue that their hopes are not misplaced.

Ours is a country open to experimentation and innovation. It is fundamentally compassionate—one reason why Bush was shrewd to seize that word—and it reveres the underdog. It sometimes admires tycoons, but never trusts them too much. It respects both equality and achievement. Its people complain about government, but look to government to act wisely and sometimes forcefully. It is a middle-class nation that wants the poor to rise and wants the rich to know they will be respected as long as they don't seek to dominate. It is a proud nation whose nationalism is restrained by its ethnic diversity and its democratic tradition.

All this means that the United States is not naturally a right-wing nation. Its impulse is to seek alternatives to reaction, to concentrated economic power, and to social indifference. At this moment, it falls to the Democratic Party to offer those alternatives and to speak for a moderate and progressive country. There are many reasons why the party has lost its voice, and they are explored in this book. But if this generation of Democrats fails to challenge itself and the direction of the nation, it will miss its calling and its opportunity. It will miss, if one may quote a famous Democrat, its rendezvous with destiny.

1. Put on a Compassionate Face

How an Idea Got Bush Elected and Got Him into Trouble

> President Bush—you'll enjoy this—he says he needs a month off to unwind. Unwind? When the hell does this guy wind? Come on!
>
> David Letterman, August 20, 2001

> Everything depends on whether he is seen as taking charge when there's something to take charge of. But there is a view of Bush that he's a total lightweight. This makes it an easy shot, so it was a risk for him.
>
> Richard E. Neustadt, author of *Presidential Power*, quoted in
> *The Washington Post*, August 29, 2001, on that long Bush vacation

The day before planes piloted by terrorists crashed into the World Trade Center, the Pentagon, and the Pennsylvania countryside, George W. Bush was, if not a failed president, then a floundering leader who had lost the initiative and faced a miserable autumn. David Frum was serving at the time as a White House speechwriter. Frum admitted in *The Right Man,* a book as friendly to Bush as its title suggests, that he was planning to leave the White House before the events of 9/11 happened because he did not want to watch as the Bush presidency "unraveled."

Bush was in trouble courtesy of a problem that will always plague his presidency: having persuaded many Americans during his campaign that he was moderate in spirit, he governed from the right. His deep, instinctive conservatism and his impatience with moderate Republicans led to the great debacle of his first months in office, the defection of Senator Jim Jeffords of Vermont from the Republican Party. On May 24—just four months after Bush took office—Jeffords flipped control of the Senate to the Democrats. It was the most important political moment of the Bush presidency before 9/11.

The Jeffords switch was, in retrospect, a logical response to how Bush chose to manage his presidency. After the disputed election of 2000, Bush faced the choice of governing as a moderate and healing the wounds left by the Florida debacle, or governing as an uncompromising conservative and bulling his way to a series of ideological victories. He chose the aggressive strategy. It worked reasonably well until Jeffords decided he had had enough. Jeffords's defection was a rebuke not only to Bush's strategy but also to a conservative movement that assumed for many years that it could trash, ridicule, intimidate, and denounce Republican moderates— and still count on their votes at crucial moments.

The strategy had succeeded for at least a decade, and it ultimately succeeded on Bush's big tax cut when most moderates (including Jeffords) fell into line. Because the moderate Republicans rarely rebelled when it mattered, conservatives could overlook the inconvenient fact that without the progressives from the Northeast and Middle West, the Republican majority in Congress would disappear.

The funny thing is that Jeffords did exactly what conservatives, for years, had told him he should do. Over and over, they denounced him as a crypto-Democrat who had no business wearing the Republican label. Even as Jeffords was preparing to leave, conservative leaders and their supporters were saying, "good riddance."

"Sen. James Jeffords of Vermont is not a moderate," declared *National Review* in an editorial e-mailed around the land. "He is a liberal." The magazine that guards conservative orthodoxy said the party switch "makes it clear that the Republicans are the conservative party and the

Democrats are the liberal party." Jeffords's decision, they said, was "a clarifying one."

Indeed it was. Jeffords realized it made no sense to serve in a Republican majority that had made itself the servant of the Bush program when, as Jeffords put it, "I can see more and more instances where I will disagree with the president on very fundamental issues."

The Jeffords defection was played as a breakdown of Bush's much-praised political operation, and that was true enough. Bush's advisers never saw the defection coming, perhaps because they focused so relentlessly on the right wing of the party. But above all, Jeffords's departure marked the failure of Bush's strategy. Once in office, the president acted as if he had won a mandate despite his loss of the popular vote. He assumed he could win on issue after issue by getting votes from Democratic moderates in states he had carried. The president's apparatus figured that pressure, digs, and threats leaked to conservative journalists would keep moderate Democrats and potentially rebellious Republicans in line.

But Republicans from the states carried by Al Gore knew perfectly well that their own voters were in no mood for anything but a middle-of-the-road program from Bush. Jeffords's decision to walk away could thus be seen as the real American majority, moderately progressive in temperament, striking back.

John Grenier, a leader of Barry Goldwater's 1964 campaign, said at the time that the central question in Republican politics was: "What are you willing to pay for the South?" Quite a lot, it turned out, and the payoff came in the defection of millions of conservative southern Democrats. They included such Republican senators as Strom Thurmond of South Carolina, Phil Gramm of Texas, and Richard Shelby of Alabama, all of whom lost power in the Senate when Jeffords switched.

The steady "southernization" of Republican politics—Bush was part of that trend—eventually called forth a reaction in the old Republican bastions of the North. There was a poignant moment when Jeffords announced his switch. He chose to refer to his political ancestors as "Lincoln Republicans." That was a quiet rebel's yell against the new Republican Confederacy.

Jeffords's voluntary departure was, finally, the revenge of Republican moderates and liberals who had been driven from power involuntarily over the years. Distinguished Republicans such as Jacob Javits of New York, Clifford Case of New Jersey, and Thomas Kuchel of California were beaten in Republican primaries. The battle against moderates continued under Bush as conservative groups such as the Club for Growth staged primary challenges against Republican mavericks. The idea was that the offending moderates would be defeated—or brought into line.

For a moment, at least, Jeffords brought to life an alternative possibility: that if moderates were attacked often enough, they might just pack up and leave. It was a dreadful portent for Bush's efforts to create a new Republican majority.

II

From the beginning of Bush's quest for the presidency, both he and his top political adviser Karl Rove understood the delicacy of the situation they confronted. On the one hand, Bush and Rove were determined not to repeat what they saw as the core mistake of the first Bush presidency: the failure to enunciate a vision that appealed to the conservative base of the Republican Party. But they were also determined not to repeat the mistakes Newt Gingrich made during his Republican Revolution after the 1994 election. "Compassionate conservatism" was born out of this tension. It proved to be a brilliant construction. Conservatives already thought they were compassionate and thus, in principle, would not be offended by the adjective, even if some resented that it was needed at all. But moderates heard something very new—though that something was far less new than it seemed.

Not repeating his father's errors was an obsession for Bush. When I interviewed George W. Bush for a magazine piece before the 2000 campaign, I asked him about his family's tradition of public service. Bush spoke respectfully of his father—and quickly got to the political point.

"Obviously it's a proud tradition," George W. said. Then he immediately identified himself with his brother, Florida governor Jeb Bush—and, effectively, against his father. "I believe we have that sense of service, but I believe that we're both driven as well by ideas and philosophy," he said. "That we have come to realize, particularly in our respective roles as governors, how powerful an idea can be. And that it's important to serve but it's also important to achieve results. To set goals, clear and measurable goals, and to lead." As president, Bush was determined to lead to the right.

Yet Bush knew that was not enough. When I asked him what the Republican Party had done wrong since 1994, he had a quick answer. "It hasn't put a compassionate face on our conservative philosophy," he replied. "People think oftentimes that Republicans are mean-spirited folks. Which is not true, but that's what people think." Note that Bush spoke of putting a compassionate *face* on conservatism. That was not the same as transforming it. On the contrary, Bush seemed to be saying there was nothing wrong with the Republican Party that a different face wouldn't cure—and he knew whose face he had in mind.

David Frum, the Bush speechwriter, offered this puckish take on Bush's creed: "Bush described himself as a 'compassionate conservative,' " Frum wrote, "which sounded less like a philosophy than a marketing slogan: Love conservatism but hate arguing about abortion? Try our new compassionate conservatism—great ideological taste, now with less controversy."

But whether compassionate conservatism was primarily a philosophy, a marketing slogan, or merely a dodge, it was the product of prodigious work and careful thinking. Bush did the work, but his assignments often came from Rove, whose relationship with his candidate (and president) cannot simply be defined by the words "political adviser."

When Rove first met Bush, he seems to have realized almost immediately that his own skills as a gut fighter, a visionary, and a self-made intellectual were perfectly complemented by Bush's ease with people and his upper-crust connections. ("Bush is the kind of candidate and officeholder political hacks like me wait a lifetime to be associated with," Rove once said.) What Rove has never said—publicly at least—is that Bush badly needed his boy genius, as Bush called him, on absolutely everything related to the substance of politics: policy, strategy, tactics, and, when necessary, a willingness to execute, without much apparent scruple, whatever political attack was necessary.

"Rove was cerebral; Bush never liked going too deeply into the homework," James C. Moore and Wayne Slater write in their important Rove biography, *Bush's Brain.* "Rove had an encyclopedic mind and a gift for campaign arithmetic; Bush had engaging people skills, a knack for winning over opponents with pure charm. If Rove approached politics as a blood sport, Bush's instinct was to search out compromise and agreement." If ever a relationship deserved to be called co-dependent, this was it.

But Rove was not simply a tough guy. He was also a political visionary. He could play the low road, but it was in pursuit of a grand dream. Compassionate conservatism was one important plank to be used in a much larger project. Rove's dream was to create a dominant Republican majority for the next two decades or more. And he had a model: the success of turn-of-the-century Republican president William McKinley, who became the master of political fund-raising from the corporate world—exactly what Bush would become. McKinley identified with the rising interests of industrial capital, just as Bush identifies with capital's leaders today. Rove sees in the current moment the same epoch-making potential that existed at the time of the election of 1896, when McKinley produced a new Republican majority that endured, with the interruption of the Woodrow Wilson years, until the Great Depression.

Rove argues that McKinley understood that the issues surrounding the Civil War, which had dominated politics for three decades, were no longer relevant to a large and growing segment of the electorate. McKinley also realized that immigration and industrialization had changed the character of the country. If Republicans did not make a bid for the votes of immigrants and the working class generally, they would lose preeminence. Rove, for whom archival research is a hobby, can cite letters McKinley wrote describing the party's problem and meetings he held with immigrant leaders to bring them around to the Republicans' promise of the "full dinner pail."

Rove's analysis represented a sharp break with the popular conservative assumption that all that was required for a Republican victory was to recreate Ronald Reagan's appeal and to reassemble his coalition. The electorate had changed enormously from the time of Reagan's last election. Baby boomers and younger voters were now at its heart. And in 2000, at least, Reagan's best issues were gone. The Cold War was over and hostility to government programs ebbed.

It was not hard to see how Rove would play out the McKinley parallel. Bush's quest for Latino votes—a large factor in California, Texas, Florida, New Jersey, and Illinois—was directly comparable to McKinley's wooing of the Czechs, the Slovaks, the Italians, and the Irish. Similarly, Bush's minuets on social issues such as abortion and affirmative action—and his more general pledge to a compassionate conservatism—reflected Rove's sense that creating a durable Republican majority required converting suburban independents and Democrats whose social and moral views are more moderate than conservative.

Rove also liked to quote Napoleon's adage: "The whole art of war consists in a well-reasoned and extremely circumspect defensive, followed by rapid and audacious attack." Compassionate conservatism might be seen as the "well-reasoned and extremely circumspect defensive." The "rapid and audacious attack" was situational. In 2002, as we'll see, it used Iraq and homeland security as its weapons.

Rove seemed to have the Republican coalition—and the hope of a larger one—built into both his conscious and subconscious minds. He lives and breathes with his potential majority. He always understood, for example, that cultural conservatives would be a linchpin of Bush's constituency, even as he also understood that Republicans would, by conviction and necessity, always be the party of business. "To govern on behalf of the corporate right, they would have to appease the Christian right," write Lou Dubose, Jan Reid, and Carl Cannon in their Rove biography, *Boy Genius*. "The marriage of the Christian conservatives had to be made to work if the party was to work."

Yet Rove also understood the importance of wooing middle-class voters who were not right-wing. He wrote a memo to Republican governor Bill Clements of Texas in the 1980s that perfectly described the strategy he would later pursue for Bush. He did not expect to get votes from liberal constituencies, but he did want to win over moderates who shared some of the liberals' concerns. "The purpose of saying you gave teachers a record pay increase is to reassure suburban voters with kids, not to win the votes of teachers," Rove wrote to Clements. "Similarly, emphasizing your appointments of women and minorities will not win you the support of feminists and the leaders of the minority community; but it will bolster your support among Republican primary voters and urban independents." Welcome to compassionate conservatism before it was cool.

Bush knew perfectly well how cool the idea could be—and how important it was to his advancement. Even though Bush shared the conservatives' anti-government creed, especially where environmental, labor, and business regulation were concerned, he had learned from Gingrich's failures. The former House Speaker's conservatism had clearly been too combative, too devoted to an anti-government rhetoric that could never, in practice, deliver as small a government as it promised. It was also, perhaps, too honest. Bush found a rhetorical style that, at least in principle, made him a friend, not an enemy, of government.

"In this present crisis, government isn't the solution to our problem. Government is the problem," Ronald Reagan had said. George W. Bush has put his case much more modestly. "Government if necessary," Bush said, "but not necessarily government."

"Too often, my party has confused the need for limited government with a disdain for government itself," Bush declared. He criticized "the destructive mind-set," holding "that if government would only get out of the way, all our problems would be solved."

Here was "a well-reasoned and extremely circumspect defensive." Here, also, was the essence and the paradox of Bushism. By rejecting pure anti-government rhetoric, Bush left himself more room than Reagan had to reduce the size of government. Because Bush was not a government basher, he was given more leeway to limit its scope. Because Bush proclaimed his conservatism as "compassionate," he could pursue conservative goals with more vigor. And after 9/11, because Bush so increased the size of government where defense and homeland security were concerned, his broader anti-government purposes went unnoticed—even, until the fiscal picture turned bleak in 2004, among most conservatives.

This rhetorical shift led many to credit Bush with having made his party more moderate. "Bush's Moderate Steps Bring Change to GOP," read a *Philadelphia Inquirer* headline on a story about a Republican National Committee meeting in Austin on January 20, 2002. "He's taken the hard edge off the party," Bill Cobey, the GOP state chairman in North Carolina, told reporter Steven Thomma.

But Bush was no Rockefeller Republican. He was, in many ways, more conservative than Reagan—and that should have been obvious before he became president. Unlike Bush, Reagan never pushed to repeal the inheritance tax, even if he loathed it. Reagan didn't propose a partial privatization of Social Security, even if he saw Social Security as a socialist program. Reagan praised religion, but never contemplated a faith-based initiative.

Paul Weyrich, the president of the Free Congress Foundation and a veteran leader of the right, had qualms about whether Reagan was conservative enough. He definitely had problems with Bush I. But he loved Bush II. In an open letter to the second President Bush in January 2002, Weyrich praised him as "one of the finest men to have ever served as president." Weyrich was speaking for the conservative base, which had been overwhelmingly sympathetic to Bush from the outset. That's because they knew he was one of them. They understood—as some moderate voters and many in media did not—that Bushism (or in deference to his father, should we call it "W-ism"?) offered the best chance for a new conservative ascendancy.

Since at least the end of World War II, American conservatism has confronted a political and philosophical split between libertarians and traditionalists. The libertarians prize the free market above everything and see human liberty as the highest calling. The traditionalists emphasize community over individualism, values over profits, self-discipline over consumerism. "Conservatism is something more than mere solicitude for tidy incomes," wrote the traditionalist thinker Russell Kirk in 1954. "Economic self-interest is ridiculously inadequate to hold an economic system together, and even less adequate to preserve order."

In the 1950s, William F. Buckley, Jr., then a young editor, and his ally Frank Meyer sought to meld these two strands of conservatism. They created what came to be known as "fusionism." Donald Devine, a political scientist who served in the Reagan administration, has argued that fusionism saw America as, at heart, a conservative nation that would use the freedom libertarians preached in defense of traditional values. Whether fusionism ever worked philosophically, it worked politically by uniting conservatives behind a common cause: beating the liberals at home and the Communists abroad. This is the consensus that nurtured Ronald Reagan. His victory was a triumph of fusionism.

But Reagan's triumph also brought home fusionism's limits. In practice, traditionalists and libertarians still disagreed on many questions. Moreover, after Reagan won and prospered, the liberal enemy came to seem far less fearsome. And the collapse of the Soviet Union robbed conservatives of the anti-Communist solvent that could heal so many wounds and divisions.

George W. Bush made himself the instrument of a new fusionism. Like libertarians, he made tax cuts a central article of his creed. His devotion to business was reflected in his efforts to roll back environmental and labor regulations from the Clinton era and to open federal lands to energy development. Bush was a corporate conservative, and proud of it. But he called himself a compassionate conservative because he, like the traditionalists, understood that most people do not draw meaning from the marketplace alone. Oddly, as we'll see later, Bush was more alive to the limits of market thinking than were liberals, who feared saying anything that might invite attack from *The Wall Street Journal*'s editorial page.

"The invisible hand works many miracles, but it cannot touch the human heart," Bush declared in July 1999. "We are a nation of rugged individuals. But we are also the country of a second chance—tied together by bonds of friendship and community and solidarity." Soothing words, indeed. Yet it is wrong to see compassionate conservatism as a capitulation to liberalism. On the contrary, it was designed to undermine and replace liberalism.

"Reducing problems to economics is simply materialism," Bush declared in 1999, when he was inaugurated for the second time as governor of Texas. "The real answer is found in the hearts of decent, caring people who have heard the call to love their neighbors as they would like to be loved themselves. We must rally the armies of compassion in every community of this state. We must encourage them to love, to nurture, to mentor, to help and thus to offer hope to those who have none."

Or consider these words: "Our national resources are not only material supplies and material wealth but a spiritual and moral wealth in kindliness, in compassion, in a sense of obligation of neighbor to neighbor, and a realization of responsibility by industry, by business and by the community for its social security and its social welfare." The speaker went on: "We can take courage and pride in the effective work of thousands of voluntary organizations for the provision of employment, for the relief of distress, that have sprung up over the entire nation."

George W. Bush again? No, Herbert Hoover, in 1931, in the midst of the Great Depression. Hoover was the first compassionate conservative. The similarities are a reminder that Bush was operating very much within his party's conservative tradition.

When Bush took the presidential oath of office on January 20, 2001, his inaugural address was a brilliant distillation of his approach. "In the quiet of the American conscience, we know that deep persistent poverty is unworthy of our nation's promise. And whatever our views of its cause, we can agree that children at risk are not at fault." So far, he had everybody around the table with him, from left to right.

Bush went on to say: "Abandonment and abuse are not acts of God, they are failures of love. And the proliferation of prisons, however necessary, is no substitute for hope and order in our souls." His language here is very important. The root causes of poverty, he's saying, are *personal* and *moral*, not *social* and *economic*. Given Bush's record on law and order issues, it was moving for him even to bring up the proliferation of prisons as a problem. Yet consider that not poverty or discrimination but *abandonment* and *abuse* were the problems poor children faced. "Hope and order in our souls" is the solution to the problem of criminality, not job opportunities or reducing inequality. Thus did Bush shift the focus of the argument over poverty from the economy, government, and society to individuals and their shortcomings.

In the same speech, Bush declared: "Compassion is the work of a nation, not just a government. And some needs and hurts are so deep that they will only respond to a mentor's touch or a pastor's prayer. Church and charity, synagogue and mosque lend our communities their humanity, and they will have an honored place in our plans and in our laws." Whatever this was, it was not the New Deal. It was not the Great Society. It was conservatism, and of a rather old and traditional sort.

The tension within Bushism was on display again when he gave his first big speech after his inauguration, an address to a joint session of Congress on February 27, 2001. Bush made clear that he would act as if he had received a mandate from the voters for his big tax cuts. But he would *talk* as if he knew perfectly well that the country was in no mood for his reprise of Reaganism.

Much of the speech read as if a gremlin from the Democratic National Committee had snuck an Al Gore speech into the TelePrompTer. The grace notes were composed as Clintonian flourishes. What were Bush's priorities? Democratic priorities: "excellent schools, quality health care, a secure retirement, a cleaner environment." For good measure, there was also talk of a patient's bill of rights, a prescription drug benefit for the elderly, and a slew of smaller government programs that would have done Lyndon B. Johnson proud.

As for Clintonism, old Bill couldn't have done better. "Year after year in Washington," Bush declared, "budget debates seem to come down to an old, tired argument: on one side, those who want more government, regardless of the cost; on the other, those who want less government, regardless of the need."

If your enemies are those who are unconcerned about costs and indifferent to needs, you must be in the political center. You could almost hear Clinton's patented attacks on "the brain dead politics of both parties."

But after invoking all the centrist stuff, Bush offered his one, large priority: a tax cut of $1.6 trillion. And even on taxes, Bush actually made a case for the Democrats' middle-class tax cuts, not his own. The president didn't try to sell his plan as a tax cut for the wealthy—which it was—because he knew the voters didn't like the idea.

As Senate Democratic leader Tom Daschle noted in his rebuttal to Bush, 43 percent of the tax cut went to the wealthiest 1 percent of Americans. But did Bush haul out a millionaire investment banker or an oil baron to show whom he would be helping? No. Instead, there were Steven and Josefina Ramos from Pennsylvania, respectively a school administrator and a teacher. And he mentioned a hypothetical waitress who would also benefit.

Hiding the wealthy behind waitresses' skirts seemed like good politics. But it was an evasion that would come back to haunt Bush. It would feed the perception—which grew when the administration's prewar claims about Iraq were shown to be untrue or exaggerated—that Bush was always willing to say the convenient thing and hide inconvenient truths.

Bush wanted a supply-side tax cut without having to make a supply-side case. Where he had sold his tax cut during the campaign as affordable because the economy was booming, he sold it after he was elected as a response to the downturn. Boom, bust—whatever.

III

Compassionate conservatism required squaring so many circles that it inevitably inspired mistrust. Bush's first eight months in office were designed to get a long-term tax cut in place and cause as little short-term political pain as possible. This became clear when he released his budget in April.

Bush chose to evade a first-year ruckus by avoiding big spending cuts. Instead, he created a framework that would force such cuts in the years ahead. Ronald Reagan and Newt Gingrich could never get all the spending cuts they wanted right away. Instead of picking a losing fight, Bush turned necessity into a virtue: he would push his pleasant product, the tax cuts, first. Once he reduced government revenues, deficits would work their magic and force the large spending cuts later. Bush shrewdly put his faith in what Martin Luther King, Jr., once called, in a different context, "the tranquilizing drug of gradualism." He thus limited his cutbacks to a few areas: the environment, some housing and health programs, and agriculture.

But the cutbacks down the road were hidden in the small print. In the first year, his plan allowed for increases of 4 percent for programs other than the big entitlements such as Social Security. But by 2004, he allowed an increase of only 2.5 percent. Bush's initial budget did not even take into account his plans for new defense spending—and this was before 9/11. Conveniently, the administration launched a defense review that put off final decisions on the military until after Bush proposed his budget and big tax cut.

Long before Iraq, in other words, Bush's opponents perceived a pattern of evasion. "Rather than one year of big cuts, he's willing to wait and achieve what he wants over several years," one congressional budget specialist said of Bush at the time. "You've got two jaws to a vise—the declining revenues from the tax cut, and this consensus that we can't run a deficit." Of course it was the anti-deficit consensus that broke and, predictably, the deficit soared later in Bush's term.

The Bush tax cut was structured shrewdly to affect politics for years to come and to let conservatives set the political agenda. Many conservative activists were more direct about this than Bush. Grover Norquist, one of the right's most important organizers and a close ally of Rove's, was straightforward in saying that the goal was to reduce government revenues to force a reduction in government's size. The ultimate purpose, said the outspoken Norquist, was to get government "down to the size where we can drown it in the bathtub." Conservative columnist Donald Lambro acknowledged candidly that Bush's tax cuts "are, in effect, Mr. Bush's stealth initiative to curb future spending—big time."

By creating large deficits, Bush and his allies put advocates of more energetic government on the defensive. In the future, they would have to argue for rescinding or repealing tax cuts already passed. This is what Democrats were forced to do in 2004.

In the end, the final Bush tax cut was constructed in such a contorted and deceptive way—this was also Congress's work, not just Bush's—that the entire tax cut was scheduled to expire at the end of a decade. But this was a great victory for Bush. It concealed the real cost of the tax cut. And few expected that Congress would ever let the entire tax proposal die. Were it to remain in effect, the fiscal problems after Bush left office would be enormous. For the decade beginning in 2012, the cost of his 2001 tax cut alone would total some $4 *trillion*. Conveniently, Bush would long have been out of office then; inconveniently, that is the moment when the front end of the baby boom will be reaching retirement age.

In one area, though, Bush knew that compassionate conservatism had to deliver something tangible. Bush's approach to negotiating his education reform bill was sharply at odds with the way he negotiated almost everything else. Instead of pursuing a narrow majority of Republicans and conservative Democrats, he went straight to the most liberal Democrats in Congress and worked out a deal—to the dismay, it should be said, of some of his more conservative supporters. In getting the "No Child Left Behind Act" passed, Bush threw overboard many conservative commitments, notably to private school vouchers for children in failing public schools.

If there was any reality to compassionate conservatism, it lay in the education issue. This was a Rove imperative: if Bush could reduce the Democrats' advantage on education—before Bush came along, polls showed the public vastly preferring Democrats to Republicans on the question—he would remove one of the GOP's greatest weaknesses from the political calculus. But education was also a matter on which Bush had taken some political risks as governor of Texas. He had incurred the wrath of some on the right by proposing a tax plan that swapped certain tax cuts for tax increases.

And Bush's principles were hard to disagree with. The schools should be more accountable to parents and children. Testing students nationwide was a way to advance accountability. If this required more money, Bush said he was prepared to spend it.

Moreover, the ground for a cross-party deal on reforming education had been prepared over many years. During the 2000 campaign, Bush and Gore agreed on far more than met the eye. Bush wanted to force failing schools to change. So did Gore. Bush wanted to discipline poor schools by offering modest vouchers to parents so they could move their children to private schools. Gore wanted to require such schools to get rid of failing staffs and to reorganize.

In Congress, many Democrats had shown increasing impatience with educational failure. Representative George Miller of California and Senator Jeff Bingaman of New Mexico often defied their own party's interest groups by pushing hard for raising teacher standards. Senators Joe Lieberman, Evan Bayh, and John Kerry—funny, isn't it, that all three wanted to be president some day?—offered comprehensive education reform bills. Bush drew from a Bayh-Lieberman proposal in fashioning his own plans.

On education, as on almost no other issue, Bush negotiated in what seemed like good faith with the most liberal members of Congress, beginning with the favorite senator of almost every liberal, Edward M. Kennedy of Massachusetts. Kennedy displayed remarkable amiability in bargaining with Bush, and Bush returned the favor. Bush's staff and Kennedy regularly exchanged compliments and Kennedy urged Democrats to resist the temptation to obstruct Bush on one of his most important campaign promises. "It's an opportunity now and we shouldn't miss it," Kennedy said in April 2001. "If this program goes through properly funded, he ought to get credit for it, and Democrats ought to get credit for its being properly funded so it can come to life." The repetition of those words "properly funded" was to prove important.

During the discussions, each side gave ground. Kennedy moved closer to Bush (and to Lieberman and Bayh) in accepting that states should be given more flexibility in spending federal money. Bush moved away from vouchers and accepted some rather Gore-like ways of disciplining poor schools. And both sides fashioned a compromise through which children who failed could get help, including tutoring, outside the public school system. It was not vouchers, so Democrats could be satisfied. But Republicans could claim a concession to the principle that when public schools failed, outside forces should be allowed to help children to succeed.

The passage of the education bill was a great victory for Bush, and not a bad achievement for the Democrats who helped him. Yet there is a postscript that underscores the extent to which, when choices had to be made, Bush would make spending cuts before he would ever endanger his tax cuts. By the fall of 2003, governors were complaining that Bush had not adequately financed programs to help schools meet the federal law's exacting standards. And Kennedy was in exactly the same place he was when, in happier days, he had negotiated with Bush. "The law made proven, effective reform a priority for all schools," Kennedy told *The Washington Post* in October 2003, and he returned to his refrain: "To make it a reality, we must fund it." Republican pollster David Winston told the *Post* at the time that Bush and the Republicans were trailing Democrats by 50 percent to 36 percent on the education issue that fall—a 14-point drop for the G.O.P. from January 2002, when Bush had signed his education bill.

Bush belied his sympathetic comments about government in other areas. He proposed to weaken its regulations on the environment, on worker safety, on overtime pay. Most of the budget cuts Bush proposed were in programs for the poor and near poor. (Bush did propose a more responsible and less costly agriculture program, but acceded to Congress in supporting an expensive one. Most of the agricultural states had been painted red for Bush on election night, 2000.)

A stealthy redistribution upward became the hidden theme of Bush's domestic program. Under the cover of promoting growth, Bush shifted more and more of the tax burden from the wealthy. That was the effect of his first tax cut, but the tilt in favor of the rich was even more dramatic in his later proposal to cut the tax on stock dividends.

In the meantime, after the first year of his administration was safely behind him, Bush began offering proposals that created long-term incentives for states to cut their programs to help the poor. A revealing example was Bush's Medicaid reform, proposed in 2003. Bush suggested giving states modest short-term Medicaid relief, but only if they agreed to transform Medicaid into a block grant program. This would lead to cuts in federal help in later years, but the cuts were disguised. Whatever short-term Medicaid relief the states got in advance would be counted as a "loan" to be paid back within the next decade—meaning states would receive less federal help down the road as they paid back their "loans."

"The federal government is acting like a loan shark," said Ron Pollack, executive director of Families USA, a group that supports expanding health insurance coverage. "The federal government is dangling a little money before the states now, and then takes it back."

In later years, the federal government would get out of the business of giving the states automatic protections against increased health care costs or an increase in the number of the uninsured. The result, Pollack said, would be "waiting lists, a reduction in services, and higher premiums, deductibles and co-payments."

Robert Greenstein, executive director of the Center on Budget and Policy Priorities, a think tank that advocates programs for the needy, said states would inevitably be pressured to reduce medical coverage for the working poor—the very people the president praises over and over again for their responsibility. This was but one, very revealing policy choice of an administration whose agenda was radical in its stealthy way and threatened to undermine the federal government's rather modest commitment to helping states and cities assist their poorest residents.

Also revealing of the tensions and contradictions within compassionate conservatism was the fate of the president's faith-based initiative, designed to expand federal help to religious charities and social services. In principle, the initiative had broad appeal. During the 2000 campaign, both Al Gore and Joe Lieberman had spoken of the work of faith-based groups and endorsed more partnerships between the government and religious organizations. Liberal skepticism about any program that might erode the "wall of separation" between church and state did not disappear, and some liberals criticized Gore as well as Bush for embracing the idea. But at least some religious liberals saw great possibility in helping religious groups, many of which were passionate in their advocacy on behalf of the poor.

Yet the initiative had effectively collapsed by the summer of 2001. A version of the bill passed in the House, largely with Republican votes, hewed to a far more conservative approach than was acceptable to Democrats in the Senate. More fundamentally, the initiative lacked a constituency committed to its success. And every move the administration made to appease the idea's critics weakened support from likely allies. It was the ultimate irony for compassionate conservatism. An idea Bush had used so effectively began drawing assaults from left to right.

In the campaign, religious conservatives warmed to Bush's arguments that programs rooted in faith could fight poverty by changing hearts. Moderate voters appreciated a Republican who said he wanted to promote compassion and not just tax cuts. But as compassion took a backseat to tax cuts and little new money for the poor actually materialized, the faith-based initiative came to be seen by its critics as a cover for inaction.

One small clue: In his original tax cut package, Bush did not include a proposal (and campaign promise) to allow those who filed the short income tax form—i.e., Americans of modest incomes—to deduct their charitable contributions. By delaying action on this tax break, Bush signaled that repealing the inheritance tax for large fortunes mattered more to him than mobilizing his "armies of compassion."

The curious thing about the broader faith-based initiative was that if it had worked well, it almost certainly would have directed money to neighborhoods and religious institutions far outside the Republican base. A 1998 survey of more than 1,200 congregations by Mark Chaves of the University of Arizona found that moderate and liberal congregations were more likely than conservative congregations to express interest in applying for government money under existing "charitable choice" programs. Predominantly African-American congregations were far more likely to seek such funds than predominantly white congregations.

That was Bush's political problem. Many white, conservative religious leaders were unenthusiastic about the Bush initiative. They never wanted the government money Bush proposed to put on the table, and some of them feared that accepting any federal dollars would inevitably mean accepting abhorrent federal regulations. African-Americans, the natural constituency for Bush's idea, were split. Some black church leaders endorsed Bush's plan. But many in the African-American community were so mistrustful of the administration that they were unwilling to make common cause with Bush, even if the faith-based plan might have helped black churches. Many leaders of the black church were suspicious that the proposal was simply an effort to buy off influential ministers who had proven their ability to deliver votes—to the Democrats.

And then came a story in *The Washington Post* reporting that the Salvation Army had agreed to lobby for the president's initiative in exchange for federal protections against state and local gay rights statutes. What had been a soothing issue during the campaign was suddenly pushed into the thicket of culture war politics.

In the end, compassionate conservatism was a brilliant construction. There are, in fact, millions of conservatives—especially in the churches, synagogues, and mosques—who do feel a special responsibility to the poor. And compassionate conservatism did exactly the political work Bush hoped it would. For a while, it delivered, if not much content, then at least that compassionate *face* that Bush thought was so important. Those who wanted to see Bush as a moderate could listen to the compassion talk and turn their attention away from the heart of Bush's program.

Bush's problem was that he could not be a moderate and satisfy his political base at the same time. To the extent that he satisfied his base, he would disappoint those who thought—wrongly—that his new language of compassion marked a genuine break from the old conservatism. In the end, Bush chose his conservative base and fought for the issue dearest to its members.

That Bush ultimately won his tax cuts, it should be said, was a tribute not only to his skill and Republican unity but also to the utter flaccidity of moderate Democrats. Anger at Washington Democrats over their failure to challenge Bush on Iraq led to a flood of support in 2003 for Howard Dean's rebellion. A similar rebellion was, if anything, even more justified in 2001 when twelve Senate Democrats voted to push through an only slightly modified version of the Bush tax cut. Republicans, it seemed, had a greater desire to win and much more determination than Democrats.

Yes, the Democrats forced Bush to cut back the size of his tax cut, from $1.6 trillion to $1.25 trillion. Senate Democratic leader Tom Daschle struggled gamely at the time to argue that Bush "was dragged kicking and screaming" into a budget compromise. Daschle credited moderates in both parties for forcing the president in that direction. But Daschle also admitted that the reduction in the tax cut "wasn't as much as I would have liked."

That was putting it mildly.

The moderate cave-in to Bush suggested a double standard when it came to defining "centrism." Moderate Democrats—notably Louisiana Senator John Breaux, who supported the tax cut—had argued regularly during the Clinton years that a president's obligation had to create coalitions "from the center out." They meant that he should start with moderate ideas and seek votes from both sides of the political spectrum and the party divide.

But Bush disdained the very "center out" strategy the moderates claimed to believe in. He proposed proudly and without apology a stoutly conservative plan. Far from paying a price for his refusal to reach out, Bush managed to move the entire tax debate to the right. The moderates briefly showed signs of a fight when they forced down the size of the tax cut on the Senate floor. But the moderates quickly went along with a "compromise" that would produce a much bigger tax cut than any Democrat had said was reasonable even a few months earlier.

The episode suggested that when anyone in Washington used big abstractions—"center out," "bipartisanship," etc.—the words were irrelevant. The real issue was *who* was trying to push policy *where*. If "moderation" was good for Clinton but unnecessary for Bush, it was hard to escape the conclusion that those who used the word were trying to foil progressive initiatives and shove policy in a conservative direction. In the case of the Bush tax cut, a genuinely moderate approach would have produced a smaller, more fairly distributed tax cut. By caving so early and so easily, the moderates foiled moderation and suggested that the definition of a "moderate" was a conservative who lacked Tom DeLay's guts or candor.

The polarization of politics—later to be interrupted by 9/11 and then to reappear with a vengeance after the Iraq War—can be traced in significant part to the politics of the tax cut and the abandonment of any serious "compassion agenda." Bush angered liberals of even a moderate disposition, while many of the moderates gave moderation a bad name. And Bush's tax policies did not resonate outside his political base.

IV

The Jeffords switch destroyed any immediate political benefit Bush might have picked up from his tax victory. The Bush machine, which had seemed so powerful, crashed into a wall of moderate resistance. Bush's efforts to blame Bill Clinton for the faltering economy didn't work. Bush's energy plan developed by Vice President Dick Cheney through a process that, in its secrecy, closely resembled the workings of Hillary Clinton's health care task force, aroused intense opposition from environmentalists. The popular issues of the moment were a prescription drug benefit for seniors and a patient's bill of rights—both Democratic issues. In the summer of 2001, the talk was of a fall congressional session in which Bush might find himself playing defense.

In light of the long period after 9/11 during which Bush was regularly painted in the media as a brilliant and heroic leader, it's worth recalling that the press turned very tough on Bush in his summer of discontent in 2001. The widespread view was that his presidency was in jeopardy. Consider Dick Polman's report in the July 25 *Philadelphia Inquirer:*

> As George W. Bush marks the midpoint of his first year in the world's most powerful post, he undoubtedly has discovered the same hard truths that dogged his predecessors. Perks and prerogatives aside, presidents are often besieged by hostile political forces who can't be induced to surrender. They are sometimes hostage to events beyond their control, and they are powerless to do anything about it. Six months after taking the oath on a storm-tossed Saturday, the second President Bush has a stiff wind in his face, and even allies grudgingly agree that he will spend the next six months steering through similar weather. . . .
>
> Already Bush's pro-industry energy initiative has been sliced and diced by moderate congressional Republicans who want less drilling and more conservation. His bid to give federal money to faith-based charities has passed the House but could be treated rudely by the Democratic Senate. And his efforts to cap new federal education spending have been quashed by Democrats. . . . Even his big tax cut is likely to draw fresh scrutiny now that the economic slowdown is shrinking the projected budget surplus.

Polman did find a silver lining. "Things could be worse for Bush," he wrote. "He has been spared a foreign crisis that could trigger a major loss of life."

In an analysis published on July 5, the *Los Angeles Times*'s shrewd political writer Ronald Brownstein stressed the extent to which the Jeffords switch had emboldened Democrats.

"When Republicans controlled both houses of Congress, the White House could keep the public focus solely on the issues it wanted to highlight," Brownstein wrote. "Now, even as aides work to sharpen Bush's agenda for the fall, it must also develop a defensive strategy for responding to Democratic ideas.

"That need has grown more urgent as Bush's public support—particularly among centrist voters—has drooped in recent weeks," Brownstein went on. "Though he continues to enjoy overwhelming approval from Republicans, recent polls show him suffering unusually high disapproval ratings among Democrats and attracting only tepid backing from independents and moderates."

Brownstein noted that Bush's "overall approval rating has sagged from the 55% to 60% range earlier this year to around 50% in several recent surveys." This was bad news, indeed. "Among past presidents over the last 50 years," Brownstein added, "only Bill Clinton and Jimmy Carter saw their approval ratings fall this early in their term, according to Gallup polls. The sharpest declines have come among moderates and independents; Bush has been hurt with both groups by the perception that he is more conservative than he appeared during the campaign and favors special interests on issues such as the energy debate."

The negative view of Bush's stewardship prevailed right to the eve of September 11. "If congressional Republicans seem worried these days, they have reason to be," wrote the respected non-partisan political analyst Charlie Cook in the September 8 issue of the *National Journal*. "If the economy were on a heart-rate monitor, the results would be awfully close to a flat line. The budget surplus is history, unless Social Security and Medicare funds are included. The economic downturn and President Bush's tax cut share the blame. . . . Factor in a strong history of midterm congressional election losses for the party in control of the White House, and any Republican stalwart should be concerned."

On September 10, Wayne Washington wrote in the *Boston Globe:* "With the weak American economy rising to the top of Americans' concerns, President Bush is trying to limit the political damage, while Democrats look on skeptically." Washington quoted veteran White House adviser David Gergen's rather dismal view of Bush's prospects: "A downward spiraling economy is very likely to cost him seats in the 2002 election, which will hurt his power in the following two years and could well cost him the election."

Nor was Bush's foreign policy winning him any respect. "When it comes to foreign policy, we have a tongue-tied administration," wrote Morton Abramowitz, former president of the Carnegie Endowment for International Peace. "It is hard to think of another administration that has done so little to explain what it wants to do in foreign policy." The administration view, said Abramowitz, seemed to be: "the less talk, the fewer problems."

Abramowitz's critique appeared in *The Washington Post* on the morning of September 11, 2001.

2. "He's Ours. He's All We've Got"

How 9/11 United Us—and Divided Us Again

All of us stand with the president and support every effort to
bring to justice those responsible for these despicable crimes.

Senator Joseph R. Biden, Democrat of Delaware, September 11, 2001

We will speak with one voice.

Senate Majority Leader Tom Daschle, September 11, 2001

The fact that the administration used 9/11 in the last election, that they seemed intent on using the president's role as
commander-in-chief as a way of soliciting votes, has created a
hardening of partisan lines that will be felt until the end of
this administration.

Democratic Congressman Chakah Fatah of Philadelphia, January 2003

In light of the bitter partisan divisions that now characterize our politics,
it is hard to remember the depth of national unity that immediately followed the attacks on the World Trade Center and the Pentagon. It seems
fanciful that there was once a time when Democrats blunted all criticisms of George W. Bush, united behind him, and prayed for his success.
Literally: prayed.

I will never forget a conversation I had shortly after 9/11 with a Democratic consultant, a happy warrior who loves to defeat Republicans and has no particular sympathy for the president. Asked about his attitude toward Bush in the wake of the attack, he replied: "I actually went into church and knelt down and prayed that he'd be successful. He's ours. He's all we've got. Pray God that he's going to do what's best for our country."

The national crisis meant that Republicans and Democrats stopped throwing loaded lockboxes at each other. They stopped challenging each other's moral standing. The talk—of which I was part—was of a new seriousness in politics and the possibility of rolling back the bitterness of the last decade.

Bush himself seemed to change. His foreign policy in the months immediately after 9/11 lost some of the unilateralist tinge that colored so many of his early foreign policy choices and statements—and later ones. Winning the battle against terror required an end to unilateralism and the construction of a broad international coalition. The fact that the world rallied to the United States made hopes for such a coalition realistic. And the need for such an alliance immediately raised the profile and operational responsibilities of Secretary of State Colin Powell. This, too, had positive political effects. Powell, the quintessential coalition-builder, was the cabinet officer most popular among independents and Democrats.

A president who had said he was not "into" nation-building showed signs of understanding that nation-building was exactly what Afghanistan needed. The United States's failure to help rebuild Afghanistan after the defeat of the Soviet invasion in the 1980s laid the groundwork for the rise of the very forces the United States confronted on September 12, 2001. It turned out there was a practical side to humanitarianism. This sentiment was shared across party lines, but it was especially important to Bush's new Democratic allies.

Bush's post-9/11 rhetoric had particular appeal to his ideological adversaries. Early on, Bush stood up in defense of the rights of America's Muslim community. In assailing the Taliban, the president emphasized the aspects of its rule—its denials of religious liberty, its repression of political opponents, and, especially, its war against gender equality—most offensive to liberals and the political left. In his speeches, Bush grafted the language of Franklin Roosevelt and Harry Truman to the martial rhythms of Ronald Reagan.

Bush even seemed to abandon his pre–September 11 approach to domestic issues. Instead of trying to win legislative battles by uniting his own party and picking off as few Democrats as narrow victories required, he sought broad majorities on emergency spending and war policy. He won over not only dissidents but also the Democratic leadership. For a moment, at least, Bush transformed a partisan administration into a kind of coalition presidency. Representative Tom Davis, a Virginia Republican and one of his party's best political analysts, saw Bush as having the opportunity "to reshape the image of the party from the top down." One could even imagine the reappearance of something like Eisenhower Republicanism.

The evidence of a new, less confrontational politics was everywhere. House Speaker Dennis Hastert and House Democratic leader Richard Gephardt had almost nothing to do with each other until they were brought together by the need to agree on measures to combat terrorism. Suddenly, Republicans and the administration were rewriting the emergency anti-terror spending bills to accommodate the Democrats. Gephardt and Hastert joined to shepherd the $40 billion anti-terror appropriation to passage. In both houses, Democrats worked with Republicans to pass a war resolution promising retaliation for the attacks. Initially, Republicans hoped to ram through their own versions of both measures. Instead, they made concessions. "They could have rolled over us," said a very loyal and partisan Democratic leadership aide who resented the Republicans' initial approach but appreciated the spirit of compromise.

These were typical of the kind words longtime political adversaries were saying about each other—and all seemed to mean what they said. The mood was all the more striking because no one was prepared for it. "This fall was lined up to be the most divisive congressional fall in history," Representative Jim Leach, an Iowa Republican, said at the time.

"Now, the prospect of bickering has turned into a great sense of unity."
He added, as it turns out shrewdly: "Whether it's sustainable, I have no
idea."

Even dissent became bipartisan. It was inspiring to see Representative
Maxine Waters, a left-wing California Democrat, stand with Representative Robert L. Barr, Jr., a right-wing Georgia Republican, to ask hard
questions about the effect of the new anti-terrorism bill (it had an Or-
wellian name, the Patriot Act) on civil liberties.

Most astonishing of all, the tough guys of politics—the political consultants whose first, second, and third jobs involve winning elections—
were suggesting that politics might have turned a corner. At the time,
they said they were advising their clients to be very prudent in picking
fights.

"One of the things you've seen is a desire for a very different kind of
discourse," said Republican pollster David Winston, speaking a few
weeks after the attacks. Americans, he said, wanted to know that leaders
(and preachers and even comedians) understood how much the world
has changed. He argued that the post-9/11 criticisms of controversial
statements by the Reverend Jerry Falwell and Bill Maher of TV's *Politically Incorrect* were not so much an attack on free speech as an assertion
of new public norms. Only later did it become clear that curbing what
was, or seemed, outrageous speech could turn into a broader effort to
curb all criticism of the administration.

"The public sees there is a different political debate, that it can be
done differently and with more civility," a hopeful Winston said then.
This, he predicted, would create pressure for a different kind of political
campaign. "Politicians are going to do tit-for-tat at their own risk."

Democratic pollsters took a similar view. The country, said Mark
Penn, who later polled for Joe Lieberman's presidential campaign, had declared: "This is America, we hold together in the face of such a tragedy."
Guy Molyneux, another Democratic pollster, predicted that in the short
run, at least, politicians would try to define their position as "the sensible
bipartisan solution" and their opponents as "breaking the bipartisan
coalition." But that was tricky, as Molyneux pointed out. Politicians, he

said, would be tempted to tie all their proposals to the crisis created by September 11—and they faced the prospect of being assailed as cynics if they seemed to be using the attacks to advance the agenda they had before the planes hit the buildings. Molyneux said this in October 2001. He was prescient in explaining why, much later, Bush's use of 9/11 for his own purposes would inspire such fury among rank-and-file Democrats.

In the immediate aftermath of 9/11, politicians were operating in a climate of public opinion that was changing before their eyes. Polls showed a reversal in the anti-government sentiment that has been so powerful for so long. The mood shift confirmed a favorite adage of former Defense Secretary and Senator William Cohen: "Government is the enemy until you need a friend."

And, paradoxically at a time of increased anxiety, many more Americans thought the nation was on the "right track" than did so before the attacks.

Winston pointed to immediate post-9/11 polling results showing that Americans, while worried about the future, were gratified by the country's new sense of community. "People saw this as a horrible event," he said. "They think the economy is going to get worse. They think life is going to be tougher. But they also saw these firefighters stepping up to the plate. These were good people. They saw millions of Americans reaching into their pockets to make contributions. They saw people crashing that plane into the ground in order to save the lives of others. They saw people who acted as Americans who made them feel proud." If a new fear was one product of September 11, a new solidarity was another. That new solidarity also solidified support for Bush.

The crisis made the old slogans of the left and right seem stale, sometimes shamefully so. Only the most contorted analysis could lay the blame for the slaughter of 9/11 on "American imperialism." The rhetoric of free market omnipotence, so dominant for so long, became a bit less believable when Republicans and Democrats in Congress agreed that the marketplace couldn't keep the airlines flying; only the government could do that.

Complaints about America's alleged "moral bankruptcy" or "hedonism" were laid low, as Winston noted, by the community spirit and self-lessness of countless firefighters, rescue workers, and volunteers. Our celebrities, suddenly, were not high-tech wizards, Hollywood beautiful people, or hotshot investors, but public employees who soared in our esteem by simply doing their jobs, and ordinary citizens who simply behaved as citizens should. Arnold Schwarzenegger would eventually give Hollywood celebrity its day again. But that was much later.

Finally, and most powerfully, patriotism was spoken of without irony. The American flag, a politically contested symbol in the forty years' culture war that began in the 1960s, was restored as the banner representing the entire American community. This was not a trivial change. It suggested at least the possibility that Americans might come to believe again in common endeavor and public life.

Given how nasty politics have become, it is almost impossible to remember the soul-searching that followed 9/11 or the embrace of patriotism on the left end of the political spectrum. Todd Gitlin, a Columbia University professor who was a student radical in the 1960s and who never abandoned his affiliation with the left, captured the spirit of the moment with poignancy:

> Patriotism is not only a gift to others, it is a self-declaration: It affirms that who you are extends beyond—far beyond—yourself, or the limited being that you thought was yourself. You are not only an isolate. Just as you have a given name and a family name, you also have a national name. It gives you a past and a future. You are in solidarity with strangers: Their losses are your own. One deep truth about September 11 is that a community was attacked, not an assortment of individuals.
>
> . . . After September 11, 2001, millions of Americans wanted to enlist in nation building *at home*. They wanted to fight the horror, to take their fate in their hands, to make community palpable. They wanted to rescue, save, rebuild, restore, recover, rise up, go on . . .

It was, says Gitlin, "no surprise" that a few days after 9/11, "my wife and I decided to hang an American flag from our terrace. . . . The flag was a plain affirmation of membership . . . an affirmation of membership with an injured and resolute people."

The hope of the moment was not for an end to partisanship, but for the beginning of a new partisanship, a debate over real differences with less meanness and manipulation. There seemed to be a consensus that politics, public life, and public service had become too important to be trivialized or denigrated. That these hopes seemed realistic at the time only heightened the anger and disappointment when partisanship later reasserted itself with such a vengeance.

Even at the height of that solidarity, Linda DiVall, a Republican pollster, viewed its staying power with some skepticism. The rise in the "right track" numbers, she argued, involved a rallying of the country, and especially Republicans, to the president in this time of crisis. Of the bipartisanship, she said in words that now look prophetic: "I don't think it's going to last."

At the time, the signs were there to support DiVall's view. When the parties argued about whether the federal government should take over airport security, they divided largely along predictable lines—Republicans mostly against, Democrats mostly for. When they debated the elements of an economic stimulus package, they did so in their usual ways.

Indeed, within only a couple of weeks of 9/11, it was clear that some Republicans wanted to use the slaughter to run the table on behalf of their favored initiatives, especially tax cuts. They pushed, for example, a cut in the capital gains tax and the rest of the economic agenda they had been advocating for the past decade. Representative John Spratt, a South Carolina Democrat and budget committee leader, was incredulous: "We've lost 5,000 people and now we need a capital gains tax cut? It's unconscionable that they'd even bring it up."

Yet eight days after 9/11, the *Wall Street Journal* editorial page was urging Bush to advance his whole conservative domestic agenda right away because "the bloody attacks have created a unique political moment when

Americans of all stars and stripes are uniting behind their president." Drill for oil in the Arctic, the *Journal* preached, speed up the tax cut—this while the country was spending tens of billions more than anyone anticipated before the crisis—and even insist on pushing through confirmation of conservative judges. What did judges have to do with this war? Nothing, but the *Journal's* editorial writers saw political opportunity: "Democrats in the Senate will hesitate to carry out borkings that clearly undercut Mr. Bush's leadership." Bush, they concluded, should "use the moment to press a broad agenda that he believes is in the national interest."

So much for national unity.

Democrats lamented that such an approach would inevitably court bitterness. "To use this crisis as a launching pad for objectives that are unrelated" to the war on terror, said Representative Sandy Levin, a Michigan Democrat, "would unravel the bipartisanship that's needed even before it had a chance to work." And that is what happened.

II

For there was a flip side to the politics of national unity. It was the politics of terrorism. The new war on terror afforded Republicans a chance to regain all the advantages they had enjoyed during the last decade of the Cold War and then lost when it ended.

"Mr. President, the only way you are ever going to get this is to make a speech and scare the hell out of the country." So said Senator Arthur Vandenberg to President Harry Truman in 1947. Vandenberg, a Republican, was giving Truman advice on how to get Congress to vote for aid to help Turkey and Greece in their fight against Communist insurgents. Vandenberg might as well have been laying out rule number one in the politics of the Cold War. From 1947 until the fall of the Soviet Union in 1991, the country was scared as hell about Soviet power and the threat of nuclear war. And these fears dominated political life.

If Vandenberg's words have a familiar ring, it's because the new politics of terrorism were remarkably similar to the old politics of the Cold War. Fear once again became a powerful tool and motivator.

Consider President Bush's speech to religious broadcasters in February 2003 as he built the case for war against Iraq. "Chemical agents, lethal viruses and shadowy terrorist networks are not easily contained," he declared. "Secretly, without fingerprints, Saddam Hussein could provide one of his hidden weapons to terrorists or help them develop their own. Saddam Hussein is a threat. He's a threat to the United States of America."

Bush scared the hell out of the country, and we followed him to Iraq. Vandenberg might have approved.

Fear provides political actors—especially incumbents—with new ways of beating back and intimidating opposition. In the post-9/11 period, Republicans became experts at the political version of Whack-a-Mole. Any time Democrats poked up their heads to challenge the president, especially on terrorism, they were beaten down and accused of lacking patriotism.

Leading Democrats—Senators Tom Daschle and John Kerry and Representative Richard Gephardt—all received this treatment. Typical was House Speaker Dennis Hastert's comment about Daschle's criticism of Bush's diplomacy before the Iraq War. Daschle, Hastert said, had "come mighty close" to "giv[ing] comfort to our adversaries." That is Cold War talk—guilt by association. This time, the bad associations were with Saddam and the French, not the Soviets.

The Cold War metaphor also applied to intellectuals and activists on the left. Because the terrorism threat was real, as the Soviet threat was, even Bush's staunchest opponents took it seriously. Many on the left, like Todd Gitlin, supported the war in Afghanistan and defended Bush's use of the word "totalitarian" to define the terrorist enemy.

Much of the left had also rallied to the American cause at the start of the Cold War. But the united front against terrorism was even stronger than the unity mustered in the earlier struggle. In the Cold War years, some on the left—a minority that shrank as time went on—still insisted that the Soviet Union was a "progressive" force. No one could argue that the Taliban or Osama bin Laden's marriage of medievalism and fascism were in the least bit "progressive." A "Liberals for the Taliban" organization was as improbable as a group called "Conservatives for Permissiveness and Socialism."

Obsession with secrecy was another trait that the war on terrorism and the Cold War shared. Many of the great controversies of the early Cold War era—the spying convictions of the Rosenbergs and Alger Hiss, for example—were about the disclosure of secrets to the Communist enemy. The new politics of terrorism reinforced the Bush administration's preexisting penchant to keep secret as much as possible—witness Vice President Cheney's refusal to disclose the interests and individuals with whom his energy task force had consulted. For months, the administration postponed a serious inquiry on the intelligence failures preceding 9/11 on the grounds that such a probe might inform terrorists of our weak points.

The new politics of terrorism also revived the issues that had naturally favored Republicans. For three consecutive presidential elections beginning in 1980, foreign policy toughness was a central pillar of Republican strategy, causing defections to the GOP among neoconservative intellectuals and working-class New Dealers alike.

The importance of the Cold War to Republicans was underscored by the differences between the last election of the Cold War, in 1988, and the first post–Cold War election, in 1992. In both elections, George H.W. Bush was the GOP nominee. In both elections, he won large majorities among voters who listed foreign policy as a primary concern. The big difference? By the time Bush was running for reelection, foreign policy had receded as a central issue for most voters, despite the military victory that Bush had orchestrated in Kuwait. In 1992, most of the country voted on economics and other domestic issues. The Republicans were routed. George Will, the conservative columnist, captured the elder Bush's problem perfectly: "George Bush prepared all his life to conduct the Cold War, only to have it end, leaving him (almost literally) speechless." The president's son was to gain back some of the advantages his father lost when the Berlin Wall came tumbling down.

A national threat served George W. Bush in another way: When voters look for security, especially from foreign enemies, they look to the executive branch of government. Franklin D. Roosevelt understood this in 1940 as war raged across Europe. His reelection slogan then was, "Don't change horses in midstream." In 1940, the horse was a Democrat; this time, the horse is a Republican.

There is one important difference between Roosevelt's approach and Bush's. FDR saw fear as something that could paralyze a nation and prevent action. Bush (like Harry Truman and Vandenberg before him) saw fear as moving the nation to action. Each new terrorist alert reminded the nation of the dangers it faced and pushed other issues to the background. A cynic might say that the only thing Republicans had to fear was the end of fear itself. Whatever doubts Americans had about Bush's handling of the economy, polls showed—at least until 2004 and despite doubts about the Iraq venture—that they saw him as a strong and steadfast leader facing down the menace of terror.

And because the war on terrorism, like the Cold War, would be long, shadowy, and difficult, there was no telling when it would be declared over. The toppling of those Saddam statues was not like the fall of the Berlin Wall. The capture of Saddam was not like the hanging of Mussolini. After Saddam, even after Osama bin Laden, there would be other enemies to slay, other terror cells to break up.

An open-ended campaign served Bush's political interests far better than a shorter but all-consuming conflict. World War II had demanded the total mobilization of American resources and sacrifices from all sectors of society. The sacrifices in the war on terrorism were asked mostly of members of the military, police, and firefighters—and of few others. Bush could give patriotic speeches on even days and tax-cutting speeches on odd ones. War, it was presumed, could coexist with tax cuts without end.

In the narrowest political terms, Bush was shrewd to avoid total mobilization or anything close to it. Consider, after all, the fate of Winston Churchill. Despite his brilliant leadership, the British prime minister was bounced from office in 1945 by voters whose wartime sacrifice and solidarity encouraged them to embrace the Labor Party's program of so-cial reform. Bush's rhetoric gave nods to the ideas of service and sacrifice but demanded little—and certainly none at all from his political base. There was no talk from the White House of the sort of social solidarity that paved the way for Labor's victory in Britain.

Instead, the president and his lieutenants seized advantages none of them had anticipated when Bush assumed office. Thus did a war on ter-rorism that began in national unity end in partisan division and recrimi-nation.

III

The breakdown of post-9/11 bipartisanship happened gradually. Even in this heyday of bipartisanship, there was evidence, as DiVall noted, that partisanship would come back. As we've seen, Republicans and Demo-crats split largely along party lines over whether security personnel at the airports should become part of the federal government. But as Washing-ton fights go, this one was relatively civilized and even predictable. More problematic—and more disturbing to Democrats—were signs that Re-publicans were prepared to use the call to national unity as a means of si-lencing all criticism of Bush, especially criticism related to the handling of terrorism. If opposition is unpatriotic, what is an opposition to do?

One turning point came in May 2002, when word leaked that an in-telligence report on August 6, 2001 had warned of the possibility of ter-rorist hijackings. For the first time, Bush faced sharp questioning over what he knew and did not know in advance of the events of 9/11. One striking aspect of the immediate aftermath of 9/11 was the discipline (staunch partisans later saw it as timidity) that Democrats showed in not pressing the administration for answers on possible intelligence failures. The report that the president might have had at least some sort of warn-ing brought forth questions that another administration—Bill Clinton's, for example—might have faced immediately after the attacks.

Indeed, while Democrats were holding their tongues about Bush after 9/11, many Republicans were already blaming Clinton. "We have no choice but to address the policies and decisions, made at the very highest level of our government, which helped bring us to this point," an influential political voice said less than a month after September 11. "To do otherwise is to be irresponsible and unprepared in the face of a ruthless enemy, whose objective is to kill many more Americans."

These were not the words of an outrageously partisan Democrat seeking a high-minded rationale for bashing Bush. They were offered by Rush Limbaugh, one of the president's favorite radio talk show hosts, in a *Wall Street Journal* op-ed piece on October 4, 2001, arguing that Bill Clinton "didn't do enough to stop terrorists." Limbaugh's conclusion: "If we're serious about avoiding past mistakes and improving national security, we can't duck some serious questions about Mr. Clinton's presidency."

Limbaugh was not alone. Just days after the attacks, Republican Senator Richard Shelby of Alabama explicitly blamed Clinton for restrictions on the CIA's recruitment of informants overseas. "The Clinton curbs," Shelby said, "have hindered the work of our human intelligence agents around the world."

Democrats could not help but notice the Republican assumption. To suggest a serious inquiry into a presidency that ended eight months before September 11 was the patriotic thing to do. To suggest a comparably serious inquiry into intelligence and bureaucratic failures of the administration on whose watch the attacks actually happened was outrageous partisanship. Democrats were not only angry over the Republicans' relentless and continuing efforts to tar Clinton. They were also livid that the White House could claim political credit for Bush's handling of the September 11 attacks without ever facing any questioning or, in the president's words, "second-guessing." Second-guessing, as the Republicans argued when Clinton was president, can be another way of describing accountability. For Republicans, double standards were the order of the day, which only aggravated the politics of revenge.

The Democrat who faced the sharpest attacks that May was House Minority Leader Dick Gephardt. Even Democrats were uneasy with his use of the Watergate era "what-did-the-president-know-and-when-did-he-know-it?" formulation to challenge Bush on the August memo. But the White House's war against any and all Democrats who dared utter a critical word was so furiously partisan that it suggested a defensiveness about September 11 no one knew was there.

Vice President Dick Cheney, for example, declared that anyone who dared criticize the administration too hard was getting in the way of the war on terrorism. "Incendiary" commentary by opposition politicians, the vice president said, "is thoroughly irresponsible and totally unworthy of national leaders in a time of war."

This effort to suppress dissent was too much even for the conservative *Weekly Standard* magazine, which flatly labeled Cheney's remarks as "wrong." It added: "It's precisely because we're in a war that we need to find out where we failed."

Also infuriating to Democrats were White House efforts to avoid an independent inquiry into what went wrong before 9/11. The call for a bipartisan commission to investigate the attacks was championed by Republican John McCain and Democrats Joe Lieberman in the Senate and Tim Roemer in the House. But despite pleas from families of those who met their deaths in the attacks, the administration resisted the creation of a commission right through the 2002 elections.

"I think it's the wrong way to go," Vice President Cheney told Fox News on May 19, 2002. As Brian Montopoli put it in a definitive article on the commission fight in *The Washington Monthly,* Cheney insisted that national security concerns trumped the concerns of the families. Bush's aides claimed that the president wanted a commission, but kept negotiations going to pressure its allies in Congress not to act. The argument crawled into the fall. On October 11, with the election less than a month away, Lieberman spoke for many commission supporters: "The question we want to pose to the White House today is: 'Do you really want to allow this commission to be created? And if you don't, why not?' "

John McCain was even more scathing: "Every bureaucracy in this town is scared to death of an investigation," he said. "Remember, no one has really been held accountable. No one has lost their job, no one has been even reprimanded, nothing has happened as a result of Sept. 11. Unless responsibility is assigned, then we can't cure the problem."

A reckoning could not be postponed forever, and a commission was set up—after the election. The administration's decision to name Henry Kissinger as the commission's chairman invited more skepticism. "If you want to get to the bottom of something, you don't appoint Henry Kissinger," wrote *New York Times* columnist Maureen Dowd. "If you want to keep others from getting to the bottom of something, you appoint Henry Kissinger." Kissinger withdrew. The chairmanship went to former New Jersey governor Tom Kean, a Republican who was to struggle to get the information from the administration he thought the commission needed. "We have not gotten everything we need to do our job," he said at one point. "We expect to get everything we need to do our job." Battles between the commission and the White House continued into 2004, most dramatically over whether national security adviser Condoleezza Rice would testify in public. The White House dropped its resistance to Rice's public testimony only after the administration was sharply criticized by Richard Clarke, the administration's former terrorism adviser. Further resistance became politically untenable.

The most important political episode of 2002 began playing out in June. Bush had resisted establishing a Department of Homeland Security, which was originally proposed by Lieberman. On June 6, Bush abruptly announced on national television that he had switched sides and now embraced a new department. Why, exactly, and why then?

For weeks, the news had again been dominated by stories reporting the failures of U.S. intelligence and law enforcement in the period leading up to the terrorist attacks. Suddenly, Congress was asking the obvious question: How could this have happened?

It was not a line of inquiry the administration welcomed. Bush's speech endorsing the homeland security department happened to come on the very first day of testimony from whistle-blower Colleen Rowley, the chief legal counsel of the FBI's Minneapolis field office, who had brought her agency's pre-9/11 failures to public attention.

Not surprisingly, Bush overshadowed Rowley.

Dan Balz, chief political reporter for *The Washington Post,* noted the next day that Bush appeared on television as he was "struggling to regain the initiative" on security issues. While the president retained the confidence of the country, Balz wrote, "his administration is no longer immune from questions or criticism about what happened before Sept. 11, and whether everything is now being done to make the homeland safer.

"In recent weeks," Balz continued, "Bush has faced the first sustained scrutiny since the terrorist attacks." The result: "signs of declining public confidence in the government's ability to combat future terrorism."

Given this opening, did the Democrats respond to Bush's speech with partisanship? No. As they did so often after September 11, they turned the other cheek. Senate Majority Leader Tom Daschle, regularly vilified by the Republicans as a mad partisan, called Bush's remarks "encouraging." Representative Jane Harman of California, one of the Democrats' leading voices on security, called Bush's proposal "bold and courageous."

The natural move from here would have been authentic bipartisanship to get a bill passed. After all, the differences between Bush and the Democrats were so small that Senator Phil Gramm (R-Tex.) noted that 95 percent of the homeland security bill that was eventually approved after the 2002 elections had been written by Democrats.

But getting a department created before the election was clearly less important to the president than having a campaign issue. He picked a fight over union and civil service protections for its employees that Democrats had inserted into the bill. Republican senators filibustered various efforts to reach a compromise. In late September, Bush went so far as to charge that the Senate—meaning its Democratic majority—was "not interested in the security of the American people."

Because Bush succeeded in evading debate over what happened and what was known in the months before 9/11—and because Republicans defied tradition in the midterm elections by recapturing the Senate and gaining seats in the House—Bush's maneuverings could be seen as brilliant politics. But it was brilliance bought at a high price. More than any single episode, the homeland security maneuver broke the spirit of bipartisanship. It permanently alienated Democratic leaders and, eventually, the party's base. This happened *before* the Iraq War, which is often taken as the central cause of the political divisions in the Bush years. It was not.

In no 2002 contest did the Republicans' use of the homeland security issue more enrage Democrats than Georgia's Senate race. Republican Saxby Chambliss pilloried Democratic incumbent Max Cleland in a vicious advertisement that used pictures of Osama bin Laden and Saddam Hussein—surely the ultimate in guilt-by-association—to portray Cleland as soft on terrorism because of his insistence that the homeland security bill include civil service protections. The ad accused Cleland of voting against Bush's "vital homeland security efforts 11 times," which only meant that, in the legislative maneuverings, Cleland had insisted on the Democrats' version of the bill over Bush's.

What made the implication that Cleland was an ally of terror especially shameful was Cleland's record as a Vietnam War hero who, near the end of his tour, lost an arm and both of his legs in a grenade explosion. "I served this country, and I don't have to prove my patriotism to anybody," said an angry Cleland, who noted that Chambliss used four student deferments to escape service before receiving a medical deferment because of "an old football knee."

It is impossible to overemphasize how the attacks on Cleland hardened Democratic attitudes toward Bush—who campaigned hard for Chambliss—and the Republican Party. "This is something that gnaws at us," Senator Richard Durbin of Illinois said months after the election. "A decorated and disabled Vietnam veteran would be discredited because of his stand in the homeland security debate?"

Louisiana senator Mary Landrieu poured Tabasco on her comments about Cleland. "He left three limbs in Vietnam. He's already served his country in more ways than any of us ever will. The president came in with a very personal and very vicious attack, using the homeland security issue to unseat a man who fought on the Armed Services Committee to give the guys in the battlefield everything they need. It didn't mean a thing to this president."

Landrieu had her own issues with Bush. A Democratic hawk, she strongly supported him on Iraq, and called for even higher levels of defense spending than Bush did. She had voted for the Bush tax cut. In an early ad, she boasted of how often she had backed the president.

"Mary Landrieu really did all she could to work with this president and did all she could to reach across party lines," said Representative William Jefferson, a New Orleans Democrat, "and he [Bush] and the Republican Party still tried to come and stomp on her."

Indeed, they did. The Republicans' campaign against Landrieu confirmed that for Democrats in the House or Senate, it did not matter how they voted or what they said or how patriotic they were. The Bush machine would do all it could to defeat them anyway. A lesson was learned: there was no percentage in making nice with an administration willing to politicize security issues in pursuit of a long-term Republican majority.

Landrieu's victory only hardened her attitude toward Bush. "For Democrats who were trying to work with the president on national security issues and support a more hawkish stand than might seem natural for a Democrat, this president discounts it, ignores it, and acts as if it's not relevant," she said after the election. "Any time the country is poised for war and about to engage on behalf of the security of the country, it's very important that the president make that the priority and make everything else come in second. Unfortunately, the president has done exactly the opposite of that."

Yes, Landrieu lamented, the country was deeply polarized along partisan lines. "Unfortunately, the president has earned this polarization," she said. "It hasn't just happened. He pushed it to happen."

Landrieu's victory in the runoff was a counterpoint to Cleland's defeat. If the overall message of the 2002 election was that timidity loses, the message of Landrieu's runoff victory was that toughness wins. Bush threw everything except poisoned gumbo into the fight to defeat her. She hit back where it hurt, on the economy, and threw sugar in the president's eyes. She told the voters in a pro-Bush state that they had a choice between a Bush rubber-stamp and an independent voice. Independence beat Bush.

Landrieu had an advantage over all other Democrats running for the Senate in 2002. Under Louisiana's unusual election system, an open primary is held on Election Day, and if no candidate wins a majority, a runoff is held in December. This gave Landrieu time to digest the meaning of the November results. She defeated her Republican opponent, Suzanne Haik Terrell, because in a single month, she and her campaign changed course.

The Republican Party deluged the state with cash to support fierce attack ads against Landrieu. Even Republicans thought the tone and quantity of the spots bred a backlash. Representative John Cooksey, a Republican who lost out to Terrell in the first round of voting, told *The Advocate* of Baton Rouge that Louisiana voters rebelled against "outside money and influence telling them how to vote."

But Landrieu didn't just play the victim. She struck back hard. She used a report in a Mexican newspaper to lash the Bush administration for allegedly supporting a big increase in sugar imports from Mexico, to the detriment of the state's well-protected but ailing sugar industry. And in a bit of political eclecticism that Karl Rove must have privately admired, she also criticized the administration's own protectionist policies on steel because they hurt the Port of New Orleans. In both cases, she argued, she would stand up for Louisiana against Bush.

Al Quinlan, Landrieu's pollster, noted the change in tone between the two rounds of voting, "We ran a much more aggressive, tougher race" after realizing that the campaign "had to be sharper, had to be more focused on economic issues." It was easier for Landrieu to push economics because the homeland security issue disappeared between the two rounds of voting. Congress gave Bush the homeland security bill he wanted in a lame duck session after the November election. You could tell how much Republicans longed to keep the issue alive—and how important it had been to their takeover of the Senate—when Karen Hughes, Bush's former top aide, came to the state and criticized Landrieu for "taking a whole year to decide that she ought to work with President Bush to protect our homeland."

It didn't work, and Quinlan argued that the attacks on Landrieu for failing to support Bush on everything only reinforced her declaration of independence. It also helped bring Democrats to the polls, especially African-Americans, who had not voted in large numbers in the first round. In the runoff, Landrieu sought black votes with a new energy, and her victory speech played off on an old civil rights saying. "My feet are tired, but my soul is inspired," she declared. Yet even as Landrieu was reassuring African-Americans, she did better among white voters than she had six years earlier. Jobs and political independence proved to be themes that could reach across racial and ideological lines.

Mary Landrieu's lesson, which her party took to heart, was that losers allow their opponents to set the terms of the competition. Winners change the terms and fight back. Democrats took a long time to learn that. The tone of 2003 and 2004, the rise of Howard Dean, the toughening of the response of Democrats such as John Kerry and John Edwards to Bush—all reflected lessons learned the hard way.

IV

Changing the terms of debate was critical to George W. Bush's successes in 2002. If homeland security was one pivot point for the change, Iraq was the other. Insecurity over terrorism still loomed large as the summer of 2002 approached. But the return of domestic anxieties—over the economy and the wave of corporate scandals symbolized by the collapse of Enron—gave Democrats hope that the fall elections would be fought on issues unfavorable to Bush. Iraq would change that.

This was not immediately obvious. Even when the administration began sounding battle cries against Iraq in midsummer, the response—especially from Republican elites close to the president's father—was less than enthusiastic. A clear split emerged in the Republican Party.

Vice President Cheney, Defense Secretary Donald Rumsfeld, Deputy Defense Secretary Paul Wolfowitz, and an important group of neoconservative thinkers led by William Kristol and Robert Kagan emerged as strong supporters of bold American action to transform the Middle East. The United States, they insisted, should be unencumbered by the doubts of cautious European allies. The Iraq struggle would not simply be a war to topple Saddam Hussein—though many of its supporters had devoutly wished this for a decade. It would also transform the Middle East, alter Islam's political culture, and thus change the world.

Republicans who supported a more traditionalist approach to foreign policy—call them realists—were skeptical of such grand designs. They were especially skeptical of the neoconservative view that a war lacking support from America's traditional allies could be a long-run success. This camp was represented in the administration by Secretary of State Colin Powell. He won strong support in the 2002 summer war of newspaper opinion pieces from such close advisers to the elder Bush as Brent Scowcroft and former Secretary of State James A. Baker III.

The debate had a strange quality because the realists did not want to concede the anti-Saddam high ground to the neoconservatives. So they argued less about going to war than about which war the country should wage. The hard-liners insisted that going it alone was better than coalition-building, more weapons inspections, and delay. The realists insisted that the United States would be better off building a broad international alliance against Hussein, and that doing so required giving weapons inspections more time.

In late August, Cheney and Rumsfeld laid out the unilateralist case. Speaking to the Veterans of Foreign Wars, Cheney explicitly rejected any effort to restart weapons inspections in Iraq. "A person would be right to question any suggestion that we should just get inspectors back in Iraq, and then our worries would be over," he said. "Saddam has perfected the game of cheat-and-retreat, and is very skilled in the art of denial and deception." The danger of inspections, Cheney said, was that they "would provide false comfort that Hussein was somehow 'back in his box.' Meanwhile, he would continue to plot."

A day later, Rumsfeld declared that the administration might not wait for allied support before it launched an attack. "It is less important to have unanimity than it is making the right decision and doing the right thing, even though at the outset, it may seem lonesome," Rumsfeld told members of the 1st Marine Division. "Leadership in the right direction finds followers and supporters."

But sometimes it helps to find those followers and supporters ahead of time. That's what Baker and Richard C. Holbrooke, who was ambassador to the United Nations under Bill Clinton, suggested in important op-ed articles around the same time.

Baker chose not to break with the Bush administration. Writing in *The New York Times* before Cheney or Rumsfeld had spoken, Baker allowed that "the only realistic way to effect regime change in Iraq is through the application of military force." Yet Baker wrote as if he had seen Cheney's and Rumsfeld's arguments in advance. "We should try our best not to have to go it alone," Baker wrote, "and the president should reject the advice of those who counsel doing so. The costs in all areas will be much greater, as will the political risks, both domestic and international."

Baker endorsed the adoption of a U.N. Security Council resolution "requiring that Iraq submit to intrusive inspections anytime, anywhere, with no exceptions, and authorizing all necessary means to enforce it." Pushing for such a resolution would allow the United States to "occupy the moral high ground." Baker explicitly answered those who "will argue that this approach will give Saddam Hussein a way out because he might agree and then begin the 'cheat-and-retreat' tactics" he has used in the past. Baker's answer: "The first time he resorts to these tactics, we should apply whatever means are necessary to change the regime."

Holbrooke, writing in *The Washington Post*, also endorsed a new U.N. resolution calling for "no-notice inspections, anywhere, anytime," and argued that "a campaign against Saddam cannot be waged without allies."

The summer arguments did little to reassure congressional Republicans. When they came back to Washington in September, many reported skepticism back home. The words they used over and over about the administration's Iraq policies were "concern" and "unease." It's worth visiting with these Republicans because the doubts they expressed six months before the war suggest that it was far from inevitable. There was no public clamoring for an attack on Saddam Hussein—which helps explain why doubts about the wisdom of going to war arose in 2004.

"My sense from talking to people here is that the case hasn't been made," said Representative Dave Camp, a Michigan Republican and loyal mainstream conservative. Camp said his constituents had seen the benefit of successful coalitions in both the first Iraq war and Afghanistan. "They're concerned about a go-it-alone strategy," he said, "and that includes going it alone without the American people."

Representative Thomas Petri, a Wisconsin Republican, said his constituents expressed "concern about whether we know what we're doing or how we're going to do it," while Representative Jim Leach, an Iowa Republican, reported: "The public doesn't want to say the president is wrong, but they're very uneasy." Senator Susan Collins, a Maine Republican, said her constituents were "stressing a lot of reservations." She went on: "They want to support the president, they trust his judgment. But they're every uneasy—they're very uneasy about invading another country unless the case is very strong."

Representative Doug Bereuter, a Nebraska Republican and one of his party's leading foreign policy voices, allowed that the "hard line" put forward by Cheney and Rumsfeld might have a positive effect—"to soften up the Europeans" and push them to support tough weapons inspections. But Cheney's outspokenness also had serious costs. "There are costs in terms of confidence in the Bush administration's foreign policy," Bereuter said. "It may have fractured support for actions against al Qaeda around the world." For good measure, Bereuter noted that the conflict in Afghanistan and the fight with Al Qaeda were "far from finished"—echoing an argument that would be made months later by Democrats, especially Florida Senator Bob Graham, General Wesley Clark, and Howard Dean.

The queasiness these Republicans reported was reflected in the polls at the time. A Pew Research Center survey released on September 5 found that only 22 percent of Americans thought the military effort against terrorism was going "very well," down from 45 percent in October 2001 and 38 percent in January. An ABC News poll released a day earlier found that just 52 percent of Americans approved of Bush's handling of Iraq. And while 56 percent favored military action to depose Saddam Hussein, a quarter of those supporters dropped away when asked whether they would still favor military action in the face of opposition from American allies.

What's striking in retrospect is the political deftness, however manipulative it was, of the administration's response. Having laid out a strategy that was threatened with public rejection, even within his own party, Bush switched gears and went to the United Nations. This switch in time (without, of course, admitting any change in policy) paralleled the administration's change of position on homeland security. Changing course while insisting that no turn had been made became a characteristic of the Bush presidency.

Even before he went to the United Nations to seek the world's support, Bush backed away from his administration's swaggering lawyers' insistence that he didn't need a congressional vote to go to war with Iraq. After a September meeting with congressional leaders, Bush promised that "this administration will go to the Congress to seek approval" for actions "necessary to deal with the threat."

Politically, Bush counterattacked on two fronts. He sought a strong U.N. resolution calling for new weapons inspections and the threat of force against Iraq. And he went to Congress for a resolution to authorize force. The first move diffused the criticism. The second put the Democrats on the spot.

In fact, the administration was asking for a blank check. If the resolution Bush sought was passed, he would never again have to go back to Congress before he went to war. (And he didn't.) He was asking Democrats who would support a war under the right conditions to give him authority to wage war under *any* conditions. Yet any Democrat who dared to oppose what Bush asked for could then be accused of thwarting his efforts to win support at the United Nations. Among his major potential adversaries in the 2004 election, all but one—Senator Bob Graham of

Florida, who later dropped out of the race—decided to vote for the reso-lution. Senators Joe Lieberman and John Edwards and Representative Dick Gephardt did so with some enthusiasm. Senator John Kerry did so with considerable doubt. In a political sense, at least, Kerry's doubts were confirmed when it turned out that large numbers of Democrats were seeking an anti-war candidate. Many Democrats turned away from Kerry and embraced Howard Dean, who had the luxury of not having to vote on the resolution but came out strongly against the war. It took well over a year for Kerry to recover from the anti-war backlash.

Feeding the Democrats' perception that Bush's move was political, the president and the Republicans were not shy about using the prospect of war to improve their electoral chances. By September, Republican candi-dates in South Dakota, Minnesota, and New Mexico were already deploy-ing soft-on-Iraq charges against their Democratic opponents. Republican strategists promised more of the same elsewhere.

It was also obvious that pushing war to the center of the news shoved the Democrats' issues to the side. Senate Majority Leader Tom Daschle launched a broad attack on the administration's economic record on September 18. The speech might have been big news under other cir-cumstances. It became a sideshow.

None of this "proved" that the motivations behind the war buildup were political. But its sheer political convenience fed the opposition's doubts—and became another source of Democratic rage after the elec-tion. Bush did not ease those doubts with a remarkable mid-September criticism of Democrats who insisted on U.N. support before any Ameri-can military action. Bush characterized such members of Congress as saying, " 'I think I'm going to wait for the United Nations to make a de-cision.' "

Bush went on: "It seems like to me that if you're representing the United States, you ought to be making a decision on what's best for the United States. If I were running for office, I'm not sure how I'd explain to the American people—say, 'Vote for me, and, oh, by the way, on a mat-ter of national security, I'm going to wait for somebody else to act.' "

By distorting the arguments of others and obliquely accusing them of failing to act in American interests, Bush courted the resentment that would confront him later. On Iraq, as on homeland security, Bush was willing to do what it took to win a midterm election.

For, in truth, few of Bush's critics opposed his goals. "There's a near consensus around here on supporting the president's request that the United Nations lay down a deadline, an ultimatum, and authorize the use of force to support it," said Senator Carl Levin, a Michigan Democrat who chaired the Armed Services Committee. "Where there's a division here is over whether we should say we'll go it alone and whether we should say that at a moment when we're going to the United Nations and asking them to act."

Creating an anti-Saddam alliance in association with the United Nations, insisted Illinois Senator Richard Durbin, could "diffuse negative reactions" to the war abroad and guarantee that "the long-term commitment [to Iraq] once Hussein is gone would be a shared commitment."

In the end, both Levin and Durbin voted against the war resolution. Their arguments were vindicated when the administration's optimistic predictions of a relatively easy aftermath to the war proved badly wrong. In 2004, Bush found himself in desperate need of United Nations support, more troops, and international contributions to Iraqi reconstruction.

Still, for the short term, Bush's move worked. It transformed the 2002 election and provided him with a second punch to go along with the homeland security issue. Democrats in swing states and swing districts were petrified to oppose Bush on the war. Many in the party wanted to get the war resolution out of the way so the 2002 campaign could return to economics. They thus ceded the entire foreign policy terrain to Bush.

In late September, I traveled to South Bend, Indiana, in the state's 2nd Congressional District. It was the scene of one of the country's most competitive House races. At the time, Jill Long Thompson, a Democrat and former House member, was essentially dead even with Republican Chris Chocola. Bush and Cheney had already stumped and raised money for Chocola.

I caught up with Long Thompson at a late afternoon friends-and-neighbors party at South Bend's stately Queen Anne Inn. Long Thompson quickly defined the terrain on which she wanted to fight. She didn't pause when asked where she and Chocola differed most. "It's on domestic issues," she replied, "it wouldn't be international."

The sagging economy and unemployment, preserving Social Security against privatization, "fair trade," and a tough stand against corporate corruption—these were the staples of her meat-and-potatoes campaign. "I will come down on the side of what's right for our country," she says. "Not on the side of a handful of people who happen to be at the top of the income scale."

She would not let the war talk block this message. When a group of sympathizers raised doubts about Bush's rush to war, Long Thompson, far from encouraging them, supported the president and even defended him. And she began her answer by noting her husband's twenty-three-year career in the military and the reserves. She explained her approach with some candor in an interview after her talk. "I think people are very uneasy about a potential strike on our part," she said, "but we are very patriotic in the Second District, and we will support our president, and we will support our troops."

And that was the problem for Tom Daschle, Dick Gephardt, and the rest of the Democratic Party's leadership. They knew from polling that the public was far more ambivalent about an attack on Iraq than it had been about the war in Afghanistan. Most Americans seemed to agree with the position that some Democrats espoused publicly and many supported privately: Americans were willing to back a war against Saddam Hussein, but only after the alternatives, such as tough inspections, were exhausted—and only with the support of a strong network of allies.

Democrats were divided and paralyzed by two fears. The first was political in the very narrowest sense: many of 2002's toughest House and Senate battles were in Bush country, places where Bush had beaten Al Gore in 2000. Gephardt was loath to say anything that might endanger the chances of Long Thompson in Indiana or Democrats like her in comparable places around the country. The same was true of Daschle, whose fellow South Dakotan, Democratic senator Tim Johnson, came under heavy Republican fire in his 2002 reelection race on national security issues. (Johnson eventually prevailed by just 524 votes.)

But in the wake of 9/11, there was the additional fear—articulated indirectly by Long Thompson—that if Democrats questioned the president, Republicans would pummel them as unpatriotic. Bush went straight to that strategy in his declaration about the Senate's alleged indifference to homeland security.

This was intimidation, pure and simple—and in 2002, at least, it worked.

Chocola, Long Thompson's affable Republican opponent, was perfectly candid in saying before the election that the war issue would help him, and he criticized some of Long Thompson's defense votes from her time in Congress. Bush's visit to the district, Chocola said, "sent the message loud and clear that there is only one candidate who would stand with the president consistently." Yet when he was asked if the questions voters had put to him changed much once Iraq began dominating the news, Chocola replied: "Surprisingly not." He added: "Consistently, throughout the year, it's been about economic issues."

In the end, the 2nd Congressional District turned in a perfectly representative result: Chocola defeated Long Thompson and the Republicans added to their narrow majority in the House. The economic issues were not enough, and the Democrats' silence on the war hurt them.

But the administration's brilliant opportunism also made it harder for Democrats to respond. Long after the troops had entered Iraq, Lincoln Chafee of Rhode Island, the sole Republican senator to oppose the war, put his finger on the suspicion that became even more powerful in 2004—that the administration had not been "forthright." In the late summer of 2003, Chafee declared: "They are using whatever argument is most marketable at any given time."

In the buildup to war, the signals from the Bush team gyrated between assertions that the United States would go it alone and a quest for cooperation from the United Nations; between an insistence on "regime change" and an acceptance of the idea that simply ridding Saddam Hussein of his most dangerous weapons would be enough. The policy, it seemed, was being set one week by the go-it-alone regime-changers, Cheney and Rumsfeld, and the next by Powell, a multilateral disarmer.

When Powell brokered a unanimous U.N. Security Council vote for tough inspections, even Bush's critics cheered. "We've decided to go to the United Nations, which all of us who opposed [the congressional war resolution] argued was the right step," said Dick Durbin. "The voice of Colin Powell was drowned out in the early phases of this debate in the White House," but he won in the end. Senator Chuck Hagel, a Nebraska Republican who criticized the administration hawks but voted for the war resolution, saw the U.N. action as "a significant win for Powell" because "he was able to redirect the administration's efforts into a responsible, international channel."

In the long run, this proved to be a Pyrrhic victory. Cheney and Rumsfeld eventually got the war they wanted without the troublesome French or Germans as allies. But at the time, you could tell the inside-the-administration hawks were worried that Durbin and Hagel might be right by the response of the leading outside-the-administration hawks, William Kristol and Robert Kagan.

The "weeks of negotiations carried out by the State Department have eroded the president's position, not terminally, but worryingly," they wrote. "The inspections process on which we are to embark is a trap. . . . Will the clarity of the case for war have been compromised, perhaps fatally, by the latest round of diplomacy?" Kristol and Kagan held out hope that Bush was truly on their side—and they were right. Bush's two steps forward, one step back approach was masterly, if misleading.

An effective opposition party might have had something useful to say about all this, but too many Democrats simply wanted to push Iraq aside. Democrats complained that Bush promoted Iraq for political reasons—to underscore the Democratic divisions and uncertainties on foreign policy and bury other issues. But the very fact that this might be true underscored the Democrats' deeper problem. Why was it that national security issues inevitably favored the Republicans, even after eight years during which Bill Clinton, after some reluctance and foot-dragging in Bosnia, had shown a Democrat's willingness to use American power and American troops?

In an appropriately titled article, "War Torn," Heather Hurlburt, a former foreign policy aide in the Clinton administration, scored the "feckless, equivocal way in which the Democrats handled the debate" over Iraq.

"Democrats are in this position," she wrote in *The Washington Monthly* before the election, "precisely because we respond to matters of war politically, tactically. We worry about how to position ourselves so as not to look weak, rather than thinking through realistic, sensible Democratic principles on how and when to apply military force, and arguing particular cases, such as Iraq, from those principles."

Had the Democrats made a concerted push much earlier for a tough multilateral approach to Iraq—the approach Holbrooke had favored— the party could have claimed victory when Bush turned toward the United Nations. Instead, as Hurlburt wrote, "most hid behind 'tough questions' without offering a credible alternative." Why? Hurlburt's answer:

> There are a lot of reasons for this failure, including the long-time split within the party between hawks and doves. But we will never resolve that split, nor regain credibility with voters on national security, until we learn to think straight about war. And we will never learn to think straight about war until this generation of professional Democrats overcomes its ignorance of and indifference to military affairs.

In truth, there were many veterans of the Clinton administration who could and did think regularly about foreign and military affairs— Holbrooke was one of them and so, for that matter, was Hurlburt. Some Democrats in Congress cared passionately about foreign policy. But Hurlburt was right that when the Iraq debate was forced on the Democrats by Bush, many in the party's ranks—particularly its political consultants—simply wanted the issue to go away. It wouldn't.

V

Bush had every reason to believe that America's victory in Iraq would be the crowning achievement of his presidency and render him politically invulnerable. It was an easy initial victory, made all the more sweet for Bush and Defense Secretary Donald Rumsfeld by carping during the war about tactics and strategy—and by predictions of a long fight that did not immediately materialize. The Iraqi army gave up and dispersed. The critics of the war strategy had been wrong. Or so it appeared on May 1, 2003, when Bush flew in a military plane to the USS *Abraham Lincoln,* an aircraft carrier off the coast of California. Bush took control of the plane for part of the trip and emerged in a green flight suit, his helmet under his arm, exhilarated. "Really exciting," Bush told reporters. "I miss flying, I can tell you that."

Bush later changed into a business suit, but he was no less elated when he addressed the nation from the flight deck beneath a banner that read: MISSION ACCOMPLISHED. (Later, when the mission appeared to have been less than fully accomplished, Bush and White House aides insisted they had nothing to do with the sign.)

"The liberation of Iraq is a crucial advance in the campaign on terror," the president declared. "We have removed an ally of Al Qaeda and cut off a source of terrorist funding. And this much is certain: No terrorist network will gain weapons of mass destruction from the Iraqi regime, because the regime is no more."

In light of all the questions the administration would confront later, it's diverting to consider how the controversial statements Bush made—about Iraqi links to Al Qaeda and the regime's possession of weapons of mass destruction—seemed utterly uncontroversial at the time. And in retrospect, what seemed like a brilliantly media-savvy moment—the choreography of Bush's fly-in was compared to Ronald Reagan's very best photo ops—may have been a turning point. It was the moment when the administration's credibility first came into serious question.

Consider this report in *The New York Times* six days after Bush's trip: "The White House said today that President Bush traveled to the carrier

Abraham Lincoln last week on a small plane because he wanted to experience a landing the way carrier pilots do, not because the ship would be too far out to sea for Mr. Bush to arrive by helicopter, as his spokesman had originally maintained." The White House told a little fib about why Bush had donned that flight suit and arrived in a military plane. One can only imagine the uproar over "little lies" if President Al Gore had done the same thing.

The small flap was a sign of things to come and marked the beginning of an excruciating period for Bush. One by one, the administration's prewar claims about Iraq—its weapons capacity, its alleged nuclear capabilities, its links to Al Qaeda—came under searing examination. Once credibility is lost, it is hard to win back. Bush began losing it in the summer of 2003, at least among those who were not firmly in his corner.

There was, first, the controversy over the president's famous "sixteen words" in his January 2003 State of the Union address: "The British government has learned that Saddam Hussein recently sought significant quantities of uranium from Africa." In July, White House spokesman Ari Fleischer came right out and said the president should never have cited the British government's claim. CIA director George Tenet said he should have kept the words out of the speech. But he also told a Senate committee that his staff didn't even tell him that the questionable claim was in the address until after it was given.

Members of the administration were not on the same program. Led by Condoleezza Rice, the president's national security adviser, Bush's defenders insisted that what Bush had said was technically true because he was reporting only on what the British government had "learned." Which meant exactly what for Bush? That he was right all along? That Fleischer's statement immediately became inoperative? That the president believed British intelligence more than he believed his own CIA director?

The real story was that the administration knew perfectly well that the two arguments most likely to persuade Americans who had doubts about going to war were, first, that Saddam Hussein had some link to 9/11, and, second, that this dictator had nukes. The administration pushed the 9/11 connection as hard as it could, despite highly questionable evidence, and used the nuclear claim as an effective closing punch. Whatever works.

The administration's habit of treating arguments about national security as little more than maneuvers in a political campaign came back to bite hard. In the summer of 2003, the administration leaked the name—and blew the cover—of Valerie Plame Wilson, a CIA agent whose husband happened to be Joseph Wilson. He was the official enlisted by the CIA to test the claim that Iraq had sought nuclear material in Africa. Wilson debunked the claim publicly. The administration retaliated with the leak. And by the fall, Bush's White House found itself under investigation for violating national security statutes (written to get at leftists who outed agents) by revealing Plame's name.

Things got worse for the administration in late August when a terrorist truck bomb blew up the U.N. headquarters in Baghdad. The bomb exploded the pretensions of an arrogant strategy that assumed the United States could do nation-building on the cheap with little support from traditional allies, only a limited number of troops, and relatively modest expenditures to rebuild a shattered country. As the attacks continued to escalate, the nation debated whether the struggle in Iraq was beginning to resemble the war in Vietnam.

Perhaps even more disturbing than the administration's indifference to the truth or falsity of the various claims it made before the war was the fact that it seemed to believe its own propaganda.

In March 2003, shortly before the war began, *Meet the Press* moderator Tim Russert asked Dick Cheney: "If your analysis is not correct and we're not treated as liberators but as conquerors, and the Iraqis begin to resist, particularly in Baghdad, do you think the American people are prepared for a long, costly, bloody battle with significant American casualties?"

Cheney replied: "Well, I don't think it's likely to unfold that way, Tim, because I really do believe that we will be greeted as liberators."

The vice president said he knew this because he and the president had met with "various groups and individuals, people who have devoted their lives from the outside to trying to change things inside Iraq. . . . The read we get on the people of Iraq is there is no question but what they want to get rid of Saddam Hussein and they will welcome as liberators the United States when we come to do that."

Note the implications of those sentences: For its reading of the situation *inside* Iraq, the administration relied on people who spent their lives *outside* Iraq. The administration believed the outsiders because the outsiders, many of them associated with the Iraqi National Congress, said what the administration wanted to hear—and perhaps also because the administration had no clue as to how people inside Iraq might react.

It is astonishing in retrospect that Bush and his advisers never seemed to take seriously obvious alternative possibilities. Many Iraqis who were perfectly happy to have the United States rid their country of Saddam Hussein might want U.S. troops to leave quickly after the job was done. Many other Iraqis who could accept a longer American stay might become impatient when the wealthiest and most powerful country on earth failed to protect the streets, turn on the electricity, get the oil wells running and the economy moving, and prevent acts of terrorism.

Nor did the administration ever offer an explanation—let alone a well-deserved apology—for putting down General Eric K. Shinseki, the army's chief of staff before the war. Shinseki had told the Senate Foreign Relations Committee in early March that "something on the order of several hundred thousand soldiers" would be required to occupy a postwar Iraq.

Two days later, Deputy Defense Secretary Paul Wolfowitz described Shinseki's estimate as "way off the mark." Cheney was also dismissive. In his *Meet the Press* appearance, he insisted that "to suggest that we need several hundred thousand troops there after military operations cease, after the conflict ends, I don't think is accurate. I think that's an overstatement."

It became clear later that Shinseki knew what he was talking about.

The president only made matters worse with his statement on July 2, 2003, in response to a question about attackers targeting our troops. "Bring 'em on," Bush declared. "We've got the force necessary to deal with the security situation." They brought it on.

And when the president, on September 7, 2003, called for spending an additional $87 billion for military and reconstruction costs in Iraq, the nation was shocked. It should not have been shocking that occupying and rebuilding a nation shattered by war was an expensive proposition. Early on in the war debate, *New York Times* columnist Thomas Friedman—who supported the war—coined the phrase "if you break it, you own it" by way of warning that winning in Iraq would prove to be a very expensive proposition.

But the one place where the potential costs of the war and its aftermath were never acknowledged in advance was the White House. Before the war, the president and his lieutenants had tried to play down its price, or simply feigned ignorance. Asked by Tim Russert during that *Meet the Press* appearance whether the war might cost $100 billion, Cheney replied: "I can't say that, Tim." He would only say: "There are estimates out there." Note the denial of responsibility in that phrase "out there," as if the administration had no estimates of its own.

The entire debate leading up to the war was a travesty. The responsibility for the travesty lay first and primarily with the administration. But it also lay with Democrats who failed to be tough enough, early enough, to ask the questions that needed to be asked before the war started.*

---

*Because it's fair for readers to ask someone who is so critical of everyone else what he said at the time, I offer the following—a column I wrote published on February 18, 2003:

I have a terrible foreboding that when we look back on our debate over the impending war with Iraq, we will be disappointed in ourselves. We may end up starting a war without any real argument over what it will take to win the peace.

Like many Americans, I do not feel fully comfortable in either of the big camps lined up against each other over this war. Those of us who are doubters but not full-fledged opponents constitute, by a fair reading of the polls, about one-third of our fellow citizens.

We doubters cannot identify with those who see American power as a force for evil in the world, and we believe President Bush was right to increase pressure on Saddam Hussein to disarm. Many of us agree with British Prime Minister Tony Blair's statement over the weekend that, given the nature of the Iraqi regime, "ridding the world of Saddam would be an act of humanity."

But doubters do not share the confidence of so many of the war's supporters that victory

81

Still, facts are stubborn things. When weapons of mass destruction were not found, when the administration's claims before the war came to be seen as increasingly suspect, the public mood shifted. In the winter of Bush's discontent in 2004, *Time* magazine's cover headline marked another tipping point in his presidency: "Does Bush Have a Credibility Gap?" All that Bush had achieved politically after 9/11 began to crumble.

VI

Tom DeLay was in full cry at summer's end in 2003.

What initially set DeLay off was a statement by Senator Edward M. Kennedy on September 18 denouncing the Bush administration's policy in Iraq as "a fraud."

"There was no imminent threat," Kennedy said. "This was made up

---

will revolutionize the politics of the Middle East. We worry about the unintended consequences of military action and can't quite shake the hope that the very military buildup Bush has carried out creates opportunities to disarm and perhaps even unseat Hussein through means short of war.

My own doubts are rooted in the Bush administration's failure to prepare our country for the long commitment that will be required if this war is to achieve the results its supporters promise. We still don't know how the administration intends to handle the aftermath of what one hopes would be an American military victory. And it is not as obvious to me as it is to the war's supporters that this battle is the clear next step in our response to 9/11. It's hard to escape the feeling that those who always wanted to "finish" the last Gulf war by getting rid of Hussein are using the events of Sept. 11, 2001, as a rationale for doing what they wanted to do on Sept. 10.

Some of my doubts are, purely and simply, doubts about this administration. I find it astonishing that Bush and his lieutenants are not willing to offer a sober calculation of the long-term costs of this war, factor those costs into the nation's budget and ask Americans to pay the price. Instead, they would shuck off the costs to the next generation.

Their failure to count the costs can only make you wonder about how committed they are to what will be an arduous struggle to pacify and democratize Iraq. This is why it matters that we have allies, including, eventually, those obstreperous French and Germans. We are unlikely to want to do the job of rebuilding Iraq all by ourselves, or with the British alone.

in Texas, announced in January to the Republican leadership that the war was going to take place and was going to be good politically."

The comment, DeLay insisted, was an outrage. Democrats, he said, "have spewed more hateful rhetoric at President Bush than they ever did at Saddam Hussein.

"I call on all the vociferous Democrat critics"—here he listed two Democratic presidential candidates and, respectively, the Senate and House Democratic leaders—"from Kerry to Dean and from Daschle to [Nancy] Pelosi to have the courage to tell their hero Ted Kennedy that he went too far."

And, in what those politicians must have seen as a low blow, he added: "Are they leaders, or are they just liberal pundits?"

A year earlier, such an attack would have had Democrats cowering.

But the Democrats of late 2003 were a tougher and angrier bunch. "Tom DeLay is a bully," declared Senator John Kerry in defending his

---

God bless the Czechs and the Poles, the Portuguese, the Spanish, the Estonians and other Europeans standing with us. But it is unrealistic to think that these nations will be in a position to offer serious help, financial or military, in the postwar work of transforming Iraq.

It's easy to trash the French and the Germans. But the leaders of Germany and France are only following European public opinion. Even if you think that Jacques Chirac and Gerhard Schroeder are being opportunistic, you wonder how much the Bush administration created the opportunity they are exploiting by conditioning public opinion against us. Would we be in this fix—would millions of demonstrators have poured into European streets—if the Bush administration had not been so publicly indifferent to European views on issues ranging from global warming to the International Criminal Court?

Yet like so many of my fellow doubters, I find it hard to be a wholehearted supporter of the antiwar movement. Some in its ranks harbor reflexive anti-Israel sentiments that I find repellent, even though I am no supporter of Ariel Sharon. For all my misgivings about Bush, I find it absurd to call him a greater threat than Hussein, as some in the antiwar movement do.

By being a man of few doubts, Bush pushed a reluctant world into dealing with the dangers posed by Hussein. But that is an achievement Bush now threatens to undercut by being indifferent or dismissive toward those who lack his certainty. The danger is that he will fail to build the consensus, at home and abroad, to turn an American military victory into a genuine triumph for our national security and for democracy. More than he knows, he needs the doubters.

fellow Massachusetts Democrat. "He tried to bully Democrats in Texas and we're not going to accept his shrill partisan attacks or allow him to suggest that patriotism belongs to one political party."

And Kennedy came right back at DeLay with a recitation of the Democratic Catechism of Republican Outrages. "This is the same kind of response that the Republicans had for Max Cleland when they called him unpatriotic after he lost three limbs in Vietnam," Kennedy said. "It's the same kind of rhetoric from the Republicans that they had for Tom Daschle when he questioned the administration's policy."

The controversy over Kennedy's remarks continued for weeks. Columnist Charles Krauthammer argued in *The Washington Post* that "Kennedy's rant reflects the Democrats' blinding Bush hatred, and marks its passage from partisanship to pathology."

Not content with his initial salvo, DeLay extended his attack to all Democrats in a speech in late September at the Heritage Foundation. DeLay said that the party's current leaders lacked the "moral clarity" of John F. Kennedy and Franklin D. Roosevelt and were guilty of a "Blame America First mentality." He added: "Too many Democrats treat the war on terror as a political nuisance."

That DeLay stayed on the case reflected Republican worries that criticisms of Bush's Iraq policies were taking root with the public. DeLay gave his Heritage Foundation speech at a moment when the president was tumbling in the polls. Reaction to Bush's $87 billion request was negative. Nearly every day, the news from Iraq brought word of more bombings, assassinations, and deaths of American soldiers. DeLay could not change the facts, so he sought to silence the messengers. He failed. Even Democrats who distanced themselves from Kennedy's formulation defended his right to speak out—and their own right to probe and dissent.

This end-of-summer skirmish was the perfect bookend for the political phase—era turns out to be too strong a word—that had begun two years earlier on 9/11. Republicans played the patriotism card for political purposes once too often. Neither Democrats nor, it seemed, large parts of the public were listening. Bush went from being the most unifying leader since Dwight Eisenhower to one of the most divisive in the country's history.

In the process, Bush brought Democrats and progressives low—and then did them a large service. By using a national calamity for political purposes, he inspired anger all the way down to the Democratic grassroots and across the party's philosophical spectrum. He created a sense of unity and a sense of crisis. He mobilized what had been a somnolent political force. What conservatives saw as a moment when Democrats went off their rockers was—potentially, at least—a time when the party decided to fight and try to win.

But why did it take so long for Democrats to find their voices? Why was the party so hapless during most of 2002 and so easily rolled by Karl Rove's strategizing? It is to the problems of the Democrats that we turn next.

3. What's Wrong with the Democrats?

I don't think you ever kill any political party. Political parties
kill themselves, or are killed, not by the other political party
but by their failure to adapt to new circumstances. But do you
weaken a political party, either by turning what they see as
assets into liabilities, and/or by taking issues they consider to
be theirs, and raiding them? Absolutely!

Karl Rove, President George W. Bush's top political adviser,
quoted in *The New Yorker*

The Democratic Party lost its way because of its obsession with pointless
feuds, outdated strategies, and old arguments. Democrats complain regularly that Republicans fight unfairly, that they will say and do anything
to win. But Democrats forgot how to fight back. They didn't know what
they stood for, so they didn't know what they were fighting for.

Democrats have come to assume that their role is always to be out-
spent, outmaneuvered, and outfoxed. How, Democrats ask, can they possibly win when all three branches of government, vast financial resources,
conservative talk radio, and a rightward-drifting media are all arrayed
against them? Democrats fear defeat before it even happens.

Instead of framing new choices, Democrats run away from their old
commitments. Instead of reaching for greatness, they argue that they are

not as bad as everyone else thinks they are. The party that once galvanized a nation by declaring that there is nothing to fear but fear itself has become afraid—afraid of being too liberal, afraid of being weak on defense, afraid of being culturally permissive, afraid of being seen as apologizing for big government. Democrats are obsessed with telling people who they are not. As a result, no one knows who they are.

The Democrats' problem was described perfectly by Wendy Satterford, a fifty-year-old Democrat from San Diego who was interviewed by the *New York Times* in May 2003. "The Republicans have a clear view of what they want and are effective in promoting it," she said. "The Democrats don't have a clear vision. They seem afraid of the electorate and the apparent rising tide of conservatism. They don't seem to be able to speak out even for the middle-of-the-road things." Satterford was speaking for a large share of the country. The *New York Times*/CBS News poll in which she was a respondent found that while 53 percent of Americans said that Republicans had a clear vision of where to lead the country, only 40 percent said the same of Democrats.

The Democrats' problem was not about positioning, or the need to move farther left. As Satterford noted, Democrats couldn't even stand up for "middle-of-the-road things." Their problem was about picking the right fights and drawing the right lines. It was about having something to say about things that matter.

Each part of the Democratic Party regularly blames some other part of the party for what's wrong. The party's left accuses its center of selling out, of offering pale copies of Republican policies, of being unwilling to draw clear lines and fight urgent battles against social injustice and corporate power. The left sometimes accuses Bill Clinton of stealing the Republicans' clothes and creating an ill-fitting wardrobe. The party's center accuses the left of being out of touch, inattentive to national security, too devoted to "big government," and intent on pursuing anti-business policies that spell electoral doom in an entrepreneurial republic.

You can't seize the future if you're living in the past. Democrats were paralyzed by their eagerness to replay the same internal debates over and over again. Robust debate is good if it gets somewhere. But like the stereotypical old couple, bickering Democrats seemed to live for replays of old fights so that the memory of an ancient feud might make them feel young again.

For some Democrats, there is no way ever to forget the bitter battles between supporters of Eugene McCarthy and Robert Kennedy, the dueling anti-war candidates of 1968. For others, the anti-war movement's insistence on ruining Hubert Humphrey's chances that same year—and helping to elect Richard M. Nixon—is the unpardonable sin. George McGovern won the Democratic nomination as an anti-war candidate in 1972. That's more than three decades ago. Yet some Democrats insist that the party has never recovered from "McGovernism."

To this day, you can hear the resentments of those who were on opposite sides of Edward M. Kennedy's challenge to President Jimmy Carter in the 1980 Democratic primaries. The 1984 battle between Gary Hart and Walter Mondale left fewer footprints. But Hart's attacks on the "old arrangements" of the liberal old guard and Mondale's riposte against the "new ideas" candidate's lack of "beef" still resonate for some. You wonder occasionally if the Democratic Party is simply a Museum of Unforgotten Wars.

And all these battles get distilled in different ways when "New Democrats" square off against "Old Democrats"—or, as they'd prefer to be known, in the late Senator Paul Wellstone's memorable phrase that was picked up by Howard Dean, "the Democratic wing of the Democratic Party."

The party's hawkish wing accuses its doves of squandering the party's credentials on national security. In the debate leading up to the Iraq War, the hawks accused the doves of failing to understand the threat posed by Saddam Hussein. The doves accused the party's leadership of selling out to George W. Bush on an unnecessary, preemptive, and unilateral war and granting him a free hand to pursue dangerous dreams abroad. In the middle were Democrats prepared to wage war, but not without allies and not without United Nations support. They were forced to deal with the facts Bush created, under assault from both wings of their party, unable to locate a middle ground on which to stand. They were left homeless.

In 2003, Democrats largely united against Bush's outrageous, outsized tax cuts for the wealthy. But they could not agree on why doing so was so urgent. For some, the issue was fiscal responsibility and the need to stanch rising deficits. For others, the priority was to save the public sector, to keep Bush from depleting the federal treasury to such a degree that new initiatives in health care, child care, and education would become impossible for years to come. As a tactical matter, it was easy for both sides to agree that Bush's tax cuts were excessive, especially for the long term. But lacking a unity of purpose, Democrats could not make their case with the same forcefulness brought to the battle by Republicans for whom tax cuts are a unifying form of identity politics. And enough Democrats defected to hand Bush his tax victories.

Democrats themselves disagree about deficits. Many Democrats despise the balanced budget politics of the Clinton years. They argue that Clinton's refusal to use the 1990s surpluses for large public purposes left the party—and all that cash—vulnerable to Republican claims that surpluses should be returned to the taxpayers. The deficit hawks insist that the Clinton economic policy is the party's greatest legacy. The 1990s boom stands as testimony to the benefits of fiscal responsibility combined with careful expenditures—the Earned Income Tax Credit to boost the incomes of the working poor is the shining example. Despite the Clinton achievement, voters are confused as to whether the Democrats are the party of surpluses or deficits. Who is to blame except the Democrats themselves? In the meantime, Bush has increased the deficit at an unprecedented rate with the complicity of most of his party. Only a handful of brave Republican deficit hawks cried foul.

Health care has been a Democratic rallying cry since Harry Truman made universal coverage a revered party cause. Yet even on this cause, Democrats hack away at each other. So traumatized are Democrats over the failure of Bill and Hillary Clinton's health care plan that many in the party's leadership just assume that the words "national health insurance" are a curse. When Dick Gephardt offered a nearly universal health care proposal in the spring of 2002, he was attacked from the left and from the right. Joe Lieberman said he was entering the no-no-land of big government solutions. John Edwards said he was showering benefits on big corporations. God forbid that any Democrat would try to offer a big idea. It will be shot down within the party before Republicans even have to say a word. Later, of course, other Democrats offered their own, somewhat more modest health plans—potentially a positive sign, as we'll explore later.

The perfect model for defeat is what happened to the Democrats in the elections of 2002. The Democrats thought they could run against President Bush without actually running against him. They were wrong. They thought they could make the economy an issue without offering a coherent alternative to Bush's policies. They were wrong. They thought they could get their electoral base to turn out without explaining why it was urgent to stop Bush's program. They were wrong.

The result was an electoral catastrophe worse for Democrats than the 1994 Republican sweep. Then, at least, Democrats held the White House and could shape the political argument. After 2002, they had no power centers, no obvious leader. The 2002 election, close though it was, pointed to the weakness of the Democrats' small-bore approach to issues. As we have seen, the voters' verdict shattered the party's illusions that after 9/11, accommodation to Bush and reticence on national security were keys to success.

Democrats were complicit in the strategy pursued by White House political genius Karl Rove. By trying to work around Bush—and, in many states, by running as Bush supporters—Democrats did exactly what Bush needed. They helped keep his approval ratings high. As the conservative writer Daniel Casse put it in *Commentary* magazine, "the Democratic problem in 2002 was not just the failure to win a fight but the inability even to pick one." Bush's popularity turned out to be crucial to this outcome. With so many members of the opposition party repeatedly praising the president, voters saw no reason to doubt his virtues.

Swing voters didn't decide the 2002 election; voters in the Republican base did. Because of their affection for Bush and because they believed in their view of the world with such conviction, conservative Republicans swarmed the ballot boxes. As one Democrat put it mournfully, "They seem to believe more in their ideas than we do in ours."

The paradox of the election was that Democrats looked partisan— even as they were accommodating Bush. After Senator Paul Wellstone's tragic death in a plane crash, a memorial service held in his honor also became a memorial to his political views and a call for the election of Democrat Walter Mondale as his successor. In the final days before the election, attacking the "partisan Wellstone memorial service" became a Republican battle cry. Republicans, in the meantime, shrouded their own partisanship in the American flag.

Democratic political consultants argued for tactical campaigns. They thought they could win enough races on the edges—a little prescription drugs here, a little Social Security there. But tactics are no substitute for ideas or for courage.

Most Democrats believed that the Bush tax cuts were a disaster not only because they threatened fiscal chaos but also because they will deprive the government of revenue needed to solve urgent public problems. But too many Democrats were afraid to say that—until after the election.

Most Democrats believe that government regulation—to protect the environment and to curb business abuses—can be a good thing. But too many were afraid to say that.

Most Democrats worried that Bush's divided foreign policy team would needlessly alienate our allies and make the aftermath of a war in Iraq far more difficult than it had to be. But too many were afraid to say that.

George W. Bush used his standing after 9/11 to intimidate his opposition and to hide partisanship and ideology behind the determined face of national unity. Thus, while Bush was engaging in "fierce, relentless, highly effective partisanship"—the description came from conservative writer Jeff Bell shortly after the election in the conservative *Weekly Standard*—Democrats were bewildered. Forget left and right: they even missed chances to fight Bush hard on issues that could have united moderates and liberals.

Consider the Democrats' biggest missed opportunity. The polls made clear that while the public liked the president, it preferred a Congress that would check the more extreme enthusiasms of his party. To make this case required no sharp move leftward. It meant suggesting that on matters such as the environment, corporate abuses, workers' rights, and budget cuts, Democrats could be a powerful moderating force. The Democrats made some ads on this theme but didn't run them much and resisted nationalizing the election. They left that to Bush.

Similarly, Bush flailed Senate Democrats for blocking some of his judicial nominees. But not until after the election did Democrats move forcefully to make the counterargument: that it was in the interest of moderates as well as liberals to resist packing the judiciary with right-wingers. Making this case loudly and often could have united moderates and liberals.

On the homeland security issue, so effective for Bush as we have seen, the Democrats had two plausible responses: to capitulate to the president even at the risk of angering their union friends; or to go on the offensive.

They did neither.

Having stuck to the view that the rights of civil servants and union members deserved protection in a new Department of Homeland Security, the Democrats could have aggressively defended those unionized civil servants. Imagine news conferences featuring firefighters, police officers, and other public employees who are now national heroes. Were they unpatriotic for wanting some on-the-job protections? Instead, the Democrats moved to—well, to what other issue, exactly?—and let Bush wield his homeland security club.

Another reason for the Democrats' 2002 defeats: enormous last-minute corporate expenditures, especially from the pharmaceutical companies, on phony "issue ads" attacking Democratic candidates. Where was the outrage? More to the point, why didn't Democrats try harder to organize it? As Senator John McCain has shown, opposing the power of big special interests is good government and good politics with both moderates and liberals.

At least one Democratic candidate understood this. Shortly before his death, Minnesota's Paul Wellstone discovered that in the ten days before the election, he would face $1 million in television attack ads from a shadowy conservative group that did not disclose its contributors. Rather than just absorb the assault, Wellstone turned the campaign against him into an argument on behalf of everything he stood for. "I can tell you who these people are not," he shouted at a rally in northern Minnesota, two days before his death. "They do not represent firefighters. They do not represent teachers. They are not family farmers. They are not wage earners. They do not represent senior citizens." And on he went, listing group after group, concluding with a shout: "I can assure you: We will beat this crowd!"

There is no way of knowing for certain if Wellstone would have beaten that crowd, though the polling evidence suggested that he was in a good position to win reelection. What is clear is that by showing passion and relish for a fight on behalf of the constituencies he cared about, Wellstone used the attacks to prove that he stood for something. Wellstone was a staunch progressive, but his approach could easily have been deployed by moderate Democrats facing similar attacks. It required them only to have a sense of who they were, whom they were fighting for, and what they were fighting against.

The Democrats lost in 2002 because Bush—and Rove—were much tougher than they were, much smarter in the issues they chose. Republicans had passion and convictions. Republicans built a powerful network of fund-raisers, lobbyists, think tanks, consultants, talk show hosts, and grass-roots activists. They now have control of the federal government.

Democrats have to learn how to oppose, how to organize, and how to inspire. In 2002, they failed at all three.

II

The Democrats' timidity of recent years would seem to be a break from the intellectual effervescence that characterized the party in the years leading up to Bill Clinton's victory in 1992. Clinton developed a formula that appeared to get Democrats out from under the failures and divisions that frustrated the party in the 1970s and 1980s. He understood that the Democratic Party could not move forward unless both its wings flew in tandem. Cut off one wing and the old bird will crash into a tree every time. With a careful mix of populism and centrism, with bows to both soccer moms and gays, with balanced budgets and new programs for the poor, Clinton seemed to square the Democratic circle. He was the essential man all parts of the party would support or, at least, tolerate—sometimes with huge enthusiasm, sometimes with exasperation. He was a New Democrat proposing a Third Way.

The Third Way. Those three words arouse instant suspicion. Skeptics asked whether the Third Way was a set of real ideas or an advertising slogan. Was it a serious effort to create a new form of progressive politics, or was it, instead, a capitulation to the right, the final triumph of Ronald Reagan and Margaret Thatcher?

Ultimately, the critics asked whether the Third Way was simply a ploy that shrewd politicians such as Clinton and Britain's Tony Blair could use to distinguish themselves from some terrible "them" without ever having to define who "we" are.

The Third Way was defined largely in negative terms. It was not "the old left" or "the new right." It was not about unlimited confidence in the state, and it was not about unlimited confidence in the market.

As common sense goes, it's a good formula destined to be the starting point of any progressive revival. The electorates in most of the wealthy democracies have doubts about *both* the old left and the new right. They do not fully trust either the government or the unfettered market.

Third Way politics was also a relief for electorates that had been exhausted by ideological politics, first in the 1960s and again in the 1980s.

Voters seemed to prefer cultural peace to culture wars. They identified neither with the revolutionaries of the 1960s nor with the conservative ideologues of the 1980s. Voters sought to make peace with both decades. If not everyone was, as David Brooks cleverly suggested, a "bourgeois bohemian," most Americans created their own blend of responses to the claims of tradition and modernity—or, as some called it, postmodernity. Few Americans played a single role. NRA members were also union members. Religious Americans also loved rock 'n' roll. Feminists were also mothers of both sons and daughters. Investors were also wage earners. Parents were also the children of someone, simultaneously worried about how their kids would fare in the future and how their mothers and fathers would fare in retirement. All citizens worried about more than a single problem, and most tired of being pigeon-holed.

Third Way politics responded to the exhaustion of the old formulas by promising to replace ideological enthusiasms with problem solving. Politicians who spoke of the practical concerns of families—how to balance responsibilities at home and at work, how to improve schools, how to pay for college—came to be preferred over those who moralized about "family values." Politicians who spoke of creating jobs seemed more effective than those who offered free market bromides. Politicians who spoke of reforming government seemed more in touch than those who reflexively attacked government or defended it. In a nation of blended values, politicians who preferred "both/and" were more appealing than those who insisted upon "either/or." The Third Way was most definitely "both/and" politics.

But the Third Way has proven better as a critique of the past than as a road map to the future. Oddly, while Third Way parties and politicians relentlessly use words such as "reform" and "new," they quickly come to be seen as agents of the status quo. They are unwilling to do much to expand government *or* to cut it back in serious ways. Third Wayers support capitalism more or less as it is, though with certain reservations. They worry that even their own reforms might upset it. They warn of the dangers of deregulation, but fear too much new regulation.

Third Wayers face a constant struggle to mobilize their core constituencies. Their political base often seeks more change than the Third Way can offer. This is a politics well suited for shedding politically damaging baggage. It is not a politics that creates excitement or inspires commitment. It is, as Philip Collins of the London-based Social Market Foundation put it, a "politics without a lodestar."

Britain's old Labor Party, Collins argued, "was so cumbersome because it was so ideologically glued together." But New Labor—and by extension, the Clinton project in the United States—had its own problems. Instead of the old ideological purity, "we have a managerial state which does what works, in an endless series of partnerships with market and third sector organizations. But works to do what exactly?"

Collins insisted that Blair and the moderate left elsewhere did have a vision. It combined a yearning for high rates of achievement and social mobility with strong guarantees of help for those stuck at the bottom of the economy. The goal, as Collins put it, was "an open, socially mobile society with a high floor of social provision."

This is, in many ways, an attractive vision, combining achievement with solidarity. But it was not a vision that sent people marching in the streets. "Meritocracy," as Collins called his system, has its problems. As it is, parties of the moderate left—Democrats included—faced the prospect of being politically prudent folk who made difficult decisions and restored fiscal responsibility, only to see their opponents hijack the public's yearning for a vision with promises of low taxes and a small government utopia. That's not where the Third Way was supposed to lead.

It's entirely true, of course, that the Democrats had real image problems—witness their three presidential losses in the 1980s. Without strategic corrections and a little blurring of the past, they never would have won the White House in 1992 or 1996, or won the popular vote in 2000. There is no need in principle for Third Way politics to be empty of content or devoid of conviction. A new progressive politics will start with the Third Way, but cannot end there.

For in practice, Democrats have spent too much time running away from ghosts. No, the Democrats would say, we're not tax-and-spend liberals, we're not weak on defense, we're not soft on crime, we're not feckless on family values.

The costs of fuzziness have become plain in the face of a Bush White House determined to win, determined to bull ahead with one tax cut after another, determined to undo the progressive achievements of the previous century. As the poet suggested, passionate intensity defeats the lack of all conviction almost every time.

III

If the Democrats are in so much trouble, if they seem so hapless and fearful, why should anyone care? If the forces of history are moving against them, what's the point of resisting?

The American electorate has not given up on the Democratic Party. Perhaps despite themselves, Democrats can claim allegiance of at least a third of the electorate and typically win support from close to half the voters. That the Democrats should so often behave as losers is thus surprising and disappointing. Even in the 2000 election that brought Bush to power, Democrats won a plurality of the votes, and it took the intervention of the U.S. Supreme Court to put Bush in the White House. In the 2004 presidential primaries, Democrats even showed signs of moving toward a common vision, well captured by John Edwards. He spoke of a choice between "two Americas"—one for the privileged and one for the "rest of us." Edwards's well-tempered populism and his call for "one America" of shared opportunity offered Democrats a Reaganesque rhetoric combining a critique of the status quo with an optimistic alternative.

In principle, moreover, Democrats have achievements to call their own. Bill Clinton's economy remains a powerful legacy, and all the more so at moments of economic sluggishness. Even in 2002, the Democrats lost the overall vote only narrowly. With a switch of just 37,000 votes in the right places, they would have retained control of the Senate. At the same time, the Democrats were gaining back governorships they had lost in the 1994 Republican sweep. In 2002, they returned to power in important battlegrounds, including Pennsylvania, Michigan, Illinois, and Wisconsin. Their weakness in the South was offset by gains in the Northwest and Middle West.

There is also a strong case that demographic forces are moving the Democrats' way. In their brilliant if ill-timed 2002 book, *The Emerging Democratic Majority*, John Judis and Ruy Teixeira made a persuasive case that while core Republican groups were on the decline as a percentage of the electorate, Democratic-leaning constituencies were growing in strength.

Not only was the share of non-white minorities—Latinos especially—rising in the electorate; the class structure itself was changing in the Democrats' favor. Judis and Teixeira traced the rise of what they called "ideopolises," metropolitan areas dominated by the new knowledge and information industries. Ideopolis voters—including not only the remnants of the Democrats' old working class and minority base but also upper-middle-class professionals—were becoming Democrats. Moderate to liberal in their views on social and cultural issues, strongly environmentalist, opposed to racism and gender discrimination, these voters steadily turned away from a Republican Party that was becoming ever more conservative. If Republicans were losing their hold on the professional classes, once a GOP bastion, then Republicans, not Democrats, were the party facing long-term decline. The Judis-Teixeira thesis was persuasive enough that conservative columnist George Will wrote a stern essay urging his party to take it seriously.

In all the talk of political realignment during the Reagan years and the brief heyday of Newt Gingrich's revolution, most of the attention had focused on the realignment of the South toward the Republican Party. But the emerging Democratic majority idea called attention to the counterrealignment toward the Democrats that began taking shape in the 1990s in suburban counties of the Northeast, the Midwest, and the West Coast. It was a shift noticed early by *Washington Post* political writer Dan Balz. As the Republican Party came to be dominated by the personalities and ideas of the South, non-southerners started moving the Democrats' way.

But if a Democratic majority was so inevitable, how can the defeat of 2002 and the current crisis in the party be explained? Had the events of 9/11 transformed the nation's political terrain? Would war and terrorism permanently disrupt the trends of the 1990s?

In an analysis written in 2003, Ruy Teixeira, perhaps not surprisingly, insisted that one election does not make (or break) a trend. "Particular elections depend on a host of contingencies—from the quality of candidates to the money at their disposal to outside events that help one party much more than the other, as in the 2002 election," Teixeira wrote. "But political trends are the product of deeper shifts within the society and the economy."

The "primary cause" of the Democrats' defeat, Teixeira acknowledged, was the rise of the national security issue, "sparked by the Iraq debate." This, he said, "mobilized Republicans, especially conservative whites in rural and exurban areas," which in turn "moved a number of close elections into the Republican column." "Democratic demobilization," he added, "due to an anemic Democratic campaign and program was also clearly a factor."

But in defending his and Judis's original claims, Teixeira noted that the Republican victory was built on a mobilization of the white vote and traditionally Republican constituencies, *not* on large-scale defections from the rising Democratic groups. "There is very little evidence," he argued, "that Republicans made headway among key Democratic groups like Hispanics."

The Judis-Teixeira thesis was strongly challenged by Matthew Dowd, President Bush's chief polling analyst. Importantly, Dowd stressed not the makeup of the overall population but the makeup of the actual electorate. "It seems obvious," he said, "but the key to understanding partisan voting trends and political dynamics is looking at election returns and who actually votes and how they voted. Analysis should not be about who might possibly vote, rather it should focus on what actually happens on Election Day."

Dowd's distinction is important. It is all well and good to say that Democratic-leaning demographic groups are growing as a proportion of the *potential* electorate. But if Republicans continue to loom large in the *actual* electorate, the Republicans will win elections. Passion, commitment, and belief matter. If they are present on one side of the partisan divide and absent on the other, the side that commands them will win.

It's true that Republicans in 2002 copied Democratic successes in 1998 and 2000 in mobilizing voters. Karl Rove and the Republicans were alarmed that Democrats, through the activism of organized labor, civil rights groups, and environmentalists, outperformed the GOP in bringing their own voters to the polls. Florida was in play in 2000 for many reasons but one of the decisive factors was a wave of African-American voting, including the appearance of substantial numbers of new voters at the polling stations on Al Gore's behalf. Surprised by Gore's showing, Republicans invested heavily in their own turnout campaign in 2002. Both the financial and organizational resources the party brought to bear increased Republican participation. So did passion, commitment, and belief.

Republicans also took seriously the threat that the rise of new demographic groups posed to their hopes for long-term dominance. Bush and the national party laid heavy stress on courting Latino voters. They insisted that candidates who received financial support from the national party invest in Latino media. In the California recall in October 2003, Arnold Schwarzenegger showed that in a state where Latinos were more hostile to Republicans than almost anywhere else, a Republican candidate, under the right circumstances and with the right campaign, could win a decent share of the Latino vote. And understanding the benefit to the Democrats from "soccer moms" in the 1990s, Republicans hoped that "security moms"—essentially the same women, this time motivated by fear of terrorism and confidence in Bush—might begin moving their way. They hoped, as well, that upper-middle-class professionals who had drifted Democratic on social issues in the 1990s might drift back to the Republicans in gratitude for the substantial tax cuts Bush threw their way.

The demographic wars will continue well beyond the Bush administration. But whether or not the Democrats are destined to prosper in the near future, the Bush administration gave the country very good reason to care about the Democrats' viability as a forceful opposition. The very aggressiveness of the Bush agenda made it urgent that a cohesive political force offer resistance, and alternatives.

Democrats have had difficulty offering those alternatives in the current political climate. The Clinton years, so promising in many respects, galvanized the right in ways few anticipated. A bitterness and anger among conservatives created a wave of new institutions and a style of attack politics not seen since the McCarthy era. The media, under relentless pressure from conservatives, shifted to the right, and so—even more so—did the new town hall of national politics, cable television. Clinton united his party in his own defense during the Monica Lewinsky scandal, but he also energized the right and alienated some of his own supporters. Both Clinton and Gore could plausibly blame each other for an election result that gave the Supreme Court its chance to pick the president. But the very language of politics—a language to which Democrats have largely capitulated—has shifted to the right, creating new barriers to progressive arguments. All this affected the world of Democratic political consultants. They were paid to be realists. But their realism was conditioned by forces working against their own candidates, causes, and interests.

4. Talking the Other Guy's Talk

Why Democrats Are Afraid of Their Own Principles

> Hell, make 'em cry, or make 'em laugh, make 'em think
> you're their weak and erring pal, or make 'em think you're
> God-Almighty. . . . Tell 'em anything. But for Sweet Jesus'
> sake don't try to improve their minds.
>
> Robert Penn Warren, *All the King's Men*

> If thought corrupts language, language also corrupts thought.
>
> George Orwell, in "Politics and the English Language"

Opposition is almost always underrated in high-minded assessments of politics. Oppositionists inevitably face the question: "Where are your constructive alternatives?" In the mid-1960s, when Republicans were in the minority and beleaguered, their leaders felt compelled to speak of Constructive Republican Alternative Policies. The word "policies" got dropped when some shrewd adviser realized the acronym would not do.

In fact, the first duty of an opposition is to oppose. The first and best argument for changing leaders and political direction is that there is something defective in the status quo. Bipartisanship is certainly honorable in the right cause. It is dishonorable when it serves as a way of dressing up extreme and partisan policies in the false colors of moderation. Honest opposition is always better than timid capitulation.

But if anger, properly directed, can be politically useful and even necessary, it cannot, all by itself, create a political movement or inspire a country. As Todd Gitlin put it—he was talking about the dangers of anti-Americanism—"You can fall in love with your outrage."

The Democratic failures over the last four years cannot be explained simply by Bush's shrewdness or because of September 11. Democrats also failed because, since the 1970s, they—and, by extension, liberals and progressives—have gone on the intellectual defensive. They have so internalized the attacks of their opponents that their first response is to seek ways of fending off criticism (sometimes before it's even made) rather than to propose moving forward. Being a Democrat has come to mean reciting a catechism of "I'm not's," as in, "I'm not a big spender," "I'm not a big taxer," "I'm not against the family," "I'm not against a strong defense"—and on and on and on.

A team that stays on defense can't score and a party that thinks first of defense cannot inspire.

This is not to say that the rounds of self-criticism the party has undergone in the last three decades were useless or unnecessary. Having engaged in some of it myself—the first third of my book *Why Americans Hate Politics* was devoted to the shortcoming of liberals and Democrats since the 1960s—I am in no position to say that, and would, in any event, assert the opposite. The self-critical period was essential to the rebuilding that culminated in the results of the presidential elections of 1992 and 1996. In their era of dominance after the triumph of the New Deal, liberals did become arrogant. To understand how overpowering liberalism once was, it is always important to recall the words of Lionel Trilling, a discerning intellectual who was, in fact, a self-critical liberal. "In the United States at this time, liberalism is not only the dominant, but even the sole intellectual tradition," Trilling wrote in *The Liberal Imagination*. "For it is a plain fact that nowadays, there are no conservative or reactionary ideas in general circulation." Trilling wrote in 1954, and his view prevailed long afterward. Liberals did not take the rising conservative movement seriously until much too late.

The catalogue of liberal and Democratic failures, both real and alleged, is so well known as to be shopworn. There is no need to belabor them here—and, in any event, readers can tune in to any right-wing talk show on any day, anywhere, to hear the old list trotted out and applied to today's news.

But there is a lesson in that: the arrogance that once characterized liberalism now characterizes conservatism. Liberals may now fail from too much self-doubt, but conservatives allow themselves too little. Republicans once felt they were required to adjust and respond to the dominant liberal ethos of the New Deal heyday. Now, Democrats and even liberals feel required to accommodate to the demands of a conservative era.

II

The most subtle yet most important effect of the politics of accommodation is a shift in the nation's political language to the right. It is hard to express your own beliefs if you are forced to speak in the tongue of your opponents. Arguments are lost before they begin because the terms of debate are skewed in advance. That is the position in which Democrats, liberals, and even moderates now find themselves.

One telltale sign of the shift is the extent to which the language of the economic marketplace now dominates the political discussion. We are at a point where any action that might seem good or wise on other grounds must nonetheless be defended in the market's terms. The tongue-in-cheek comment of Ann Lewis, a veteran of Democratic campaigns and administrations, is exceptionally revealing: "We used to call for immunizing little children against disease. Now we call it an investment in human capital."

Distorting language in this way—that was Lewis's point—concedes what should not be conceded: that the market represents the one and only proper measure of a public action. As the columnist and economics writer Robert Kuttner has argued, the idea that everything should *not* be for sale reflects a deep popular wisdom. Immunizing little children is, indeed, a wise investment in "human capital." But it would be a good idea whether a careful market analysis justified its economic value or not. We don't measure the moral rights of children on the same basis as we might calculate the value of a stock or the purchase price of a car.

Despite the explorations of certain market economists on the subjects of love, child rearing, and the allegedly self-serving aspects of altruism, we could all produce our own catalogues of areas where the moral sense drives us to resist the calculus of the marketplace. Where public policy is concerned, consider the imperatives of strengthening family life, educating the next generation, and reducing suffering and need among the elderly, the sick, and others who are vulnerable. All are things worth doing whether or not some economist tells us they'll pay off. We do them because our consciences tell us they are right.

It's entirely true that acts on behalf of the public good are also helpful—even essential—to the proper functioning of the market. Universal education has certainly proven its worth and promoted economic growth. So has a system of free labor. But if a radical economist put forth airtight arguments that the economy would grow faster if children went to work at age eight or that the buying and selling of human beings would produce a more efficient labor market, would we not reject these proposals out of hand despite his findings? Allowing narrow economic arguments an unassailable place in the political realm undermines moral claims rooted in any aspirations that defy economic calculation.

These shifts in language are self-reinforcing. Appeals to moral arguments are made to seem "soft"—an important word that will come up again—when compared with the supposedly hardheaded assessments of the market. As a result, advocates of a particular moral course gradually stop making moral arguments at all. Or they make them apologetically. "Well, uh, yes, I think it's right to help the poor, but forget that: just think of all that lost productivity if we don't help the poor get more skills." Consider the concession that has just been made: if it could be shown with reasonable certainty that helping the poor does little for productivity—or promotes productivity less than, say, doubling education spending on rich kids—the case is lost.

It turns out that it's not "softheaded" to make moral arguments. What is soft—and also timid and ineffectual—is to be so fearful of *looking* soft as to abandon the strongest arguments one can make and instead make whatever claims are in fashion at any given time. This has happened again and again. As liberals and progressives lost faith in their own moral compass, they turned to the standards of their opponents.

The reluctance of liberals and progressives to make arguments on straightforwardly moral grounds has the corrosive effect of ceding *all* moral argument to the right. Liberals and Democrats, center and left, are unwilling to turn to the traditional sources of moral guidance—including religious traditions. By default, they leave the impression that tradition and religion always point rightward. The public domain of "moral" talk is narrowed, usually to the personal and the sexual. But morality speaks to the social as well as the personal. The social, in turn, affects the personal. Lectures about "family values" can be valuable; sometimes they're even necessary. But support for families, especially in a society in which so many mothers and fathers both work outside the home, requires more than talk. How society organizes pay, leave time, health care, and child care powerfully affects the ability of families to cope and stay together. These questions implicate morality no less than do discussions of sex, adultery, abortion, divorce, and homosexuality. Yet if someone says that he or she is going to talk about "morality," most people these days are certain they're about to hear a commentary on sex. The practical questions that face parents, spouses, and children every day about work, the quality of the schools, and putting food on the table are every bit as "moral." But we rarely think of them that way.

In recent years, religious voices have been raised on behalf of the poor and the necessity of social justice. Groups such as Call to Renewal have rallied religious liberals, moderates, and even conservatives across the lines of faith and denomination to the moral imperative to lift up the poor. Many of these groups expressed sympathy for Bush's faith-based initiative and clearly shared certain values with the president.

That made it all the more powerful when some thirty religious leaders, led by the Reverend Jim Wallis, sent a letter to Bush in June 2003 protesting his policies toward the poor. The signers noted that they had supported his faith-based initiative "from the beginning of the administration," and had also sympathized with "the proposals of your administration to strengthen marriage and family as effective antipoverty measures." But after noting the president's kind words for "the good people" in community groups that help the poor, the signers offered these sobering thoughts: "Mr. President, 'the good people' who provide such services are feeling overwhelmed by increasing need and diminished resources. And many are feeling betrayed. The lack of consistent, coherent and integrated domestic policy that benefits low-income people makes our continued support for your faith-based initiative increasingly untenable. Mr. President, the poor are suffering, and without serious changes in the policies of your administration, they will suffer more."

The energy and commitment of such progressive religious people rarely receive the attention they deserve. When the institutions of the mass media bring on "religious voices," their reflex is to talk with representatives of the Religious Right. The assumption is that religion lives on the right. This ignores the majority of religious people who are moderate or liberal in their political views. The African-American church is rarely dealt with as a spiritual entity. African-American preachers are typically dealt with as "civil rights leaders," which leaves aside the fact that their views on social and racial justice are rooted in the scriptures and in commitments that are just as "religious" and "moral" as the views of conservative religious leaders.

The problem here can certainly be blamed on the existence of media stereotypes. Oddly, the very "secularism" that the right condemns in the media actually leads to the marginalization of *liberal* religious voices. The secularist usually assumes that religion cannot be progressive. Therefore, "religious" must mean "conservative."

But these media stereotypes also point to weaknesses in liberalism and in the Democratic Party. The assumption that religion lives on the right cuts progressives off from many of their most vital traditions: the anti-slavery and civil rights movements; the turn-of-the-century settlement houses; the neighborhood-based community organizing that so often grew out of the churches; and more than a century's worth of social justice activism on the part of priests and rabbis, ministers, nuns, and imams. The fear of moral talk among liberals and Democrats and their acquiescence to the language of materialism and the market are an implicit, if unintended, concession that the progressive agenda lacks a moral core and a moral basis.

Even to make arguments critical of the market of the sort I just offered is seen as risky. After all, has not the market proven itself to be an efficient creator of wealth and a shrewd allocator of resources? Doesn't the death of communism prove that capitalism is the only system that works? Surely someone who raises any questions about the market runs the danger of being accused of dangerous radicalism. Why take that chance?

The paradox is that it's precisely because the market has triumphed that it is now in such need of serious criticism. Because no one with any likelihood of taking power wants to upend capitalism, criticisms of the system are both as safe as ever—and more urgent. What needs to be opposed is not the market itself, but claims that the market can do things that it can't.

As the thoughtful moderate writer Matthew Miller has pointed out, even though the economy grew by 40 percent in the decade between 1992 and 2002, the persistence of deep social problems proved that economic growth is not an "elixir."

"How can it be," Miller wrote, "when even after this boom, we have 40 million people without health insurance, 15 million family members of full-time workers in poverty and schools that are as desperate as ever." Miller is no enemy of markets. On the contrary, he suggests that the most effective programs may well be those based on "market friendly" approaches. But he insists that even market friendly programs require government action, government spending, and government support.

Why can't the market alone solve the problems that it leaves behind? On this question, oddly, the market's critics have more faith in its capacities than the market's apologists. Because the market is efficient, it can be assumed that if there is money to be made solving any given problem, the market will solve it. No one is talking about the "problem" of a shortage of automobiles or software or hotel rooms. The market does just fine providing such things to all who can pay for them—and provides these goods at different prices and different levels of quality.

But if there is no reasonable expectation of profit to be earned from selling health insurance to poor Americans who cannot afford the premiums, market participants will move on to areas where they *can* make money—for example, by selling health insurance to the healthy and the wealthy. To deny this is to deny the very genius of capitalism: it is very good at measuring the potential for profit. It is absurd to ask capitalism to do things that it can't—a conclusion most democratic countries, including our own, reached long ago.

I stress the importance of the dominance of market language because market talk increasingly crowds out so many other kinds of talk. One can notice this in the proliferation of cable television programs devoted to business. There is nothing inherently wrong with such programs, some of which I enjoy myself. But their multiplication constitutes a moral choice. It not only sends the message that the primary business of America is business but also that the language and logic of business is superior to other languages and other forms of logic. Given the priority that the currently dominant form of conservatism places on leaving the market as free as possible from regulation and taxation, allowing market logic to penetrate all corners of the political debate leaves those who would challenge the status quo at an overwhelming disadvantage.

The tentativeness of Democrats and liberals can be traced to their increasing reluctance to challenge market language. An alternative language and logic would insist that markets are valuable but insufficient, that market values are not the *only* values. This alternative would assert that free societies, including free markets, thrive only when they are supported by strong communities and vibrant public institutions.

Surely that is one of the lessons of the recent financial scandals. Even the market depends on the idea that there is such a thing as the public good. Markets require the enforcement of honesty and openness—or, in the currently popular word, transparency. Ultimately, as the philosopher Francis Fukuyama has argued, they depend upon trust, upon "the social virtues" behind "the creation of prosperity." And trust is built only when actors in the marketplace know they are dealing with others whose values include not only the expected desire for material gain but also virtues that existed long before capitalism became dominant. These include simple but essential virtues such as honesty, decency, and a concern for one's good name. If such virtues do not temper the market's natural "animal spirits," the human spirit is overwhelmed, and markets fail.

One of the striking aspects of Bush era conservatism, as William Greider has noted, is the extent to which it is an effort to move *backward*. It is an attempt to weaken or obliterate the legacies of the Fair Deal, the New Deal, and the Progressive Era and take the country to something closer to the unconstrained capitalism of the late nineteenth century.

Consider the historian Richard Hofstadter's description of that earlier era in his classic book *The American Political Tradition:*

> There is no other period in the nation's history when politics seems so completely dwarfed by economic changes, none in which the life of the country rests so completely in the hands of the industrial entrepreneur. The industrialists of the Gilded Age were . . . men of heroic audacity and magnificent exploitative talents—shrewd, energetic, aggressive, rapacious, domineering, insatiable. They directed the proliferation of the country's wealth, they seized its opportunities, they managed its corruption, and from them the era took its tone and color.

Change the "industrial" references to "high tech" and Hofstadter's description of the late nineteenth century sounds like a brilliant evocation of our own time. Read the great historian's passage with the Enron scandal in mind. Is a single word out of place? The period Hofstadter describes was followed by the Progressive Era, when Americans reacted against the power of "rapacious, domineering, insatiable" capitalism and pushed the country toward a more reasonable version of the system.

Hofstadter accepted that the big capitalists of the earlier era were brilliant—"shrewd, energetic, aggressive"—just as we accept that the capitalists of our age are no slouches. But if our forebears came to understand that something was terribly wrong with the sharp guys, so do we. Until the last few years, those who questioned the brilliance of the people who ran Enron or various profit-free high-tech companies were often met with the response: "You just don't get it." It turned out that the people who supposedly didn't get it were posing questions that needed to be asked.

The era that's ending—or should—saw regulators as nothing but meddlers getting in the way of genius. But capitalism cannot work without regulation, which is simply a fancy word for rules and laws. Powerful people will often take advantage of their muscle unless someone—like it or not, that someone usually works for the government—keeps an eye on them.

Let's pick an extreme example of why the "self-regulating" capacity of the market is insufficient. Imagine that many people die because a fast-food chain sells tainted hamburgers. Word would, indeed, get out. Customers would stop eating the hamburgers. The market would eventually pummel the company's stock.

But if the market "worked" in this little tale, it surely didn't work for the people who ate the bad burgers. Does anyone think that the market's "genius" in punishing the company *eventually* means we can repeal the Pure Food and Drug Act? Are not both entrepreneurs and consumers better off because they can rely on the rules to guarantee that the hamburger the chain buys is safe? And when problems do arise—*E coli,* mad cow disease—isn't the market rendered *more* efficient when regulators act with dispatch to restore the supply of safe meat?

In Enron's case, its fall simply cannot be used to prove that the market worked when so much avoidable damage was done before the market acted. For a very long time, we've assumed that the fundamental conflict in capitalism was between owners and workers. Enron proves that the real conflict is between *insiders* and *outsiders.* The losers in the Enron case were stockholders *and* employees. This suggests a new form of politics both inside corporations and in the country as a whole.

"It used to be said that because so many people had 401(k)s, you couldn't do class politics anymore," says David Dreyer, a former Treasury Department official and Democratic activist. "Now, with Enron, because so many people have 401(k)s, you *can* do class politics."

This new class politics between insiders and outsiders is good for capitalism. It insists that corruption and insiderism distort both the market and politics. It asserts, in Hofstadter's terms, that when democratic and deliberative politics are overwhelmed by powerful economic actors, we are in danger of forgetting the value of prudent rules and regulations enforced by an honest government.

In the modern corporation, enormous power has been vested in top executives. These insiders, when supported by pliant boards of directors, can reap benefits through staggering salaries and extravagant stock option plans. The old assumptions were: (1) All the benefits heaped on top management would benefit stockholders; and (2) pushing CEOs to do whatever it took to produce profits in the next quarter would benefit shareholders and employees in the long run. After Enron, it can never again be taken for granted that big benefits for people at the top of companies are consistently in the interest of shareholders. Enron's manic efforts to hide losses to keep pushing up stock prices were harmful to the interests of everyone except the insiders. Might this mean that the era of the swaggering capitalist is over?

The biggest signal of a change in the culture is the extent to which capitalism's strongest defenders have begun to express doubts about how the current corporate system works. Few publications are more committed to capitalism than the London-based *Economist*. Yet in the fall of 2003, it ran a cover story on "The Problem with Executive Pay."

"For many," the magazine maintained, "top bosses are not the toughest or most talented people in business, just the greediest." This decidedly non-Marxist publication continued:

What is now causing the most indignation, in Europe as well as in America, are "golden parachutes" and other payments which reward bosses even when they fail. Not only does it seem that bosses are being fed even bigger carrots, but also that if the stick is finally applied to their backside, they walk away with yet another sackful of carrots to cushion the blow. Bugs Bunny couldn't ask for more.

The highest-profile cases of excessive pay, unfortunately, are not isolated exceptions. . . . In 1980, the average pay for CEO's of America's biggest companies was about 40 times that of the average production worker. In 1990, it was about 85 times. Now this ratio is thought to be about 400. Profits of big firms fell last year and shares are still down on their record high, but the average remuneration of America's companies rose by over 6%.

If such friends of the market as the editors of *The Economist* are willing to challenge its failures and excesses, surely Democrats (and Republicans who claim to be progressive) should lose some of their fear. They might then stop capitulating to a language and a logic in which they do not really believe.

True to its own beliefs, *The Economist* suggested that shareholders rather than government should challenge excessive executive pay. Shareholders should certainly be empowered to act—and it needs to be said that the rules under which they exercise their power are set by government regulations. Consider what was the country's first response to the corporate scandals. It was the response of both parties: they turned to government. Congress enacted new rules to prevent abuses. State regulators such as New York attorney general Eliot Spitzer stepped in to enforce the old rules. Big government is said to be terrible for capitalism—until the moment when government is called in to save it.

III

This points to the second large shift in the language of politics. The assumption that pervades political discourse is a view that government is, at best, a necessary evil, a lumbering, inefficient giant that breaks more things than it builds.

Just examine the popular press: the term "government waste" is ubiquitous. We hear far less about "economic waste" or "corporate waste."

Critics of government say there is no need to talk about private waste because the market always punishes it. But that is not true. If a company is badly mismanaged, its stock price might collapse, and the company might well go out of business. But the market itself does not measure or account for the human costs of this failure—the lives disrupted and sometimes shattered by unemployment, the communities that undergo great distress and sometimes die when a large employer goes bust. The costs of such failures are typically covered by government through unemployment insurance, welfare, job training, and assistance to troubled communities. The system seems to be built on privatizing profits and socializing losses. Taxpayers pick up the costs of private failure; but that does not protect the politicians who run governments from being attacked whenever they raise taxes to pay the bills.

Here again, Democrats and liberals have become afraid to say what they really believe. They believe in affirmative government. But they claim to be against "big government." They believe that taxation to achieve public purposes is in the public interest, and they believe in progressive taxes that ask the wealthiest—who benefit the most from society and, in the end, from government itself—to bear a larger share of the burden. But they are always looking over their shoulders, fearing that the tax-and-spend charge is about to ruin their day.

No one believes—and no one should—that government is a perfect institution. On the contrary, it is capable of inefficiencies and corruption. One of the most important tasks of those who believe in government's purposes is to reform it and make it work. Al Gore's "reinventing government" project was an underrated achievement of the last administration, and could usefully have been pushed even farther.

And it is one of the central principles of liberalism that government should be limited. One of the odd paradoxes of our politics is that supposedly anti-government conservatives are often willing to grant government exceptional powers in the area of law enforcement. The arguments over the Patriot Act and U.S. Attorney General John Ashcroft's eagerness to use its authority pit liberals who want to limit government against conservatives who would expand its reach.

Yet liberals and Democrats will never win their argument with conservatives and Republicans unless they also insist that democratic government has the power to *expand* the rights of individuals. It is no accident that African-Americans have been more faithful to Democrats and liberals than any other group. African-Americans understand that their emancipation first from slavery and then from segregation was achieved only when the federal government was pushed to act forcefully to enforce and defend their rights.

Democrats and liberals have lost the will to make the case for government as a vehicle through which the rights of individuals and communities can be enforced and enhanced. Conservatives and Republicans argue incessantly that government is guilty of "overregulation." But it is regulation that guarantees individuals clean air and water. It is regulation that protects the rights of individual workers in the workplace. It is regulation that protects individual consumers from fraud. It is regulation that protects individual investors from being plundered. It is regulation (and government deposit insurance) that allows individuals to engage in that quintessentially capitalist act of saving money in banks and other financial institutions with some sense of safety.

Democrats and liberals have become so obsessed with the successes of Republicans in attacking government that they have begun to think in the opposition's terms: that government is only about bureaucracies and "redistribution." Put aside that "redistribution" has allowed elderly Americans to retire in security with decent health care, and that this is an achievement. The narrow focus on redistribution misses that government, by the way it writes the rules, can empower individuals to act, alone and in concert with fellow citizens, on their own behalf. As Robert Kuttner has pointed out, no single piece of legislation did more to create the great American middle class than the Wagner Act, which facilitated the formation of unions. Workers were empowered to bargain collectively, which raised their wages and the living standards of their families.

This social change required almost no spending by government beyond the enforcement of the law. Yet the amount of money this single act allowed to flow to previously low-income families transformed a nation.

Organized workers did not need government handouts because they gained the power to bargain within a capitalist economy on behalf of themselves. Doing so enhanced their living standards, allowed them to become owners of property—and thus strengthened capitalism.

Democrats and liberals have forgotten this legacy—or have been fearful to claim it. Yes, they accept the help of unions at election time. But they have largely forgotten how to make arguments on behalf of the principles that lie behind the union movement. Conservatives and Republicans, on the other hand, never forget how to make arguments for their own vision of a highly individualistic and corporate version of capitalism.

Anyone who doubted government's importance had only to look to Iraq. In the immediate aftermath of Saddam's fall, the television pictures showed us looters ransacking homes, hotels, even hospitals. The lesson the looters taught was basic: The alternative to tyranny is not the abolition of government. Absent a government committed to the protection of rights, there are no rights. Without government, individuals have no way to vindicate their claims to property, to personal liberty, to life itself. And in the fall of 2003, there was the great irony of a conservative, Republican president proposing what amounted to a vast New Deal spending program to rebuild Iraq and put its people to work. It was George W. Bush, not some liberal, who argued that American taxpayers should be willing to foot the bill for the construction of schools, roads, energy grids, new postal and telephone systems, and job creation—in Iraq.

What goes undiscussed—and this is the fault of Democrats and liberals—is the extent to which our personal and collective prosperity as a property-owning, enterprising people depends on strong and effective government. No government, no property. No government, no security from looting, theft, or violence. No government, no national defense. No government, no social stability. No government, no securities law. No government, no food inspections, no consumer and environmental protection, no safeguards for workplace rights, no social insurance.

"Americans seem easily to forget that individual rights and freedoms depend fundamentally on vigorous state action," write law professors

Stephen Holmes and Cass Sunstein in their powerful book, *The Cost of Rights: Why Liberty Depends on Taxes.*

"Without effective government," they say, "American citizens would not be able to enjoy their private property in the way they do. Indeed, they would enjoy few or none of their constitutionally guaranteed individual rights. Personal liberty, as Americans value and experience it, presupposes social cooperation managed by government officials. The private realm we rightly prize is sustained, indeed created, by public action."

Take the particularly neuralgic issue of whether the rich are asked to give too much to government through income and inheritance taxes. Because the well-off account for such a large share of total income tax receipts—and more still of inheritance levies—conservatives argue that our beleaguered, best-off citizens should be the most generously provided for in any tax cut proposal. This leaves aside the fact that payroll, sales, and property taxes hit the middle class and the poor much harder. But there is an even more basic point: Our legal and social orders disproportionately benefit the well-off. Both the police and the courts safeguard their holdings. Our system is designed to protect and preserve the current distribution of property and wealth.

"Property rights are meaningful only if public authorities use coercion to exclude nonowners, who, in the abuses of law, might well trespass on property that owners wish to maintain as an inviolable sanctuary," Holmes and Sunstein write. Markets themselves could not function outside the law; "they function well only with reliable legislative and judicial assistance."

Holmes and Sunstein are not Marxists. They vigorously defend property rights and the value of a society that "encourages personal initiative, social cooperation and self-improvement." But they also note that public programs commonly described as "redistributive" are essential to the social stability on which property owners depend. Welfare rights, they argue, "compensate the indigent for receiving less value than the rich from the rights ostensibly guaranteed equally to all Americans." And, especially in the case of education, government expenditures promote both initiative and self-improvement.

If Democrats doubt that a case can be made for government, they should consider compassionate conservatism and the efforts of George W. Bush, described earlier, to protect his party from being seen as too hostile to government. Bush's rhetorical shuffle suggests that the president was shrewder than his opponents. He understood the limits of the anti-government argument.

There are many lessons from Bush's clever two-step on government and taxes. It's clear that even anti-government Republicans now recognize that attacks on government must be oblique. During Newt Gingrich's high tide, Clinton demonstrated with his M2E2 strategy—the defense of "Medicare, Medicaid, Education and the Environment" —that certain essential government functions command broad public support. As Bush himself showed with his constant invocation of the word "compassionate," Americans are not socially indifferent. And as the public response to the corporate scandals showed, Americans want government to step in to prevent bad actors from exploiting capitalism on behalf of insiders and against the public interest.

One of the most revealing episodes during the Bush presidency was the reaction of politicians—including Bush himself—to the decisions of first one and then another judge striking down federal rules aimed at stopping telemarketers from interfering with the American family's evening at home. At issue was the "do-not-call" list established by the Federal Trade Commission. Put your name on the list, and telemarketers who call you risk an $11,000 fine. Between July and September 2003, some 50 million Americans signed up for the list. Here was a classic case of individuals gaining rights over commercial entities, courtesy of the federal government.

When a judge struck down the rule, Congress acted within a day—a single day—and across partisan lines to restore the right of Americans to shut down the calls. Representative Elliott Engel, a New York Democrat, thanked the judge for creating a moment during which the bitter partisan acrimony that characterized almost everything else in Washington was swept aside. And Bush rushed to sign the bill. As Matt Richtel and Richard W. Stevenson put it in *The New York Times,* "Mr. Bush generally supports reducing regulation of business. But in this case, political strategists said, public opinion in favor of limiting telemarketers' calls is so strong that Mr. Bush had little choice but to support the legislation."

Bush chose to be the paladin of the people and was prepared to use big government to enforce their will. He said that the "conclusion of the American people and the legislative branch and the executive branch is beyond question" and that "the public is understandably losing patience with these unwanted phone calls, unwanted intrusions."

Yes, it's hard to find a better enemy than telemarketers. But the principle is clear enough: government can empower, and when it does, it turns from enemy to friend. By being so timid in defending government's empowering role, Democrats and liberals give up one of their most powerful assets in the public debate. Republicans will always attack Democrats as the party of "big government." Democrats can cower in the corner and try to deny the charge. Or they can stand up and accept their role as defenders of an institution that, in our history at least, has served as a countervailing power to domineering private interests on behalf of the public interest and the rights of individuals.

IV

The third shift in the language of politics goes back a long way, but is also of more recent vintage. It has to do with what constitutes being "tough" in dealing with enemies, both foreign and domestic. Since World War II, liberals and Democrats have faced regular accusations of being "soft" about something, sometimes many things. This is ironic, since the victory of 1945 was won under the leadership of two liberal and Democratic presidents, Franklin D. Roosevelt and Harry Truman.

That didn't stop the attacks. In the late 1940s and 1950s, liberals were accused of being "soft on Communism," a charge that came around again when most Democrats came to oppose the Vietnam War after

Richard Nixon's 1968 victory. And the view that Democrats were "soft on foreign policy" was successfully sold at the end of Jimmy Carter's administration. The apparent advance of the Soviet Union—especially after its invasion of Afghanistan in 1979—and the failure to resolve the Iranian hostage crisis made it easy to portray an America that was ineffectual, even helpless, before a hostile world. As the journalist Michael Tomasky put it: "Carter's paralysis over Iran *was* humiliating. Ascendant conservatives and neo-conservatives made short work of converting Carter's failure into a symbol of American anemia." Ronald Reagan defeated Carter handily in 1980 and his defense spending increases (along with an economic recovery) restored popular confidence.

Former U.N. Ambassador Jeanne Kirkpatrick highlighted the contrast between allegedly strong Republicans and allegedly weak Democrats at the 1984 Republican National Convention. Her attack was all the more pointed because of her standing as a former Democrat. Repeatedly, she assailed the "San Francisco Democrats"—the party held its 1984 convention that year in that very liberal city—who "blame America first."

During the wave of urban violence that began in the late 1960s, Democrats were accused of being "soft on crime"—here again, Nixon played a key role in the attack—and too sympathetic to the rights of the accused, always rendered as "the rights of criminals." The symbol of such "softness" became opposition to the death penalty. The first President Bush was singularly successful in using softness to win election in 1988 against Democrat Michael Dukakis. The Bush victory was built on a softness double-whammy. Dukakis was attacked for both softness and incompetence because a criminal named William Horton raped a woman in Maryland while on furlough from a Massachusetts prison. (Horton happened to be black, which added to the political kick of the assault on the state's furlough program.) And Dukakis's alleged lack of fitness to lead the country militarily was dramatized by unfortunate footage—created by the Democrat's own campaign—showing the Massachusetts governor riding ineffectually around in a tank and looking for all the world, chortled the Republicans, like Rocket J. Squirrel.

After 1988 especially, combating the image of "softness" became a high Democratic priority. Democrats tried to argue that all the allegations of squishy softness were unfair and contrived for political purposes. And most of the time, the charges *were* manufactured. Most Democrats, from Harry Truman forward, were anti-Communists and mistrustful of the Soviet Union. Truman, often facing opposition from the Republicans, built the key anti-Soviet institutions of the Cold War. That did not stop Senator Joseph R. McCarthy from accusing the Truman administration of harboring Communists.

Democrats were again accused of advocating policies of "cut-and-run" during the Vietnam War. The charge was in some ways ironic, since the Vietnam conflict first escalated not under Republican presidents, but in the administrations of John F. Kennedy and Lyndon B. Johnson. As student radicals would say at the time, it was in many ways a "liberal war." Many Democrats later decided the war was a mistake not because they discovered a sudden sympathy for the Viet Cong or the Stalinists of North Vietnam, but because they came to believe—plausibly, in retrospect—that it ill-served American interests.

Conservative Republicans (joined, it should be said, by some hawkish Democrats such as the late Senator Henry "Scoop" Jackson) also saw arms control agreements with the Soviet Union as weakening American defenses. Yet many thoroughly hardheaded analysts in both parties supported the arms agreements. Some even understood—and history bore them out—that preserving America's social and economic superiority over the Soviet Union would matter as much as military strength.

As John Newhouse, the able foreign policy journalist, has pointed out, it was Henry Kissinger—nobody's idea of a softie—who favored arms control agreements during Gerald Ford's presidency in the mid-1970s. "Kissinger favored negotiation," wrote Newhouse, "a political process aimed at discouraging outright confrontation with the Soviet Union and infusing the relationship with some stability." As Newhouse observed, Kissinger's efforts to secure an arms treaty were foiled by none other than Donald Rumsfeld, Ford's chief of staff, who later became his—and then George W. Bush's—defense secretary.

Newhouse argues that Ford's failure to reach an arms agreement may have hurt his chances against Jimmy Carter in 1976. But in the long run, the softness charge gained ground against the Democrats as the Carter years progressed.

As for being "soft on crime," Democrats *were* slow to realize the power of criminal violence as a domestic political issue. They were too ready in the late 1960s to see all calls for "law and order" as a cover for racism—even if some of them were. Linking opposition to the death penalty with support for criminality was demagogic, but also effective. (I say that as an opponent of the death penalty.) Many Americans had lost patience with what seemed a failed criminal justice system and saw the death penalty as the better alternative to parole and recidivism.

Even assuming that all the softness charges were unfair, the very process of debating who was a softie moved the political argument to Republican and conservative turf. A dialogue based on endless renditions of "You guys are soft"/"No, we're not" puts all the initiative in the hands of the accuser.

After Bush defeated Dukakis in 1988, the quest for toughness became a high Democratic priority. In December 1991, I wrote an article arguing—only partly tongue-in-cheek—that the Democratic Party and liberalism had never been the same since Humphrey Bogart was lost as the symbol for what it meant to belong to FDR's party and to support his worldview. Woody Allen, Robert Redford, and Alan Alda were all very amusing, but Democrats and liberals were dying from an overdose of irony and detachment. In Bogart, they had the perfect symbol: a tough guy with a heart, and convictions.

The serious point was that Bogart symbolized a different kind of liberalism from the sort that was so easily parodied after the 1960s. It was a liberalism that asked something of citizens (even, as I pointed out back then, hard things like giving up Ingrid Bergman in *Casablanca*). Bogart's message was that you didn't do the right thing because you wanted to be nice or sensitive or feel good. You did right because it was right. And by usually winning in the end, Bogart proved that doing the right thing was rewarded.

Robert Reich made a similar point in less cinematic terms in his book *The Resurgent Liberal.* Writing in 1989, Reich maintained that contemporary liberalism was rooted in the values of altruism and conciliation. While perfectly worthy goals, Reich argued, both easily collapsed into "an overwhelming preference for smoothing over rather than settling conflict," which in turn contributed "to an environment in which unaccountability flourished."

In the New Deal era—in my terms, the Bogart era—liberalism was held together by stronger glue. The imperatives then were ending the depression and beating the Axis powers. "The goals of reviving the economy and winning the war, and the sacrifices implied in achieving them, were well-understood and widely endorsed," Reich says. "The public was motivated less by altruism than by its direct and palpable stake in the outcome of what were ineluctably social endeavors." In other words, altruism is a virtue, but it was more defensible—and certainly much *tougher*—when it was married to the principle of solidarity. Solidarity implied social generosity; but, as Reich noted, it was a generosity rooted in a shared concern for the success of a community in which individuals felt they were invested.

Reich's theory was important at the time, and it fit neatly with his old friend Bill Clinton's emphasis on a trio of political values, "Opportunity, Responsibility and Community." But Reich's idea, as we'll explore again later, may be even more relevant to a political environment shaped by 9/11.

In the 1992 presidential campaign, Clinton certainly took the question of "softness" seriously. He was so concerned about appearing tough on crime that he not only devoted time and attention to "community policing"—a good idea—but was determined to show how strongly he believed in the death penalty. One of the least edifying moments in his political career was his decision during the 1992 campaign to put Ricky Ray Rector to death. Rector was mentally retarded and, even in the view of many death penalty supporters, should never have been executed.

Clinton was tough as well on welfare, though his position was carefully calibrated to appeal to liberals and moderates as well as conservatives. His promise to "end welfare as we know it" appealed to the tough-minded, as did his pledge to put welfare recipients to work. But Clinton's toughness was matched by a commitment to spending substantial sums on job training and child care for welfare mothers and on increasing the incomes of the working poor. More conservative voters heard the "tough" part about ending welfare. More liberal voters welcomed the commitment to additional assistance to the needy.

Since the welfare system was a failure, new departures in favor of work were sensible on policy as well as political grounds. Clinton's original welfare proposals were more compassionate than the existing program. But when the Republican Congress kept passing welfare reform bills as the 1996 election approached, Clinton finally signed a version of their less generous plan. He was not about to look soft on the issue.

And on foreign policy, Clinton chose, early on, to embrace the legacy of—Ronald Reagan. In mid-October 1991, long before he emerged as the front-runner for the Democratic nomination, Clinton met with a group of reporters and editors at *The Washington Post*. He startled many of us in the room (and won himself a story in the next day's newspaper) when he said that Reagan's defense buildup had hastened the fall of Soviet communism. Clinton praised Reagan's "rhetoric in defense of freedom" and his role in "advancing the idea that communism could be rolled back.

"The idea that we were going to stand firm and reaffirm our containment strategy, and the fact that we forced them to spend even more when they were already producing a Cadillac defense system and a dinosaur economy, I think that hastened their undoing," Clinton added. Reagan deserved credit, he said, for "the idea that he wanted to stand up to them."

To back up his tough Reaganite rhetoric, Clinton actively courted conservatives who had cooled to the first President Bush. For good measure, Clinton went to the first President Bush's "right"—and, considering that human rights are a liberal issue, simultaneously to his "left"—by criticizing Bush's response to the massacre at Beijing's Tiananmen Square as "woefully inadequate" and "inconsistent with our sense of values."

Thus did Clinton beat back the trifecta of "softness"—on defense and foreign policy, on crime, and on the poor. And because he did, he was often accused of stealing ideas from the other side, even if his welfare and community policing proposals were based on a marriage of liberal and conservatives themes. Clinton's gift for neutralizing historically effective Republican attacks was one reason why so many of his opponents despised him and dubbed him "Slick Willie."

What's not in doubt is that Clinton's approach worked. There is no reason in principle why other Democrats and liberals could not find their own ways of undercutting the softness charge. In the fall of 2003, thousands of Democrats rallied to the presidential candidacy of retired General Wesley K. Clark precisely because they felt that his military background—and that word "General" in front of his name—would give him immunity from charges of foreign policy weakness. Who better than a former general to raise doubts about George W. Bush's military policies? Clark's candidacy failed, but John Kerry's took off in part because his standing as a Vietnam War hero seemed the perfect antidote to all charges of softness—and contrasted with the incumbent's Vietnam War record. Many Democrats rallied to the candidacy of former Vermont governor Howard Dean because he opposed the Iraq War. But their attraction to Dean was also based on the presumption that he, more than his rivals, was tough enough to challenge Bush and fearless enough to speak his mind. Liberals, it turns out, like toughness too—and retain a hankering for the Bogart model.

But this points to the fundamental problem with the discussion of "softness." Softness and toughness are not *issues*. They are not *ideas*. They are *dispositions*. They relate to character. In the end, there is no surefire way to "win" the debate over toughness except by being tough-minded. And being tough-minded means holding to principles—even on occasions when the other side claims that such principles are "soft."

How, for example, have Democrats and liberals largely pushed aside charges that they are soft on crime? Partly through opportunism—so many of them have abandoned their opposition to the death penalty. But the "soft on crime" charge went away for another reason. The crime rate went down. Fear of crime went down along with the crime rate. The crime rate dropped for many reasons, but two of them were entirely consistent with liberal and Democratic principles. Leaders in both parties—and Clinton was among the first—embraced the ideas behind "community policing." All over the country, notably in Rudy Giuliani's New York City, mayors deployed police officers in innovative ways, fought petty as well as violent crime, and put more cops where crime actually happened. At the federal level, Clinton successfully pushed for funding to support 100,000 new police officers around the country. This is a classic case in which government, thinking anew, dealt with a public problem—the very definition of the government's job. "Soft" or "tough" matters less than being successful and effective.

And the crime rate dropped in tandem with a sharp drop in unemployment. The late 1990s were the best period for employment in over thirty years. Low unemployment was accompanied by improvements in the wages paid to the least well-off workers. No, this does not "prove" that unemployment causes crime. It does show that high levels of employment combined with rising wages for the poor can create a social climate in which many good things happen. The falling crime rate was one of those good things.

The welfare example is more complicated because the welfare reform bill Clinton finally signed provided less help to the poor moving off the welfare rolls than it should have. But the principles behind welfare reform—a preference for work and a belief that Americans who work should not be poor—combined toughness with compassion. Here again, it took progressive and compassionate measures to make toughness work. It's better to be tough and smart than tough and dumb. The Earned Income Tax Credit provided income supplements to the working poor, and low unemployment created the circumstances in which poor people previously left out of the labor market could find jobs. In times of high unemployment, less skilled and experienced workers are the last people employers want to hire. They don't have to hire them because so many more experienced workers are looking for work. When unemployment is low, employers in need of workers give the previously excluded a chance. Thus did the oldest of liberal commitments, the promise of full employment, give life to the conservative pledge to end welfare as we know it.

Yes, a cynic might say, that's all very nice. But policy can only take you so far in the toughness wars. That's true. Toughness wins the toughness wars. Toughness requires confidence, which is different from arrogance. The primary characteristic of the contemporary Republican right is its certainty that its convictions are right and that its opponents are wrong, unpatriotic, and immoral. The primary characteristic of mainstream Democrats has, until recently, been fear—fear of being attacked by the right, fear that the public does not share their convictions. The facts, including the results of the 2000 election, suggest otherwise: that the public is closely split in its political orientation and that the battle for the future is open. Winning that battle requires changing minds and changing the direction of the political debate—exactly what conservatives started doing on their own behalf in the 1960s. The Democratic problem is not primarily about "positioning"—and no one who is obsessed with "positioning" will ever look tough.

V

That was the problem with the Democrats' response to George W. Bush's push for war in Iraq in the summer of 2002. The issue was not simply whether Democrats as a party or liberals as a movement should have supported or opposed Bush. More dispiriting was the Democrats' fear—with honorable exceptions on both sides of the issue—of taking any position at all. Democrats were indeed furious that Bush chose to inject the Iraq issue into a campaign that they hoped would be waged on domestic questions. They were desperate, as we have seen, to move the campaign back to such issues. But the party's fear of looking less than "tough" paralyzed many in its ranks. And, paradoxically, it was their fear of speaking out that made the Democrats look weak.

The honorable exceptions—I will focus on the Senate—deserve

mention here simply to make the point that at a difficult moment, it was possible to be clear and consistent. Senator Joe Lieberman had long supported tough action against Iraq and he was unequivocal in backing Bush. Senators such as the late Paul Wellstone and Ted Kennedy were equally clear in opposing him. Senators Carl Levin and Dick Durbin were both deeply skeptical of unilateral action. As we've seen, they tried to shape a congressional resolution that would not give the president unbridled authority to wage war without international support—and without further action by Congress. And Senator Joe Biden—more sympathetic to war than many in his party—tried to work with his Republican colleagues, Richard Lugar and Chuck Hagel, to put some constraints on the president.

Yet avoiding the Iraq issue in the 2002 election became gospel among virtually all of the Democratic Party's political consultants, and it was the policy on the ground, as we saw earlier in the case of Jill Long Thompson's campaign in Indiana. The party's policy was to "get back" to issues the pollsters thought were Democratic winners: health care, the economy, prescription drugs for the elderly, and education.

It can be claimed that before Bush's standing on foreign policy had been dented in the messy aftermath of the Iraq War, Democrats could not possibly have won by challenging Bush on the issues that were his strength. It's certainly true, as we've seen, that the Republican calculation was to change the subject of the election to homeland security and Iraq in order to reduce the importance of the Democrats' issues.

Yet the cost of Democratic evasion turned out to be very high. Criticizing the party's political consultants after the election, Noam Scheiber noted in *The New Republic* that a Gallup poll conducted three days after the election showed only 34 percent of Americans saying Democrats were "tough enough" when it came to dealing with terrorism, compared with 64 percent who said this of the GOP. Did this suggest that the Democrats were shrewd in avoiding the issue, or that Democrats lost the election because they never dealt with it at all?

Yes, a few thousand votes the other way in a few places and the Democratic strategists might have looked as smart as Karl Rove. But in retrospect, the list of issues the Democrats did run on proved easy enough for the Republicans to bat back since, as Scheiber put it, "the issue that performs best in a poll is usually easiest for the other side to co-opt."

The set of issues the Democrats chose to run on was "so obvious and well-known that Republicans had long since figured out how to counter them." Indeed, the drug companies through a front group poured millions of dollars into close races touting the credentials of Republican candidates on the prescription drug question. The irony here—that these companies were backing Republicans who opposed legislation that might inconvenience drug makers—did not matter on Election Day. (And Democrats, with a few exceptions such as Wellstone, were ineffective in challenging their opponents for being the beneficiaries of such corporate largesse.)

On Social Security, Scheiber told the story of the Senate campaign in North Carolina, where the Democratic campaign committee ran an advertisement in September accusing Elizabeth Dole of wanting to "gamble Social Security money in the stock market, even though it would reduce guaranteed benefits for retirees."

Scheiber continues the tale: "Dole responded with three straight ads over the next week accusing her opponent, Erskine Bowles, of distorting her record and telling voters that her Social Security plan 'helps their grandchildren increase their benefits without raising taxes.' Republicans wound up with a twelve-point advantage among senior citizens by the time Dole and her fellow Republicans finished flooding the airwaves with counterattack ads on Social Security and prescription drugs."

Narrow tactical campaigns sometimes work. But they rarely work in a time of national crisis, and they are hard to pull off when the president of the United States successfully fuses policy and politics to transform the national conversation. The proof was in the results: in a substantial majority of the critical contests of 2002, the Republicans won.

The Democrats' problem was not only that they feared criticizing Bush but also that their party lacked anything approaching a coherent basis for an alternative policy. What needed to be challenged was not the idea that Saddam Hussein was a bad or potentially dangerous man, but rather the plausibility of Bush's strategy and the thinking behind it. Despite Powell's involvement, the administration's approach was rooted far more in the beliefs of Dick Cheney and Donald Rumsfeld. As Michael Tomasky has argued, their views were rooted in unilateralism, in a belief that the United States should act preemptively, and in a suspicion of collective arrangements. Such arrangements served the United States rather well in the years after World War II, and helped Bush's father build the alliance that won the first Iraq war. As Tomasky put it:

> Compared with his son, George H. W. Bush, who took care in the fall of 1990 to assemble an international coalition against Iraq and who refused to press for a politicized war-resolution vote in the heat of that year's midterm elections, practically looks like George McGovern, or at least Hubert Humphrey. And here, perhaps, the administration has created an opening for a liberal counterargument that can persuade American public opinion over time.
>
> The counterargument is essentially a simple one: America is not an empire, it is a democracy. A democracy leads the world, but it does not seek to rule it.

But the counterargument was not made, Tomasky continued, because of a "failure of nerve that has typified liberalism for years." The best sign that the argument could be won, Tomasky noted, is that the administration preferred to evade debate over the underlying ideas and purposes of its policy and relied instead on "inconsistent excuses for moving against Iraq."

There is nothing "soft" about the course Tomasky suggests. He is critical of "generalities" about "multilateralism," since "too much blather about multilateralism just makes people think that the person doing the blathering isn't quite serious about the problem." Tomasky insists that the challenges after 9/11 demand both a new toughness and a new ingenuity. "Applying the old Vietnam-era schema to these situations makes no sense, and rejecting such a worldview is not a matter of moving to the right, as some would have it; it's a matter of adapting to the world as it now is. . . . Liberalism needs to assert anew that American power can be employed to good ends." Yet those ends, Tomasky argues, should be defined by "making democratic values a real priority in the world" and at the same time "surround[ing] and neutraliz[ing] terror and the fundamentalism from which it grows."

The differences between this vision and the Cheney-Rumsfeld approach have to do not just with unilateral versus collective action or how the United States defines itself to the rest of the world. Yes, this view would be critical of relying almost solely on American power and American decisions backed by weak and fluctuating "coalitions of the willing." But the alternative would also call for the same creativity the United States showed after World War II and early in the Cold War. Led by Harry Truman, the United States helped to build a series of institutions and organizations that served both national and international interests in containing the Soviet Union, expanding the world's prosperity, and promoting a degree of stability. When the world came together after the attacks of September 11, the opportunity existed for a new round of such creativity. The world was ready and the United States was in a position to lead. That moment was squandered because of the divisions created by the way the Bush administration chose to take the United States to war in Iraq. But the opportunity can be retrieved.

The core difference between these two views has nothing to do with "softness" or "toughness." But it may reflect, as the political writer John Judis argued in a perceptive essay, the difference between optimism and pessimism. Writing in May 2002, before Bush launched the buildup to Iraq, Judis maintained that:

Bush, influenced by his Pentagon rather than by his more internationalist State Department, has adopted a foreign policy based on a cramped view of American interests and a deeply pessimistic outlook on international relations. Bush officials such as Deputy Defense Secretary Paul Wolfowitz envisage an America surrounded by adversaries and potential adversaries who must be deterred by superior U.S. military power. Bush officials do not reject coalitions per se, but they do reject any idea of collective security. They have opposed both arms control and environmental agreements. They favor overseas intervention, but only when it is tied to a narrow definition of U.S. national interest.

They don't like committing America to "nation-building," whether in the Balkans, Afghanistan, or the West Bank. For them, the September 11 attacks confirmed their views that a Hobbesian state of nature stirs beneath the post–Cold War calm. They see the war on terrorism not as a collective effort to rid the world of al-Qaeda but as an American effort, aided by other countries, to destroy worldwide enemies.

Most Democrats, Judis argued, disagree with this approach:

Democrats have not merely favored coalitions, they have seen alliances and international treaties as an essential aspect of U.S. foreign policy. Democrats seek collective security in order to create the economic and political stability in which America, as well as other nations, can prosper. They do not see a U.S. military monopoly as a prerequisite for security but rather as a waste of precious resources—and an invitation to future conflict. They believe that September 11 demonstrated that such security cannot be achieved unilaterally. But they also see the outbreak of Islamic terrorism as an eruption that—like that of Nazism—can be overcome. Theirs is a Lockean view of international relations—of a world that eventually can be governed by social contracts rather than by the threat of force.

As Judis noted, "it's not likely that the discussion between the Democrats and the Bush administration will plumb these philosophical abstractions—Hobbes and Locke aren't commonly discussed on *Face the*

Nation. " But Judis was right to argue that core differences on foreign policy can be explained by "a larger disagreement about where the world is going, and how Americans should try to shape it."

It is possible, in other words, to believe that the United States faces enemies who must be defeated without believing that the world is headed in the wrong direction. It makes more sense to see the forces behind those who blew up the World Trade Center and the Pentagon not as the wave of the future, but as marginal figures whose very extremism is an expression of frustration at the failure of their ideas. The evidence of the last fifteen years suggests that the power of those who support free societies and democratic values is on the ascendancy, not the decline. The most *realistic* view is that the United States will have more than enough allies in the battles it must fight and the work it must do—if it seriously seeks them out. Battling misguided pessimism is an essential task because when pessimists are wrong, they often bring about the very results they most fear.

VI

Recall Karl Rove's love for the circumspect defense and the audacious offense. Note that the two went together. And then consider the plight of progressives and Democrats.

Democrats and liberals have chosen to live in a world in which playing defense is the preferred art. More than they realize, they have capitulated to conservative views of the market and government. They have become obsessed with the categories of "soft" and "tough." They worry that they will sound anti-capitalist, even when they know that capitalism has survived as long as it has only because its critics successfully insisted on reform. They shy away from defending government, even when they know that much of what they want to do depends upon a government that is both efficient and active. And they worry about looking soft when their very timidity only contributes to the image they are trying to combat.

In the process, they have lost the gift for the audacious offense. Their

political consultants live in a world whose boundaries are set by their opponents. And in truth, the consultants are only responding to the wishes
of the politicians who hire them. In 2002, it was not just the consultants
who feared taking the Iraq or homeland securities issues head-on. It was
not just the consultants who were worried that taking on Bush's tax cuts
would make his opponents look like "big taxers." The politicians were
wary, too.

Successful politicians, as Rove knows, pick the fights they ought to
pick. Defense is sometimes necessary. There is the odd matched political
set of Clinton declaring the era of big government over—to defend
against charges that he supported too much government; and of Bush declaring himself a friend of government—to defend against charges that
he, like the anti-government Gingrich Congress, supported too little.

But Rove chose his audacious offense on Iraq and homeland security
because he knew not only that Democrats would have trouble responding but also that they would be reluctant to respond at all. The field was
left to Republicans to use their best issues to mobilize their electorate.
Democrats did not respond and did not mobilize their own.

All these experiences have toughened Democrats and progressives.
Throughout 2003 and early 2004, the tone of their response changed.
There was more audaciousness, a greater willingness to challenge.
Howard Dean's success in mobilizing angry and impatient Democrats
had something to do with that. But the party's own leadership also
learned lessons from defeat, and so did the party's other presidential candidates. Dick Gephardt struck early, proposing to repeal Bush's tax cut
and to use the proceeds to finance an ambitious program to provide universal health coverage. Senator John Edwards explicitly challenged Bush
for pursuing policies that preferred "wealth" over "work." Joe Lieberman
proposed a bold tax program that combined tax cuts for middle-class
Americans with a repeal of Bush's tax cuts for the wealthiest. Here was a
moderate Democrat willing explicitly to raise questions of distribution
and fairness. General Wesley Clark used his standing as a former NATO
commander to bolster his criticism of Bush's policies abroad, particularly

in Iraq. And John Kerry scored in the end by explicitly welcoming a debate on national security. If Bush wanted the election to be decided on that issue, Kerry would say, mocking the president's earlier swagger, "Bring it on!"

These are beginnings. But there were forces reinforcing the predominance of the right in politics and aggravating the politics of revenge. It is to those that we turn next.

5. We're All in This Together

How the Right Won with the Media,
the Think Tanks, and the Loudmouths

> We come with a strong point of view, and people like point-of-view journalism. While all these hand-wringing Freedom Forum types talk about objectivity, the conservative media likes to rap the liberal media on the knuckles for not being objective. We've created this cottage industry in which it pays to be unobjective. It pays to be subjective as much as possible. It's a great way to have your cake and eat it, too. Criticize other people for not being objective. Be as subjective as you want. It's a great little racket. I'm glad we found it, actually.
>
> Matt Labash of *The Weekly Standard*

Liberals and Democrats perennially claim that their side is too "nice" to win, that liberals live by the rules and that conservatives break them.

It is well documented—check out the recent books by Al Franken and Eric Alterman, among others—that there are conservative propagandists who have been quite willing to stretch or ignore the truth. Conservative politicians such as House Majority Leader Tom DeLay are regularly willing to push the limits. The right's behavior during the Clinton impeachment, the battle over Florida in 2000, and the 2002 elections set a very high standard for aggression.

But the truth is that liberals and Democrats are not always "nice."

They, too, have been known to fight to win in political campaigns and judicial nomination battles. Republicans certainly have no monopoly when it comes to nasty political ads. What's going on in our political life is deeper than whether one side is "nicer." It has to do with a systematic failure of liberal institutions and the conservatives' success in building institutions of their own. There is the liberals' loss of nerve. There are the ambiguous legacy of the Clinton years and the conservatives' genius in labeling institutions as "liberal" when they plainly are not. This last tactic has worked especially well with the media.

Above all, the shift in our politics is about a solidarity that exists on the right that does not exist in any comparable way on the center-left. It is not just that conservatives built strong institutions. They linked those institutions to the partisan fray. They assumed effective control over the Republican Party and turned it into their instrument. Far more effectively than liberals and the left who invented the idea, conservatives have forged a united front—and with it a sense of momentum.

If "niceness" isn't the issue, blaming the current crop of Democratic politicians for all that has gone wrong is also too easy. The rise of the right was a long time in the making. There were good reasons why so many of the dominant assumptions of our politics changed and why Democrats and liberals found themselves fighting uphill as they were forced to battle on their adversaries' terrain and to speak in the tongues of their opponents.

Conservatives have worked in a disciplined, steady, and, at times, ruthless way. They enjoy enormous financial advantages. After all, they are fighting for those who are doing very well under the existing system, and they battle, openly, for programs (such as Bush's tax cuts) that would help the best-off do even better. Yet conservatives are also attuned to the moral rhythms of rural and small-town America, which can be heard too in many suburbs—the rhythms of the conservative churches, the NASCAR loyalists, the country music fans. Thus do conservatives operate with conviction, moral fervor, and a confidence that they will win—and deserve to win. Moral fervor plus money plus toughness is a good equation for victory.

As the admirably candid Matt Labash shows in the remark cited in the epigraph to this chapter, conservatives are perfectly aware that their "great little racket" is designed to hold their potential critics to standards to which they do not hold themselves. Conservatives regularly criticize "establishment" institutions for being "liberal" and "elitist," and then demand that those same institutions be more hospitable to conservatives. The fact that most establishment institutions are not, in fact, "liberal" is intentionally ignored. Because these institutions need, as conservative activist Grover Norquist shrewdly noted, "to be critical of both sides," they respond with apologies and even groveling when they are attacked by conservatives as biased. That's especially true of mainstream media in television and print, but it can also be true at foundations and all other institutions that hanker after the label "non-partisan." They rush to prove how fair they are to conservatives, often by attacking liberals. And conservatives chuckle at how easy these institutions are to roll. Yes, it *is* a nice little racket.

But liberals and Democrats make a great mistake when they simply whine over the conservative achievement. Modern conservatism's success at institution-building is worthy of respect. It reflects the clarity of a movement that has understood where it was starting from—it *was* in a weak position in the 1950s—and understood how much work needed to be done. The conservatives showed great tactical nimbleness. They saw the need to operate both at the highbrow level of intellectual work and at the middlebrow level of the mass media. Building a movement required enlisting those who wrote scholarly tomes and the authors of direct mail screeds. It required erudite lecturers and talk radio screechers. It took research and sophisticated propaganda techniques, those who go for rational analysis and those who are excited by conspiracy theories. It required finding a usable philosophical past *and* creating the image of something new. It sometimes required working outside the Republican Party, though it was always designed to influence the party and turn it into the primary vehicle for conservative aspirations. This is why conservative organizations, as Norquist has said, have less fear of being labeled partisan. That is especially true of the conservative press: "The conservative press is self-consciously conservative," Norquist said. "The liberal press is larger, but at the same time it sees itself as the establishment press. So it's conflicted."

The results of the enterprise are there for all to see.

Liberals and Democrats were not slothful over the last forty years, but neither were they as focused, united, or strategic as their competitors. Liberals long mistakenly presumed their dominance in the political and intellectual realm and therefore lacked the urgency of the come-from-behind conservative movement. Moreover, liberalism splintered along the lines of race, class, ethnicity, gender, sexual preference, and religion. Todd Gitlin captured the problem in the title of his brilliant book *The Twilight of Common Dreams*. The balkanization Gitlin describes is ironic because the war against race prejudice and restrictions faced by women represents a great and enduring legacy of liberalism, an achievement that should bring liberals together. It is odd that a movement rooted in the Enlightenment and the promise of human liberation should have such difficulty finding and embracing common dreams.

Liberals can simultaneously exhibit arrogance *and* a lack of self-confidence. The arrogance lies in the liberals' difficulty in taking conservative ideas seriously. The lack of self-confidence comes, as we saw earlier, in an increasing defensiveness as conservative ideas gained sway. Yes, there were many kinds of conservatives, just as there were many kinds of liberals. In the 1990s especially, conservatism faced a crack-up as its wings (particularly the libertarians and the traditionalists) no longer operated in tandem. But as the conservative movement regained its footing, the opposition—liberals, yes, but also moderates and the larger Democratic Party—seemed increasingly confused. It was unclear whether their primary goal was to stop conservative assaults on a status quo shaped by liberalism (Social Security, Medicare, environmental and civil rights legislation) or to offer new departures. Liberals and Democrats were torn over playing defense or playing offense. Sometimes, they ended up playing neither.

This chapter deals primarily with the two areas in which the conservative institutional offensive achieved its most important victories: the development of ideas and the transformation of the mass media. In both instances, conservatives pursued a two-pronged strategy of building their own institutions and subjecting existing institutions—all encompassed under the mantle of "the liberal establishment"—to withering criticism. I pay particular attention to the media because it is in this arena that the conservative offensive has made the largest difference in the day-to-day struggles of politics. It is also the area in which conservative strength has grown the most over the last decade.

The rise of a conservative "counter-establishment," as the writer Sidney Blumenthal called it in the mid-1980s, would not have had the political impact it has enjoyed since the late 1990s without the increasingly close cooperation between conservative institutions and the actors in Republican politics. Here is where Newt Gingrich, despite his subsequent downfall, played a critical role in leading us to the current moment.

The 1994 congressional elections in which Gingrich was the central player gave the Republicans control of both houses of Congress. From this base, they were able to block Clinton's program and harass his administration. The Gingrich victory—for that is what the 1994 election was—also put conservatives firmly in control of the Republican Party's political machinery. Even Ronald Reagan's election as president in 1980 had not fully accomplished this, as the elder George Bush's success in winning the 1988 Republican presidential nomination shows. The first Bush bowed to conservatives when necessary, but he was not a person of the right. He demonstrated his moderation (and alienated the right) through his willingness to raise taxes to balance the federal budget and to support strong environmental and disabilities rights legislation.

Bush's defeat by Bill Clinton in 1992 opened the way for the completion of the conservative takeover of the Republican Party. Conservatives moved quickly to argue that Bush lost not because conservative ideas had failed him but because Bush had failed conservatism. Many conservatives saw a great opportunity in defeat. "Republicans in Congress are liberated now that they no longer have to worry about a Bush agenda," Adam Meyerson, the editor of the Heritage Foundation's intellectual journal, declared shortly after the election. Conservatives were quick to say that Clinton won because he mastered conservative language about free enterprise, welfare reform, personal responsibility, and the need to be tough on crime and the bureaucracies. "What do you mean that conservative ideas didn't work in the 1992 election?" asked Kate Walsh O'Beirne, then a top Heritage Foundation official. "They worked for Clinton." In fact, both sides kept stealing from each other's notebooks—and that process has not ended yet. And the truth was that Clinton often used conservative rhetoric on behalf of liberal ideas.

With Congress firmly under conservative Republican control, the party's moderate voices were marginalized and voices from the right and the South were ascendant. Even among conservatives, the harder-edged were preferred over the gentlemanly. Gingrich's approach was consciously different from that of the courtly, conciliatory, old-school leadership of his predecessor as Republican leader, Robert Michel. Tom DeLay would not have won his position of power in the House with Gingrich. DeLay would not have had the capacity to force the Clinton impeachment and to browbeat so many moderates who had quietly opposed it—and then turned around and voted for it.

Gingrich built a sturdy bridge between the politics of ideas that engaged the conservative scholars and the politics of attack that worked so well in the media, especially in the new conservative media. Unlike some conservative thinkers and politicians, Gingrich did not worry that he would sully his reputation as a thinker by getting into the trenches and assailing his opposition. Indeed, he prided himself on his toughness and his willingness to do what it took to ensure the triumph of his ideas. "I think that because I'm so systematically purposeful about changing our world, I'm a much tougher partisan than they've seen," he said. He described himself as "much more intense, much more persistent, much more willing to take risks to get it done." Years earlier, Gingrich had told a group of young Republicans that "one of the great problems in the Republican Party" was the extent to which its leaders encouraged new activists to be "neat and obedient and loyal and faithful, and all those Boy Scout words which can be great around the campfire but are lousy in politics." Gingrich disdained the Boy Scout approach to politics. "You're fighting a war," he told his Republican recruits. "It is a war for power."

One other fact about Gingrich is worthy of note in light of the younger Bush's presidency: Gingrich, like Karl Rove, shared an admiration for Mark Hanna, the man who organized William McKinley's rise to the presidency in 1896. Gingrich and Rove both respected the McKinley-Hanna vision that created a new Republican majority by combining the power and money of a new business class with a strategy that cast the Democrats as a backward-looking minority. Interestingly, McKinley solidified his coalition with a foreign policy adventure, the Spanish-American War in 1898. That war led to an explicit debate on the merits of imperialism, with McKinley defending American territorial acquisitions in a re-run against Democrat William Jennings Bryan in the 1900 election. Imperialism won out as McKinley expanded his majority. The irony, as we have seen, is that the very Rove-Gingrich strategy that is about building future Republican dominance is also backward-looking in seeking inspiration from the Gilded Age.

And so it was in the 1990s that decades of conservative work came together. The conservatives produced a new Republican Party marked by toughness and solidarity, and supported by a well-financed and thoroughly integrated political machine. This machine proved remarkably effective in the great political battles of the late 1990s with Bill Clinton and Al Gore.

The Clinton presidency began as an explicit (and, in many ways, successful) response to the conservative offensive. Because so much emphasis is put on Clinton's intellectual larceny, it's important to look at what he actually did in 1992. In large part, of course, Clinton won the election because of hard economic times. But he also won because he ignored both left-wing and right-wing conventional wisdoms. Clinton was a "New Democrat" because he went left and right at the same time.

The talk about Clinton simply offering conservatism-lite ignores the fact that he called openly for higher taxes on the rich, condemned "trickle-down economics," saw economic salvation from the bottom up—through a better-trained, more skilled workforce—and thought government spending ("investment") could make things better. He also embraced gay rights, supported abortion rights (though he pledged to try to make abortion "rare"), and promised more liberal Supreme Court justices, though without reference to the L-word.

At the same time, Clinton denounced the "tax-and-spend" policies of the past, called for welfare reform emphasizing work, took a tough line on crime, opposed foreign policy isolationism, said he'd "reinvent" a less bureaucratic government, spoke often of family responsibility, and condemned "deadbeat dads" who refuse to pay their child support.

Even those aspects of Clintonism that seemed like rhetorical tricks carried specific messages. To be for large-scale government "investment" and against "tax-and-spend" sounded like a sleight-of-hand to Clinton's critics. It was also Clinton's way of telling voters he understood their instinct that much government spending was wasteful and that he would hold himself to the higher standard embodied in the word "investment."

Better than almost any other Democrat, Clinton understood the need to respond to the innovations of conservatives. If conservatives stole some of the organizational tools of liberal think tanks and public interest groups, Clinton would steal back some of the conservatives' rhetoric and put it to use for different purposes. During his tenure as a leader of the National Governors Association and the centrist Democratic Leadership Council, Clinton was obsessed—as many liberals were not—with finding *politically useful* ideas. By stealing and repackaging some conservative notions and blending them with liberal themes, Clinton appeared to blunt the conservatives' progress. It was one of the many things he did that made conservatives despise him.

Yet Clinton created a decidedly mixed legacy. He strengthened the Democratic Party (he was the first Democrat since FDR to win two full terms) and he weakened the Democratic Party (under Clinton, it lost the House for the first time in forty years, lost the Senate, and was decimated in governorships). His Third Way ideas were bold departures from the Democratic past. They were also cautious adjustments to a more conservative political climate. Clinton made it safe to be a liberal again by proving that Democrats could balance budgets and preside over economic growth while still raising taxes on the rich and spending more on the poor, education, and health care. He made it less safe to be a liberal by declaring the era of big government over and insisting that centrism was the wave of the future. He spoke openly about his own religious faith and about the concerns of families (including those famous "soccer moms"). By speaking in moderate tones on cultural questions, he sought to end the culture wars. Yet his encounter with Monica Lewinsky helped reignite them.

Most Democrats still have affection for Clinton, partly because they see him as a victim of implacable enemies who were willing to go to any lengths to drive him from office. Democrats—and, for that matter, many other Americans—still look back fondly on the peace and prosperity of the Clinton years and pray that those happy days might come again. And Democrats view Clinton as a master politician who understood better than anyone in their party how to defeat Republicans and the right, and how to defend the party's core legacy of social programs and a more or less progressive orientation.

Yet Democrats are aware of the lost opportunity of the Clinton presidency. They see a rare political leader who could have used his talent to build a new majority on the basis of his successes. Instead, he squandered so much of that talent—and so much *time*—on saving himself from what would have been, for most mere mortals, a lethal political situation. Clinton gave his enemies ammunition he should have known they would use. Many Democrats still cannot understand his recklessness.

The Lewinsky scandal was Clinton's great gift to conservatives, and it played out in highbrow and lowbrow ways. The conservative intellectuals focused on Clinton as an alleged example of cultural decline (Bill Bennett wrote *The Death of Outrage* to make this point) and disrespect for the rule of law. Conservative legal specialists brought lawsuits and staffed the Independent Counsel's office, creating the mechanisms that drove relentlessly toward impeachment. And the middle- and lowbrow parts of the right—particularly talk radio—had a field day with everything from a stained dress to invented conspiracies over the suicide of Clinton aide Vince Foster.

The conservatives ultimately failed in their effort to remove Clinton from office. Indeed, roughly two thirds of the country united *against* their campaign, allowing Clinton to save himself. But the scandal created great difficulties for Al Gore. Because of the scandal, Gore was hesitant to embrace the Clinton legacy that—at a time of peace and exceptional prosperity—should have been one of his greatest electoral assets.

And when election night ended in confusion over whom the voters of Florida had favored, the resulting battle illustrated the power a unified right enjoyed when it faced off against a fissured left. Conservatives grasped the stakes as soon as the narrowness of the Florida result became clear in the early morning hours of November 8, 2000. Democrats and liberals were hesitant. They grumbled about Gore's campaign. They worried about looking too aggressive. And by the time Democrats and liberals understood the stakes and began coming together, it was too late.

All this was the culmination of a great shift in the balance of power that resulted from the determined and intelligent efforts of conservatives to alter the nation's political institutions.

II

The context in which "the great little racket" described by Matt Labash operates was created by smart conservatives who understood the importance of winning the battle of ideas. "You can only beat one idea with another idea," said Irving Kristol, the neoconservative who was the center-right's most brilliant intellectual entrepreneur. He argued that "the war of ideas and ideologies will be won or lost within the new class, not against it." Conservatives regularly attacked the *new class*—the intellectuals and professionals who were idea makers and trend-setters—as elitist and out of touch. And they moved smartly to capture it.

The neoconservatives who came along in the mid-1960s were former liberals who grew dubious of liberal ideological rigidity—an irony in light of conservatism's own rigidities—and who questioned specific liberal programs. They made their appearance, as we've seen, after the older brand of conservatism had begun to break into the mainstream. William F. Buckley, Jr., founded *National Review* in 1955 with the goal of defining a new conservatism. The right began its efforts to take over the Republican Party with the movement to draft Barry Goldwater for president in 1960. He had no chance against Richard Nixon and urged conservatives to "grow up" and await their opportunity. As soon as Nixon lost to John F. Kennedy, the Goldwater movement organized in earnest, in alliance with a growing band of young conservatives who saw Buckley as a hero and formed Young Americans for Freedom at the Buckley family farm in Connecticut. In the early years, the neocons had little use for the Buckley right and many of them remained Democrats until Ronald Reagan's 1980 campaign brought the two strands of conservatism together.

But articles of confederation were already being drafted in the 1970s. From his position at the American Enterprise Institute, Irving Kristol became the ringmaster of an array of organizations and projects that brought together the insights of his own camp with those of the more traditionalist conservatives. Supply-side economics in particular provided a flashy new package for the long-standing conservative objective of reducing taxes, especially on the wealthy. Like so much of the new conservatism, the supply-side creed was based on a love affair with old ideas. (Perhaps that is just a definition of conservatism.) The supplysiders created a vogue for Calvin Coolidge and saw Coolidge's economic policies, based on low tax rates, as among the most enlightened in American history.

The network of foundations and think tanks Kristol spawned preached tax cuts, deregulation, free markets, and—when they did not conflict with the first three—traditional values. The conservative foundations and think tanks were something genuinely *new*. While earlier foundations and research organizations felt a need to put some distance between themselves and strictly partisan fights, the new conservative organizations were forthright in their efforts to change the direction of American politics. In the meantime, conservatives criticized the "liberal foundations" for pushing their own ideas in areas such as school reform, desegregation, crime, poverty, and welfare expansion. The war over the foundations bore a remarkable similarity, as we shall see, to the war on the "establishment liberal media." The "liberal foundations"—Ford and Rockefeller were always at the top of the hit list—came under relentless attack. There was much talk in conservative circles, in Congress and elsewhere, of challenging their tax-exempt status.

The difference between the larger and more established foundations and the smaller conservative upstarts lay in the conservatives' sense of urgency. "The conservative elite has been built by individuals who believe strongly, plan strategically and move collectively," Sidney Blumenthal wrote in *The Rise of the Counter-Establishment* in 1986. By contrast, many in the liberal foundations were involved in the civil war within liberalism that broke out in the 1960s over the rise of the counterculture, the failure of Lyndon Johnson's Vietnam policies, and the desire of many on the left for bold departures from New Dealism. Often, the liberal establishment found itself under attack from both the left and the right. It made sense for conservative foundations to advance the cause of a Republican Party that was coming under conservative control. Many liberals, including the ones at the foundations, found the Democratic Party an imperfect vehicle—and they frequently attacked it.

The list of conservative institutions that were born or expanded in the 1970s is long and impressive. Karen Paget offered this catalogue in *The American Prospect:* the Heritage Foundation, the American Enterprise Institute, the Free Congress Research and Education Foundation, the Cato Institute (libertarian rather than conservative), the Hudson Institute, the Hoover Institution, the Manhattan Institute, the Institute for Justice, the Washington Legal Foundation, and the Pacific, Atlantic, New England, and Southeastern Legal Foundations, as well as such magazines and journals as the *Public Interest*—it was the advance guard, having been founded in 1965—and the *National Interest.* All these institutions, as she points out, were backed by "an extensive communications and marketing capacity." And Paget's is just a partial listing.

Consider, as Paget noted, that "roughly a dozen or so foundations provide the lion's share of conservative funding." These include the John M. Olin Foundation, the Lynde and Harry Bradley Foundation, the Scaife Family Foundations, and the Smith Richardson Foundation. These four, she asserts, "give so much in tandem that they are known as the 'four sisters.' " Other key funders include the Adolph Coors Foundation, which helped launch the Heritage Foundation; the Charles G. and David H. Koch Foundations; the JM, Phillip M. McKenna, Earhart, and Carthage Foundations; and the Claude R. Lambe Charitable Foundations.

Consider also Stephan Salisbury's 1997 summary of a report by the National Committee for Responsive Philanthropy, a liberal Washington watchdog group. Writing in the *Philadelphia Inquirer*, Salisbury noted that "12 conservative foundations provided $210 million to conservative policy groups, academic organizations, legal centers, publications, critics, scholars and activists from 1992 through 1994." He continued:

> The bulk of this money—$88.9 million—supported diverse scholarship and training programs, and activist efforts aimed at reestablishing so-called traditional academic standards on college campuses. For instance, the University of Chicago, home of such conservative luminaries as economist Milton Friedman and cultural critic Allan Bloom (who died in 1992), received $10.4 million during the period studied. Much of this money, the report says, went to support legal studies opposed to government regulation of all kinds.
>
> The next-biggest chunk of funding—$79.2 million—went to high-profile think tanks and advocacy groups such as the Heritage Foundation, the American Enterprise Institute, the Cato Institute, and Citizens for a Sound Economy.
>
> An additional $16.3 million went to media groups such as the Center for the Study of Popular Culture and Accuracy in Media.

Almost $11 million went to legal organizations, several of which focus on reversing affirmative action programs, environmental regulations, and other policies of the federal government.

The remainder of the money went to state and local think tanks and advocacy groups.

More recently, the committee estimated that conservative think tanks spent roughly $1 billion promoting conservative ideas in the 1990s.

But it wasn't just that conservatives spent money. They spent it shrewdly, and with the purpose of building a movement. "Conservative philanthropists share an ideological agenda and, despite tax-exempt status that prohibits electoral activity and most lobbying, they contribute in accordance with political objectives," Paget noted. "Grant making primarily is aimed at two overriding objectives: limiting government and freeing markets from regulation—and shaping public opinion accordingly. Like good capitalists, conservative philanthropists conceive of grant making as an investment in people and institutions. Like good bondholders, they are in this for the long haul."

Liberal funders, on the other hand, are torn between "the virtues of national versus grass-roots organizing, thinkers versus doers, and so on," Paget continued. Conservative funders "are not only committed to knowledge production, marketing and communication strategies; they also place a premium on national policy concerns."

This has been a common complaint among liberals. Beth Shulman, a former vice president of the United Food and Commercial Workers union and the author of an important book on the plight of low-wage workers, argued that liberal foundations "seem intent on discouraging engagement in the policy-making process." She went on: "Their grants are awarded only for narrowly defined projects, and grantees are asked to focus completely on producing short-term, quantifiable results."

Rick Cohen, executive director of the National Committee for Responsive Philanthropy, told Shawn Zeller of the *National Journal* that whereas conservative foundations were "institution builders," liberal foundations were merely "project supporters." The conservative foundations were "unabashed" in their willingness to join Washington's battle of ideas and—speaking as a critic of those ideas—Cohen found their effectiveness "quite admirable." As the conservative activist-intellectual Clint Bollick said of the Bradley Foundation, which supported his work, it was "willing to get into the trenches with its philanthropy."

One of the best critiques of liberal philanthropy was offered by David Callahan in *The Nation* in 1995. Appropriately, Callahan later became the research director of a think tank called Demos. Callahan wrote:

At the same time that conservative foundations began investing heavily in intellectual elites during the 1970s and 1980s, foundations on the left were moving in the opposite direction. Reflecting a widespread belief among progressives that more attention should be focused on the grass roots, they placed a new emphasis on community programs and sought greater diversity in their grant recipients. They poured money into activist groups, often seeking to moderate the agenda of those groups in the process. . . . They continued to fund policy research, but they didn't expand that funding to match growing spending on the right.

The results of this starvation diet are now apparent. The left is handicapped in the war of ideas because its policy intellectuals do not have generous patrons. Today's lopsided debate over national policy stems in part from a shortage of liberal and left thinkers who can work full time to develop and sell ideas. The point is not that the side with the most policy wonks wins but that any ideological movement is in deep trouble if it fails to cultivate an energetic corps of professional thinkers.

Callahan traced the preference of liberal foundations for projects over ideas to the overconfidence of liberals in their political and intellectual dominance. "Liberal foundations have focused so much on implementation over the past twenty years," he wrote, "precisely because of their conviction that liberals knew what to do and just had to get busy doing it." But this, he says, is inappropriate to the moment.

Historically, liberal foundations have funded demonstration projects in the hope that they can be models for major government programs. However, as the right continues to win its war on the public sector and the notion of activist government becomes endangered, funding for both new and existing antipoverty efforts is fast dwindling. Better social science research and demonstration projects will not alter this trend; the ideological argument driving it must be attacked directly. To adapt a metaphor, it makes little sense for liberal foundations to labor away deep in the forest, nurturing new types of saplings and combating soil erosion, while doing little to oppose the growing power of clearcutting maniacs.

The foundation and think tank wars are only one part of the story of the troubles liberals and Democrats face. But they are revealing. Conservative foundations were clear about their political purposes and fearless in pursuing them. The conservatives understood the importance of changing the agenda of politics and creating ideas that could change the direction of politics. The liberals were often focused on social do-goodism and the development of local organizations. These were admirable enterprises that proved, as Callahan argued, largely irrelevant to the broader political battles engulfing the country. While conservatives were determined to create a new majority, liberals and those to their left were sometimes skeptical of "majoritarianism" and often enamored of "grass-roots" projects—whether or not these had any likelihood of growing into broader movements.

When conservatives did made local grants, they did it with a clear, national political goal. The Bradley Foundation and conservative philanthropist Ted Forstmann invested heavily in school voucher programs for inner-city children. Their purpose was not simply to give poor children a chance to go to private or parochial schools. The main goal was to influence national policy. They hoped to show that inner-city parents wanted out of the public school system and that vouchers were a viable public policy.

There is a critique to be made of excessively politicizing research, the academic world, and the pursuit of ideas. Ironically, given their success in harnessing the world of ideas to political activism, conservatives usually make this critique and direct it against universities and their professors. But it is the older and more liberal foundations that have resisted joining the political fray more directly and getting "into the trenches." They have done so not only out of fear, and not only because they often had politically diverse boards of directors. They have also maintained the venerable progressive faith in the value of independent research, value-neutral social science, and grass-roots creativity. These are noble commitments, and you'd like to hope there is still room for them in a highly politicized environment.

But conservatives have fundamentally altered the policy game. Steady (and well-funded) conservative work over three decades has borne fruit. Liberals can begin to compete in the battle for politically useful ideas and the struggle to define the nation's ideals. Or they can resign themselves to defeat.

Conservatives felt they were frozen out of older, established philanthropic institutions. Their response was to attack such institutions as "liberal" and then to start their own. Exactly the same thing happened with the media.

III

One of the most successful conservative tactics in the media war has been to compare conservative media institutions with neutral media institutions and declare that because the neutral institutions are not conservative, they *must* be liberal. Take just two examples.

The Fox News Channel has built its large audience by generating intense loyalty among conservatives. The network does have some very good reporters and the occasional (always outnumbered) liberal commentator. But its most important voices, from professional fire-breathers Bill O'Reilly and Sean Hannity to the more reasonable Brit Hume and Tony Snow (a former Bush I speechwriter and columnist), are conservatives. Snow, by the way, eventually moved on to other endeavors and was replaced by the less ideological Chris Wallace, a veteran journalist. The decision to hire Wallace instead of another well-established conservative suggested that liberal media criticism, when applied with the same vigor as conservative media criticism, might have an effect even on the Fox network.

The network is run by Roger Ailes. He is a tough and brilliant political consultant who has spent much of his life advising Republican presidents and presidential candidates. It is owned by Rupert Murdoch, whose publications worldwide tilt to the right—and work unabashedly on behalf of his financial interests.

Though one could wish that Fox would not try to claim that it is "fair and balanced," there is nothing wrong with having a conservative network. But it would be better for democracy if Fox were balanced by a comparably liberal network. Conservatives claim that there is a "liberal" alternative and that it's CNN. This claim is silly. There is not a single program on CNN that can be seen as liberal in the way that, for example, Bill O'Reilly's program is conservative. There are no anchors on CNN as liberal as Hume and Snow are conservative. Two of CNN's biggest stars are conservatives Robert Novak and Tucker Carlson. To the extent that liberals and Democrats appear regularly on CNN, they are balanced by conservatives. *Crossfire* and *The Capital Gang,* the network's major argument shows, are set up as 50-50 deals.

But by attacking CNN over and over again as liberal, conservatives have clearly had an effect. When Walter Isaacson, the veteran *Time* magazine journalist, took over as head of CNN in the summer of 2001—he later moved on to the Aspen Institute—he held a widely publicized meeting with Republican congressional leaders to hear their views about the network. Can one imagine the head of a network calling a comparable meeting with Democrats?

The conservatives also claim that Rush Limbaugh and his many imitators merely "balance off" National Public Radio. How does one even imagine comparing a radio news network that spends millions of dollars sending correspondents around the world with a single host in a studio who does nothing but spout conservative opinions? The answer for conservatives is: Easy. "You know," former House Speaker Newt Gingrich said in 1995, "the liberals have NPR all day. We have Rush. We pay for Rush through advertising. They pay for NPR through our taxes."

Gingrich's effort to beat back funding for public radio and television failed in the end. As the late New York *Daily News* columnist Lars-Erik Nelson wrote at the time, public broadcasting enjoyed support from "the overwhelming majority of the American people—even conservatives, who see nothing particularly liberal in National Public Radio, nothing ideological in Masterpiece Theater and nothing satanic in Barney."

But the conservative claim that conservative talk radio is simply a balance to NPR just keeps on coming, as they say on radio. "Whatever audiences Fox and Rush and the capitalist ruffians have rounded up are the product of competition," declared conservative columnist Zev Chafets in the *Daily News*. "NPR got its franchise the old fashioned way—by government fiat. NPR claims to be nonpartisan. In fact, it is a predictable organ of left-leaning news and views."

I may be said to have a bias in this matter because I have had an association with NPR for the last several years. But my experience proves my case. As a liberal, I have been free to express my views on *All Things Considered,* but partnered up with my smart conservative friend David Brooks or (when he couldn't be there) another strong conservative voice. (A truly left-wing network might have had me engage with someone to my *left.*) NPR lets liberals express their views—as long as they are arguing with conservatives. That's just fine with me. I like Brooks, and I prefer balance. None of this is the sign of a campaigning "liberal" network intent on twisting the news to fit the interests of a cause or a party.

The relentless pressure and impressive inventiveness of the right have had their effect. The case can now be made that if there is a bias in the political media, it is to the *right.*

It's important to be clear that there once was something like an "establishment liberal media"—back in the 1960s, when there existed something like a "liberal establishment." As Jack Shaffer wrote in *Slate,* "Most influential papers happily drifted with the Kennedy liberal zeitgeist," although Kennedy had his share of critics among publishers and he once canceled his subscription to the New York *Herald Tribune,* an influential liberal Republican daily. Republicans and conservatives had a fair complaint against the press for its treatment of Barry Goldwater during his 1964 campaign. "The bias against him was palpable," Shaffer wrote, and he is correct to note that the "way we argue about press bias took its modern shape in 1964."

There were other things going on. Segregationists in the South were furious over the national media's sympathetic coverage of the civil rights movement. Richard Nixon unleashed an effective anti-press campaign with Vice President Spiro T. Agnew as the point man. Agnew attacked "the nattering nabobs of negativism," a line penned by William Safire, who was to become a columnist for what the right viewed as the quintessentially liberal media outlet, *The New York Times.* Safire's hiring in the middle of the Nixon years was itself a response to the conservative campaign against the liberal media. *Times* publisher Arthur Sulzberger decided he needed a conservative voice on an op-ed page that featured such liberal lions as Anthony Lewis and Tom Wicker.

"The press wasn't Nixon's only intended audience," Shaffer notes. "He wanted to communicate a political message directly to the public: that the liberal press was out of touch with what he called middle America. Or, to put it another way, he used the age-old resentment of the press to punish the liberal elite. Nixon's message helped propel him to a landslide victory in 1972." The key to Nixon's landslide reelection was his success in bringing together his own minority share of the 1968 vote with the 13.5 percent won by the populist-segregationist Democrat-turned-Independent George Wallace. Nixon's anti-press campaign was part of a larger effort to capture the populist right.

The 1970s saw the coming together of a series of protest groups on the right animated by opposition to 1960s liberalism and radicalism. There were movements against school busing to achieve racial balance across traditional neighborhood district lines. A new anti-feminist movement led by Phyllis Schlafly, a conservative whose book *A Choice, Not an Echo* was the bible of the Goldwater right during the 1964 campaign, rose up to fight for a traditional view of women's roles. A strong movement against abortion was organized after the Supreme Court's 1973 *Roe* v. *Wade* decision. And a new Religious Right protested against the rise of what it saw as a dangerous and immoral relativism and the lack of respect shown to traditional, religious people. It can be argued that all these groups were strengthened when Nixon fell. Though rhetorically conservative, Nixon was a moderate Republican. In 1976, Nixon's successor, Gerald Ford, acknowledged the power of the right by dumping the liberal Republican hero Nelson Rockefeller as his vice president. Ford's subsequent defeat by Jimmy Carter opened the way for Ronald Reagan and the right to achieve dominance in the Republican Party.

In his brilliant book *The Populist Persuasion,* Michael Kazin lays heavy stress on the alienation this New Right felt from what it viewed as the establishment's control over the means of communication. Remember, Kazin here is writing about a movement with its roots in the 1970s:

> Like Richard Nixon, the grassroots Right was convinced that the mass media was a hostile force that might be manipulated but could not be persuaded. To get its message out, the new conservative movement turned to other outlets, some of them fresh creations, that "moral Americans" could both own and control: direct mail, radio talk shows, cable television stations, right-wing magazines and newspapers. Direct mail received the most attention—because of its emotional, polarizing style as much as for the funds it generated. Political copywriters had to alarm readers into reaching for the checkbooks instead of their wastebaskets. A letter from Jerry Falwell's Moral Majority, for example, named the television producer and liberal activist Norman Lear "the number one enemy of the American family." A solicitation for Senator Jesse Helms warned: "Your tax dollars are being used to pay for grade school education that teaches our children [that] CANNIBALISM, WIFE-SWAPPING and the MURDER of infants and the elderly are acceptable behavior."

Kazin quotes Richard Viguerie, who pioneered conservative direct mail in the 1960s and early 1970s, expressing the right's sense of estrangement from established institutions. "The liberals have had control not only of all three branches of government, but of the major universities, the three major networks, the biggest newspapers, the news weeklies and Hollywood," Viguerie said. "So our communication has had to begin at the grass roots level—by reaching individuals outside the channels of organized public opinion."

Conservatives delivered a powerful one-two punch. Steadily, with the support of the White House when Republicans were in power, conservatives gained ground in the mainstream media, which regularly responded to criticism from the right. In the meantime, conservatives built their own network of communications. What is striking is that while conservatives were constructing new institutions, liberals were complacent, acting as if they believed the conservative claim that the establishment media were on their side.

The new conservative media made no pretense to "objectivity" or "fairness." On the contrary, their goal was to mobilize the conservative grassroots and create a new majority. The establishment media, on the other hand, were living by the older rules and norms of journalism. Their task was not to mobilize but to inform. The right knew which side it was on. The established media claimed to take no side, and usually did not. Ronald Reagan got a rather good press in 1980 simply because many reporters liked him personally and, at the time, felt little warmth for Jimmy Carter.

The anti-press campaign by conservatives yielded tangible results, beginning in the 1970s. White House speechwriter Safire went to the *Times*. George Will, a thoughtful conservative political philosopher and former Republican Senate staffer, became a columnist for *The Washington Post* and a major voice on the ABC News program *This Week*. Former Nixon staffer John McLaughlin pioneered cut-and-thrust political television with *The McLaughlin Group*, giving prominent roles to conservative pundits Pat Buchanan (another Nixon staffer) and Fred Barnes. The extent to which Nixon's anti-press campaign helped his former aides to important media positions is remarkable. In the meantime, the conservative columnist Robert Novak became a major figure on CNN.

The more the establishment media responded to conservative criti-cisms, the more the conservatives attacked. Who could blame them? Their attacks were working. Conservatives built a series of organizations devoted to media "criticism." The media kept responding.

At the same time, the right continued building alternative institutions. Talk radio may be the most important. With the repeal of the Federal Communications Commission's "fairness doctrine," which required bal-ance between political points of view, radio stations no longer needed to offer multiple perspectives on public issues or election contests. Having lost music to the clearer sound of FM, the AM dial needed something new to offer. Talk radio was the answer. Freed from fairness requirements, talk jockeys could expound for hours. Where production costs are con-cerned, talk is, literally, cheap. And there was a hunger for it—especially, it turned out, on the right.

This was not the first time a political subculture on the right end of the political spectrum was built through radio. In the 1930s, Father Charles Coughlin won a vast radio audience for what were, initially, pro–New Deal sermons and then for right-wing appeals that veered toward fascism and anti-Semitism. In his important book about Cough-lin and Louisiana's populist Senator Huey Long, *Voices of Protest*, Alan Brinkley noted the irony of radio's power on the right. "The people who chafed at the intrusion of alien cultural values into their communities were often the same ones who gathered regularly before their radios, the most powerful vehicle for the transmission of those values," Brinkley wrote, in expressing a sentiment that applies equally well to Rush Lim-baugh. "Indeed, it was the radio, the greatest of all centralizing forces, that made it possible for Long and Coughlin to disseminate their appeals for decentralization." Long and Coughlin, as Brinkley notes, were espe-cially gifted at finding "individual scapegoats," another characteristic of the radio talkmeisters of our time.

Limbaugh's brilliance lies in his mastery of the art of radio developed during his years as a journeyman broadcaster. He may have been fighting those terrible liberals and their cultural decadence, but he used all the re-sources of modern entertainment, including rock 'n' roll. Although he occasionally had words of criticism for Republicans who strayed from his orthodox free market views, he unabashedly tied his fate to the fate of the Republican Party. And what he did worked. Charles Peters, the veteran editor of *The Washington Monthly*, wrote shortly after the 1994 Republican electoral sweep that "the happiest group of people in America has to be all those radio talk show hosts.

"In fact," Peters continued, "I don't think it is too much to say that Rush Limbaugh won this election. The countless hours Limbaugh and his imitators spent spewing unrelenting negativity and anti-Clinton vitriol took its toll on Democrats everywhere. On the day after the election, Limbaugh played James Brown's 'I Feel Good' and, as Howard Kurtz of the *Washington Post* noted, 'turned on his "gloat-ometer" ' to dance on Democratic graves."

Republicans never forgot how important Limbaugh was. As the party's supply-siders began pushing the flat tax in 1995, Daniel J. Mitchell, a senior fellow at the Heritage Foundation, was very clear where real power could be found. "When Rush Limbaugh is out there talking about the flat tax," Mitchell told *The Washington Post,* "that's more important than 20 think tanks here in Washington writing Op-Ed pieces for some local paper." Indeed.

Limbaugh's role during the Clinton administration was critical—and Clinton was very helpful to Limbaugh and conservative commentators like him. Limbaugh was already a going concern when Bill Clinton became president. But talk radio thrives on opposition and anger. As the first Bush presidency petered out, it was harder and harder for conservative talk jockeys to rally the troops. Bill Clinton's presidency was the gift that kept on giving.

Conservatives obviously used whatever scandals or quasi-scandals came their way—Whitewater and the White House travel office in the early going, sex later. But conservatives did not just go after Clinton on scandals. They were acutely aware of how to use scandal stories to blunt Clinton's policy successes. If Clinton was winning the war for a health care plan, conservatives could try to marshal arguments against it—and they did that. But they could also change the subject and undermine

Clinton's authority by highlighting and, if necessary, exaggerating any scandal story that came along. They did that, too. Rush Limbaugh was candid about the strategy in late April 1994:

Whitewater is about health care; Whitewater is about Bosnia; Whitewater is about crime and welfare reform; and I'll tell you why. Character—the issue of character was put on hold during the 1992 campaign. Nobody cared about it because so many people were upset with the economic situation, they wanted a change. It's now coming home to roost. Most people think that health care's a good idea, but they haven't read the plan. They're taking the president's word for it. Now I think if the president's word is what we're going to rely on for his policy—this is a debate in the arena of ideas, and this is the man setting the agenda. And if people are going to base their support for the plan on whether or not they can take his word, I think it's fair to examine whether or not he keeps his word.

This is not about getting rid of the president. This is about people who would like to stop health care in a legitimate, democratic sense—trying to compete for the minds and hearts for the American people on the basis that maybe what the president's saying isn't true. [emphasis added]

Trying to get rid of the president came later.

Shrewd Republicans always understood the political danger if Clinton managed to pass a system guaranteeing health coverage to virtually all Americans. "It will relegitimize middle class 'security' on government spending," wrote conservative intellectual and strategist William Kristol in a memo to Republicans. "It will revive the reputation of the party that spends and regulates, the Democrats, as the generous protector of middle class interests. And it will at the same time strike a punishing blow against Republican claims to defend the middle class by restraining government."

And so Republicans set out to kill the plan. Limbaugh briefly tried a syndicated television show produced by none other than Roger Ailes before Ailes started Fox. Drawing on a hit piece against the plan by conservative think tanker—and later New York lieutenant governor—Elizabeth McCaughey published in *The New Republic,* Limbaugh offered these televised words on September 30, 1993:

> Under the Clinton plan, most Americans will not be able to hold onto their personal physician or buy the kind of insurance that 77% of Americans now choose. . . . You like your health care plan now? Too bad. You probably won't be able to hold on to it. You're going to have to sacrifice it and join one of these state alliances or cooperatives and you'll be totally dependent on whatever deal they can negotiate for you. . . . Seeing a specialist and paying for it out-of-pocket will be almost impossible. The Clinton proposal is designed to drive doctors out of private practice. . . . Price controls will make private practice unfeasible. . . . There are going to be back-alley operations of all kinds because people are not going to be forced to live under this iron-curtain type of approach. . . . This is not utopia. This is an erosion—in fact, a pilfering of some of your most precious individual liberties and freedoms. We're going to be here every night helping you along with this stuff, but you're going to have to get on board with us.

The defeat of the Clinton health plan and the Republican congressional sweep in 1994 might have reduced resentment on the right. But Clinton's successful reelection in 1996 reignited Republican loathing. The outcome fed the view that Clinton was a kind of evil wizard whose corruption was matched only by his fiendish cleverness in winning political victories.

House Speaker Newt Gingrich was a partial exception. Always shrewder than his enemies conceded, Gingrich realized that his old strategy had not worked. In 1997, he moved from confrontation to conciliation and sought to reach a deal with Clinton that would balance the federal budget. It was a goal that had moved within reach because of the booming economy—booming, it might be said, despite Gingrich's earlier predictions that Clinton's tax increases would produce a "job-killing recession."

Gingrich gained something out of the deal, but so did Clinton. By January 1998, Clinton seemed finally to have achieved mastery over Washington. The last years of his second term promised to be less hyperactive than his first two years in office, but less reactive than the years after the Republicans took over Congress. The very achievement of a balanced budget, as alert conservatives understood, opened the way for liberal initiatives that had been blocked by deficits. (This was one reason Republicans were so eager to reestablish deficits when they took power again in 2000.) In early January 1998, *Wall Street Journal* columnist Paul Gigot announced the return of "the brave old world of balanced budget liberalism." As a conservative, he was issuing a warning. Gigot noted that a government that "lives within its means" is "one the public may be willing to trust with more ways and means."

This is exactly what the Clintonites hoped. "Once you start reducing the deficit, you can have an affirmative, positive view of government," Rahm Emanuel, a senior adviser to Clinton who was later elected to Congress, said around the same time. "You can raise your sights again."

Clinton was ready with a raft of new programs. Among other things, he proposed to let the near elderly buy into Medicare as a way to reduce the number of uninsured (it was the beginning of piecemeal health care reform); a $21.7 billion child care program; and new federal spending on education, including an ambitious school construction program. "I think this is an interesting week we are in," said Senator Phil Gramm, the conservative Texas Republican, in that early January of the Clinton high tide. "The president has a new idea to create new massive programs every single day."

And then came Monica Lewinsky.

The story was floating around, just below the surface, on the weekend of January 18, 1998, and finally broke to the world on the 20th. The next year would be an ugly time in American politics, the news dominated entirely by the scandal. Clinton would deny and deny, and then finally, when the denials no longer worked, grudgingly admit the truth.

Because of the scandal, the position of all of Clinton's media enemies was enhanced. Rush Limbaugh and his right-wing radio colleagues had the best story of their lives. Cable television outlets competed over which network could devote the most time to a saga that combined sex and politics. The Fox News Channel, as the voice of anti-Clinton conservatives, was well placed to soar. It did.

Journalists who had been moderate or even liberal in the past turned on Clinton with a vengeance. George Stephanopoulos, Clinton's former close aide, expressed open disappointment at the behavior of his old boss. He did so from his new perch as a commentator on ABC's *This Week,* where he arrived after leaving the Clinton White House at the end of the first term. Chris Matthews, once a press secretary to the venerable Massachusetts liberal Tip O'Neill, built his CNBC show *Hardball* on unrelenting criticism of Clinton. William Powers, the media writer for the *National Journal,* pointed to other voices raised in anger at Clinton: Maureen Dowd of *The New York Times;* the late columnist and editor Michael Kelly; *Meet the Press's* Tim Russert; and *This Week's* Cokie Roberts. Clinton single-handedly moved a substantial part of the media to the right.

And the Clinton scandal polarized the country. Somewhere from 30 to 40 percent of Americans were absolutely certain that Clinton should go. A comparable number were more furious at Clinton's enemies—Special Prosecutor Ken Starr, Representative Bob Barr, and the rest—than at Clinton himself. Fortunately for the president, Americans in the middle reached a double judgment: that Clinton had been immoral, or a fool, or both, but that his behavior did not justify driving him from office.

We are still living with the divisions created during the Clinton scandal, and they are very much part of the politics of revenge.

Clinton's survival might be seen as an achievement, proof positive that he was the political miracleworker that his friends and foes believed him to be. Could anyone but Bill Clinton have survived this? Yet Clinton's "victory" in avoiding impeachment was as much a tribute to the failure of his enemies. At every point, they made the wrong choices. They assumed if they just kept pushing to the next step—the Starr Report recommending impeachment, a partisan House vote setting up impeachment procedures, and then an even more partisan impeachment vote to force a Senate trial—victory would eventually be theirs. They were entirely mistaken. But paradoxically, by failing, they strengthened their own hand. They undermined the political legacy Clinton might bequeath, they complicated Al Gore's campaign in 2000, and they strengthened the conservative media.

The Clinton Wars set off the new kind of partisanship. As David Grann argued in a powerful 1999 piece in *The New Republic,* written shortly before the impeachment issue was settled, "the real problem with politics today is not that there is too much partisanship. It is that there is no genuine partisanship." Grann went on: "Whereas partisans once fought ruthlessly for the power to achieve the ideological goals that they truly believed in, the new nihilistic partisans are abandoning almost everything they believe in merely to obtain power for power's sake." In fact, conservatives did have an agenda they pushed with more passion than liberals would their own. But Grann's analysis was instructive about a new style of politics that in turn affected the media.

Over time, the establishment media, especially on cable television, proved itself worthy of that label. As the political establishment changed its color, so did much of the establishment media. As Republicans gained political strength, pressure from the right continued. Fox News rallied a substantial conservative audience. The other cable networks responded by reaching out more than ever to the right. With Fox increasingly cornering the right-of-center audience, its competitors might have pondered building their own market niches—in the center or among liberals, or as resolutely non-partisan. Instead, the other networks—again, particularly the cable outlets—also began searching for their own conservative ground.

One could cite many examples. MSNBC hired the racist and homophobic Michael Savage to do a talk show until he went over the top. Savage was fired in July 2003 after he referred to an apparently gay caller as a "sodomite" and told him he should "get AIDS and die." Should the network have been surprised? Joe Scaroborough, a right-wing former Republican congressman hired by MSNBC for his own show, looked positively moderate by comparison—proving once again the inanity of claiming that the media are liberal. CNN was still the most committed to a traditional, unbiased approach to news reporting, but it did add *National Review*'s Jonah Goldberg, an affable right-winger whose mother was the mastermind behind the leaking of Linda Tripp's story about Lewinsky and Clinton, as one of its political commentators.

ESPN, the sports network, went begging for the conservative audience by hiring Limbaugh as a football commentator. Limbaugh had to quit after he ascribed interest in Philadelphia Eagles star quarterback Donovan McNabb to "a little social concern in the NFL.

"I think the media has been very desirous that a black quarterback do well," Limbaugh said. "They're interested in black coaches and black quarterbacks doing well."

The sports world proved itself more interested in facts and less forgiving of ideological histrionics than the political world. Limbaugh's view that McNabb had been built up because of his race was immediately seen as nonsensical. On the Sunday Limbaugh made his comment, seven of the thirty-two starting quarterbacks were black. Two other black QB starters were sidelined with injuries. As *Washington Post* sports columnist Thomas Boswell wrote: "Sports is a world that is relentlessly reality-tested. . . . If you're in the media and analyze a daily stream of sports events with some political, religious or cultural 'agenda,' you are going to get undressed repeatedly by reality. Sports won't conform to your preferences." Are the standards of political commentary lower than those of the sports world?

There can be no doubt about the success of the right in simultaneously building its own institutions, bringing them to the mainstream, and pushing the establishment media in a conservative direction. Consider how Brian Williams, the host of his own CNBC news show and the man slated to be NBC's anchor when Tom Brokaw retires, began a report on September 24, 2002, about former Vice President Al Gore's speech criticizing Bush's Iraq policy. Here's how Williams opened:

Good evening once again and welcome back. Today our friend, Rush Limbaugh, told his radio listeners he almost stayed home from work, not due to any health reasons but because he was so livid at the speech given yesterday by former Vice President Al Gore criticizing the Bush administration's apparent march to war in Iraq. The anger that physically hobbled Mr. Limbaugh positively ignited his callers today, at least some of whom called Mr. Gore un-American for what he said yesterday. While it can't quite be called an anti-war movement, not quite yet, it could perhaps be called a loyal opposition.

Consider what is interesting here. A news anchor is describing a right-wing talk show host as "our friend." Imagine a newscaster introducing a news story with a reference to "our friend Jane Fonda"—or Molly Ivins, Al Franken, or the Dixie Chicks. The newscaster is relegating the speech of a former vice president and a man who received the most popular votes in the previous presidential election to second place behind the thoughts of a talk show host who "almost stayed home from work." And the newscaster immediately calls into question whatever argument Gore is *about to be shown making* by saying that Gore's remarks "positively ignited" Limbaugh's callers, "at least some of whom called Mr. Gore un-American." Un-American? Finally, he grudgingly concedes that what is about to be shown "could *perhaps* be called a loyal opposition." Liberal bias this is not.

There certainly was liberal bias in the media in the 1960s and conservatives had a point in their protest. That they organized to counter it is not surprising, and they have been decidedly effective. To the extent that there has been a bias in the establishment media more recently, it was less a liberal tilt than a preference for the values of the educated, professional class—which is roughly the class position of most journalists. This has meant that on social and cultural issues—abortion and religion come to mind—journalism was not particularly hospitable to conservative voices. But on economic issues—especially free trade and balanced budgets—the press found itself in the center or tilted toward a moderate conservatism. You could say that the two groups most likely to be mistreated by the media were religious conservatives and trade union leaders.

But even that view is out of date because the definition of "media" commonly used in judging these matters is too narrow. The media world now includes (1) talk radio, (2) cable television, and (3) the traditional news sources (newspapers, newsmagazines, and the old broadcast networks). The great achievement of nearly four decades of conservative campaigning and organizing is that two of these three major institutions tilt well to the right, and the third, under constant pressure to avoid even a pale hint of liberalism, has drifted rightward as well. Liberals are at an additional disadvantage because—until the relatively recent birth of a progressive presence on the Internet—they largely lacked a media aimed at mobilizing their own supporters.

What this adds up to is a media heavily biased toward conservative politics and conservative politicians. This is the context in which the political argument is now carried out. It is an environment less and less hospitable to liberal ideas.

IV

The outcome of the 2000 election was, in many ways, a perfect coda to the Clinton years. It was also a powerful commentary on the unity of the Republicans and the right and the disorganization and lack of solidarity on the Democratic center-left. Understanding the new politics of revenge and the difficulties Democrats face requires examining how Clinton's enemies used his time in office to mobilize their forces, sharpen their attacks, and develop an approach far tougher than anything practiced by either Ronald Reagan or the first President Bush.

Clinton, and especially his economy, were obviously of considerable help to Al Gore. After a difficult campaign, Gore won a plurality of the popular vote and (absent Florida's ballot snafus and the U.S. Supreme Court) a majority of the electoral vote, too.

Yet if the Clinton legacy was valuable to Gore, it also hobbled him.

Long before those debates in which he sighed, Gore went into the 2000 election trailing George W. Bush by 15 points in some polls. There was a Clinton hangover, and Gore's advisers knew it. The result was a Democratic campaign that could not figure out how to accentuate the positive side of the Clinton legacy and eliminate—or at least play down—the negative. At the 2000 Democratic Convention in Los Angeles, a Gore campaign insider described the campaign Gore would run to do both things. The idea was a two-stage campaign. First, Gore would use populist themes to rally core Democrats, beat back Ralph Nader's challenge from the left, and mark out real differences with Bush. Gore would also take some distance from Clinton to get away from his scandals. Then, in the campaign's final month, Gore would embrace the economic successes of the Clinton presidency and ask voters if they really wanted to take the risk of putting George W. Bush in the White House.

It was a smart campaign that was never fully tried. Gore was so angered by Clinton's embarrassments that he never took full advantage of Clinton's successes. As a result, Clinton blamed Gore for running a flawed campaign and Gore blamed Clinton for a legacy of moral problems. Both were right.

The result was the battle over Florida. It is impossible to understand the new politics of revenge without understanding the bitterness the Florida controversy left in its wake. Democrats were not only angry about the result and how it was achieved. They also realized—though too late for Gore's benefit—that Republicans were more united and hungrier for victory. Republicans acted. Democrats hesitated.

As Gore geared up in the days after the election to challenge Bush's narrow lead, Senator Robert Toricelli, a New Jersey Democrat, went out of his way to undercut Gore's efforts. "Ultimately," Toricelli said, "the presidency of the United States should not be decided by a judge." Senator John Breaux, a Louisiana Democrat, was more cautious, but hardly out front in supporting Gore. The right thing to do, he said, was to "count the votes and respect the decision." In the meantime, Republicans were already charging Gore with trying to "steal" the election simply because he was seeking the sort of recount that every candidate in every excruciatingly close race—from city council to governor—typically demanded.

The right went to work immediately to discredit everything about Gore. Limbaugh led the way, accusing Gore of suffering from "an unquenchable thirst for power." "It's not even a question of whether or not they're trying to steal it," Limbaugh declared in late November. "The only question is whether or not they'll succeed."

"We know the whole thing has been rigged and we've known from the get-go," Limbaugh said.

Conservative intellectuals followed the same line, suggesting that there was absolutely no difference in view between conservative talk show jockeys and conservatives with scholarly credentials. William Bennett said flatly that the election would be "illegitimate if Al Gore becomes president." Speaking on CNN (that "liberal" network), Bennett declared: "If you don't call the kind of thuggish tactics that the Gore campaign is doing right now for what they are, I think the notion of objectivity in the media is gone." Note the double whammy—against Gore and against the media. If the media did not report the story Bush's way, it was by definition biased.

Peggy Noonan, the former speechwriter for Reagan and the first President Bush, compared the recount moment to Britain's decision to break the policy of "appeasement" toward Hitler. "The Clinton-Gore operatives are trying to steal the election—and it is wrong." Warming to the theme, she also declared in her online *Wall Street Journal* column: "Every writer, scribbler, Internet Paul Revere, talker, pundit, thinker, essayist, voice, come forward and speak the truth. Howl it."

And where was that liberal establishment media, out to defeat Bush at any cost? The establishment media quickly came to a conclusion: "the country" wanted the election settled and Gore should not fight too hard because Americans were impatient to settle the contest. The establishment press, including newspapers that had endorsed Gore, warned against a lengthy process. Even though Bush's lead in Florida was narrow and even though Gore had won the popular vote, the vice president was told to be dainty. Speaking on the Fox News Channel on the Friday after the election, National Public Radio's Mara Liasson expressed the prevailing view. "I hope that Al Gore will want to preserve his viability in the system, as somebody famous once said, and give himself a shot if he wants to run again," Liasson said. "And he will graciously and honorably, you know, accept these results and not go to court and fight them. I think he will do great damage to his own political future, such as it is— such as it may be."

Throughout the process, there was the demand by the media that Gore be "gracious and honorable." No such demand was ever placed on George W. Bush.

Consider this editorial in *The New York Times* on November 10, the Friday after the election. The *Times*'s editorial page is genuinely liberal, and the paper had endorsed Gore. Yet at the moment when Gore needed all the help he could get, here is what the editorial page said:

> . . . it is worrying that Mr. Gore and a legal team led by Warren Christopher, the former secretary of state, would announce their support for a lawsuit while the mandatory recount is still going on and while seven days remain for the arrival of overseas absentee ballots. It is doubly worrying that some Gore associates are using the language of constitutional crisis and talking of efforts to block or cloud the vote of the Electoral College on Dec. 18 and of dragging out the legal battle into January. The CNN political commentator William Schneider picked apt language when he spoke of the "treacherous path" that would-be leaders choose when they talk of unraveling the finality of elections. . . . The sad reality is that ballot disputes and imperfections are a feature of every election. It will poison the political atmosphere if presidential elections, in particular, come to be seen as merely a starting point for litigation.

The efforts of Republicans to delegitimize Al Gore's insistence on a hand-recount in a very close election were remarkable, insidious—and effective. A matter of immediate convenience—Bush wanted no recounts and wished the vote tally in Florida to stay exactly where it was—was made into an issue of high doctrine. Bush supporters rhapsodized about the virtues of machines and computers in comparison with human beings who tried to count ballots by hand. Never mind that state laws, in Texas, for example, and Republican candidates had long leaned on hand-recounts to validate what voters had intended.

The Bush campaign followed a two-step strategy. Inside the counting rooms, its supporters challenged every ballot that might have been cast for Gore. The challenges, which were their legitimate right, also slowed down and complicated the vote count. Outside the counting rooms, Bush's people acted as if their supporters weren't even inside—and then seized on the complexities their own supporters were creating to discredit the process. They decried the recounts as terribly partisan, controlled by "Democrat" counties. They pretended that Democrats were just sitting there, undisturbed, making up votes for Al Gore. But if the process had not been open, they would not have had the grist for many of the charges they threw around on television.

Republicans crowed at moments when the recounts didn't immediately produce as many votes for Gore as Democrats had hoped they would. But if the counting had been as partisan as the Republicans claimed, Gore would have gone quickly ahead of Bush on the basis of votes "manufactured" by his minions in those "Democrat" counties the Bush camp kept talking about.

Bush consigliere (and Bush Sr.'s top lieutenant) James A. Baker III was the first to go into federal court. Yet Baker kept calling on Gore to drop out because, as he tried to say with a straight face, "I don't believe that the people of America want this national election turned over to lawyers and court contests."

When Bush came out to speak in late November, he infuriated Democrats with a little sermonette that made no concessions to what was taking place in Florida. "We must now show our commitment to the common good, which is bigger than any person or any party," he said. These words could only mean that Gore's commitment to the common good would be measured by his willingness to concede to the other person and the other party. "He could have done a lot more, if not to extend an olive branch, then at least to acknowledge that this has been difficult for the country, and especially for Democrats," said Representative David Price, a moderate North Carolina Democrat known for his conciliatory style. By "not sufficiently honoring a process he knows is going on and is dividing the country," said Senator John Kerry, "he poured salt into open wounds."

If the Bush partisans had been honest about what they were doing—pursuing a tough strategy aimed at minimizing the Democratic vote—they would have been operating well within the tradition of recount fights. But the Bush campaign guaranteed the continuation of the politics of revenge by claiming that Gore, in pursuing his legitimate rights as a candidate, was engaged in larceny. "We are witnessing nothing less than a theft in process," said House Majority Whip Tom DeLay. Montana's Republican Governor Marc Racicot said Gore was willing to "win at any cost."

DeLay and Racicot had no such things to say about Republican congressional candidate Dick Zimmer in New Jersey, who sought a recount in his narrow race with Representative Rush Holt, a Democrat. Zimmer was running 400 to 500 votes behind Holt in an election in which roughly 290,000 votes were cast. "I owe it to the people who voted for me to make sure that it was an accurate and legitimate count," he said. Perfectly fair—and Zimmer's deficit was proportionately larger than Gore's in Florida.

The Bush campaign was even inconsistent with itself, though no one paid much attention. In New Mexico, Gore won by a very narrow margin and Republicans wanted a recount. At one point in late November when Gore held a 368-vote lead, Republican Party lawyer Mickey Barnett demanded *hand-recounts* of ballots in Roosevelt County, New Mexico, on behalf of his party. As *The New York Times* pointed out, Barnett made exactly the same argument that Gore's lawyers made in Florida. In Roosevelt County, Barnett said, machine counts found that an unusually large number of voters skipped the race for president. Manual counting, Barnett argued, was the only way to make sure that's true.

"These ballots are not difficult to tabulate by hand," Barnett said, directly contradicting weeks of Bush propaganda in Florida. "There is, of course"—note that "of course"—"no other way to determine the accuracy of this apparent discrepancy or machine malfunction other than the board reviewing the votes by hand and comparing them with the results."

And it all ended at the United States Supreme Court. A 5-to-4 ideological majority on the Court made George W. Bush president. To get there, the Bush five contorted their own principles to achieve the result they wanted. The five who chose to intrude on Florida's election process had always claimed to be champions of the rights of states and foes of "judicial activism" and "judicial overreach." In this case, they let those principles go on behalf of the Republican candidate for president who had praised two in their ranks—Antonin Scalia and Clarence Thomas—as his favorite justices.

It was grotesque that the majority opinion invoked the equal protection doctrine to stop a recount whose very purpose was to move more closely toward equal protection of all those voters, many of them poor and members of minority groups, who lost their ballots because of confusion and unreliable voting equipment. It was remarkable that the justices who invoked the equal protection idea on behalf of Bush had been critical of that very doctrine in the past.

It was also remarkable that the Court showed an admirable concern for the need to count "overvotes" (ballots on which more than one candidate was chosen) as well as "undervotes" (ballots on which no candidate was chosen)—and then offered absolutely no remedy for either. Because the Florida court didn't fix *all* of the problems, the Supreme Court majority chose to block its efforts to fix *any* of the problems.

"Ideally, perfection would be the appropriate standard for judging the recount," Justice Ruth Bader Ginsburg wrote in her brilliantly stinging dissent. "But we live in an imperfect world, one in which thousands of votes have not been counted. I cannot agree that the recount adopted by the Florida court, flawed as it may be, would yield a result any less fair or precise than the certification that preceded that recount."

By the logic of the majority, the entire election in Florida could have been thrown out, since the certified result already included a mix of counting methods. But that wouldn't have helped Bush.

And suddenly, there was this touching bit of judicial restraint: "Our consideration is limited to the present circumstances, for the problem of equal protection in election processes generally presents many complexities." No kidding. But not so many complexities as to stop the Supreme Court majority from doing the one thing that prevented our knowing in a timely way who really won Florida.

Justices David Souter and Stephen Breyer shared the majority's concern for equal protection, but they dissented sharply when it came to stopping the count. They held what seemed on that day to be an exotic principle: The high court couldn't condemn a lower court and then offer it no opportunity to right a perceived wrong.

"There is no justification for denying the state the opportunity to try to count all disputed ballots now," wrote Justice Souter. Justice Breyer called the majority's bluff by pointing out how sweeping, interventionist, and activist its ruling really was, when he wrote that "the majority's reasoning would seem to invalidate any state provision for a manual recount of individual counties in a statewide election." So much for states' rights.

And just to make sure its decision left the bitterest possible taste in the mouths of those who disagreed with it, the majority that had abruptly stopped the recounting of ballots a few days earlier on the theory that Al Gore would suffer no "irreparable harm" proved the opposite. Oops, said the majority, sorry, that December 12 deadline Gore's lawyers were worried about is upon us. It's too late to have a recount that "comports with minimal constitutional standards."

Bush, with lots of help from the nation's highest court, was allowed to run out the clock. All those lawyers James A. Baker III had hired—and then pretended weren't there—did their jobs very well indeed. So did the conservative intellectuals and so did the conservative media. The battle over Florida was about many things. But above all, it demonstrated the power of a unified Republican Party and conservative movement—and the weakness of divided Democrats and liberals who could not stand together when it mattered.

V

Democrats and liberals now face more serious trouble than they have confronted at any time since the 1920s. All three branches of the federal government are arrayed against them. Conservatives who have regularly (and wrongly) been condemned as "the stupid party"—John Stuart Mill used the phrase a century and a half ago—now find themselves on the ascendancy in the world of ideas. They enjoy their own means of communication and have pulled the mainstream media in their direction. They did not impeach Bill Clinton, but they held back his effort to create a Democratic majority and a more progressive disposition in public policy. And in both the Clinton Wars and the battle for Florida, conservatives showed themselves to be more tenacious, united, and determined than their adversaries. They were willing to invent new doctrines, and abandon some of their most deeply held beliefs, to justify the ratification of their candidate as president of the United States.

All these developments have left American politics as polarized as they have been in the last century. Conservative Republicans struck back angrily at what they saw as their exclusion from the American mainstream and now hold the commanding heights. Liberals and Democrats, who feel as marginalized as conservatives did from the 1930s to the 1960s, are experiencing a comparable anger in the first decade of the twenty-first century—and a comparable desire to rethink, reorganize, and fight back.

6. A Fair Fight

Why Democrats and Liberals Should Stop Being Afraid

> My fellow Americans: Ask not what your country can do for you. Ask what you can do for your country. My fellow citizens of the world: Ask not what America can do for you, but what together we can do for the freedom of man.
>
> John F. Kennedy

> No matter how honest and decent we are in our private lives, if we do not have the right kind of law and the right kind of administration of the law, we cannot go forward as a nation.
>
> Theodore Roosevelt

> We have nothing to fear but fear itself.
>
> Franklin D. Roosevelt

A conservative friend called as I was completing this book with this question: Did liberals or Democrats ever wear neckties honoring an ideological hero? He was not asking about fashion choices or whether they wore ties at all. He was interested in whether progressives felt enough allegiance to a figure from the past to offer such a visible sign of commitment. Conservatives and Republicans, he noted, were proud to wear ties celebrating Adam Smith, the intellectual founder of capitalism. Some wear ties celebrating Friedrich von Hayek, the Austrian free market philosopher. A few traditionalist conservatives, he said, might wear ties celebrating the theologian St. Thomas Aquinas.

Well, I thought, there certainly are liberal heroes—Franklin D. Roosevelt and Harry Truman, JFK and LBJ all came to mind. Modern liberalism's philosophical guides included John Stuart Mill, liberty's great theorizer; Reinhold Niebuhr, the tough-minded liberal theologian; Herbert Croly, the intellectual founder of the modern progressive movement; and John Dewey, the philosopher and pragmatist who celebrated "democracy as a way of life." But not one of them is routinely celebrated by today's liberals.

After I hung up, it occurred to me: liberals and Democrats tend not to view themselves as the inheritors of a grand tradition. Almost on principle, they are suspicious of such traditions, of too much theorizing, of linking themselves too much to the past. The conclusion is inescapable: contemporary conservatives and Republicans are more ideological than today's moderates, liberals, and Democrats. Conservatives and Republicans might restate this by arguing that their movement is more interested in ideas and is more inclined to revere the past. Liberals and Democrats might restate this by saying that conservatives are more rigid and doctrinaire. Each has a point.

The strength of contemporary conservatives and the Republican Party they control is a clarity of purpose and a certainty about the moral superiority of their creed. The result is a willingness to battle to the limit. Victory is itself a moral goal because the ends for which victory is sought are seen as moral. And the objectives of the contemporary right are easily stated: less government, lower taxes, freedom for the entrepreneur, rewards for success, self-reliance.

Yes, there are certain underlying contradictions. The right-to-life movement and religious conservatives, including the Christian Right, are rather eager to use government to control certain aspects of personal behavior. On law and order questions, conservatives are quite willing to use state power against "bad guys" and—except for libertarians in their ranks—less troubled than liberals about civil liberties.

But on the whole, the conservative message is compact, and easy to apply case by case. Any bill that raises taxes is objectionable. Regulations, no matter how worthy their purpose, risk interfering with the market's efficient operation. Goods of every sort are better provided by the private sector than in the public sphere. Reducing the government's impositions on millionaires is good for society because the rich provide the capital and energy that make the economy grow. Helping the poor is very nice, but too much help promotes "dependency" and, some conservatives would say, sloth.

One paradox is that because they know where they are going, conservatives are able to compromise and find it easier to reframe their objectives. They know they cannot abolish the public schools, so instead they advocate private school vouchers. Vouchers might provide short-term fixes in a few places, but if adopted widely enough, they could weaken the entire public school system. They cannot abolish Social Security, so they try to privatize part of it by directing what is currently public money into personal accounts. They cannot abolish Medicare, so they propose a "market-based" system that will not guarantee the elderly the health care they need at any given time, as the current system does, but merely promises a certain fixed payment for buying private insurance. They knew they could not persuade the public that a grand plan to remake the Middle East by changing Iraq was practical. So they made the case for war by pointing to immediate threats of chemical and nuclear weapons (even if those threats were not as described) and linked Saddam Hussein to the horror of 9/11. They cannot get the public to buy into the big reductions of government they favor, because the biggest government programs (Medicare and Social Security, for example) are broadly popular. So they steadily shift the tax burden away from the wealthy and toward the middle class. They shrink government revenues and hope that the middle class will buy into an anti-government revolt that the wealthy cannot carry out on their own.

If the middle class and the poor were to make common cause, their numbers are overwhelming. So the conservatives fashion policies designed to ally the middle class with the wealthy, linking, for example, modest middle-class tax cuts with large tax reductions for the best off. Inch by inch, row by row, they would roll back the government by starving it. They would slowly reduce public provision for the poor, the elderly, and the out-of-luck. They would undermine the idea that there may be a common good that is more urgent, just, and desirable than individual preferences, interests, and privileges.

There is a certain elegance here that deserves respect, but there is also something terrifying about the project. For all the talk that liberals and Democrats somehow represent "the past," the conservative project is rooted not in a bold idea about the future but, as we've seen, in restoring the political order of the nineteenth century by repealing many of the political achievements of the twentieth century. It would recreate a world of unconstrained economic competition, reduce state action against monopoly and oligopoly, offer far less in the way of public provision and social insurance, limit government intervention to protect rights, and push back more recent initiatives to protect the environment, worker safety, and the consumer. It would use control of the courts to void legislative actions designed to advance such progressive ends.

All this sounds harsh because most conservatives are shrewd enough to take the hard edges off their program as they move it forward and to insist that they share liberalism's humane goals. But only if their real goals are looked at squarely will the urgency of fighting for an alternative future become obvious. The battle must be raised above the bustle of tactics, "message," and "positioning." The stakes are enormous. The polarization of American politics shows that large numbers of voters already understand the country confronts a fundamental choice. The conservatives have made their objectives clear. Their opponents must do the same.

The weaknesses and strengths of liberals and Democrats parallel each other. The weaknesses have to do with a reluctance to make their case on the grounds of principle and philosophy. This, in turn, weakens their moral position and cedes moral argument to the right. Long ago, the political analysts Lloyd Free and Hadley Cantril offered a classic analysis of the political beliefs of Americans that explains this liberal wariness.

Americans, these political scientists argued, are *ideological* philosophical conservatives but *operational* liberals. In general, Americans agree with conservatives on the need to limit government, but they tend to like the government programs that liberals have enacted. In the public debate, Democrats and liberals drink deep at the Free and Cantril well. Liberals and Democrats don't try to defend the theory behind what they do because they figure doing so is a losing proposition. They offer programs—Medicare and Social Security, environmental regulation and federal help to schools, minimum wages and family leave laws—that they know the public likes.

But avoiding the philosophical argument behind the programs—essentially, that the government can improve on the workings of the market and that public provision of social insurance can make society fairer and better—has left the ideological field to the right. Anti-government arguments (and propaganda) have not been countered. Hillary Clinton told the story of a woman who approached her during the 1994 health care fight and demanded that the government not interfere with Medicare. That this Medicare beneficiary did not see the program as a creation of government is a mark of the Democrats' failure to make their larger case.

By accepting the Free and Cantril message and stopping there, Democrats became intellectually and politically flabby. When the right attacked them on the fundamentals, Democrats were not prepared to reply in kind. In the meantime, the right understood the public's ideological proclivities and exploited them to dismantle the very programs that made Americans "operational" liberals. The flight of liberals and Democrats from philosophical arguments helps to explain the shift in the nation's political language.

Yet it is also the strength of American liberals, from both Roosevelts to Truman to Clinton, that they have never been doctrinaire. Unlike socialists, liberals and Democrats as well as progressive Republicans did not seek to overturn capitalism. Yet unlike so many free market conservatives, they never thought that capitalism, all by itself, was enough. American liberalism was experimental and (in John Dewey's sense) "pragmatic."

Liberals had a profound belief in equality, which led them to support civil rights and programs to lift up the poor. They were never committed to anything remotely close to equality of wealth or income. They thought that certain goods, such as health care and education, should be distributed in relatively equal ways. (That educational opportunity is still so unequally distributed is one of liberalism's great failures.) But they thought other goods—cars and houses are the obvious examples—could be distributed in very unequal ways, as long as those who were poor were provided with a "decent minimum." They thought that government could expand access to necessities (for example, child care and, again, health care) without necessarily being their sole provider.

This pragmatic approach squares with the common sense of a large majority of Americans. Most Americans who can afford it would prefer to make their own child care arrangements—including the option of having a parent at home. But they also accept that other Americans, including those in households in which both parents work out of choice, necessity, or both, need help in making sure their children are well cared for—and that some who don't need help today might need it tomorrow. Most Americans would like the best possible health care plan paid for by their employer, preferably, or by themselves, if they can afford it. But most Americans know the risks of losing health care, and know that the risk is growing. They also know that many of their fellow citizens simply can't afford health insurance and don't get it from their employers. They are open to health care solutions that try to preserve such freedoms they now have but also provide everyone with a degree of security. And as health coverage becomes less secure and more expensive, Americans are increasingly willing to accept in principle that trade-offs must be made.

But that phrase "in principle" is a perfect example of the problem liberals and Democrats face: squaring everyone's desire for as much coverage and choice as possible with government guarantees of health care security is difficult and expensive. It's far easier to mouth free market slogans about "choice" and "incentives."

So, sure: Solving common problems with help from government is something that's hard to talk about. It's much easier to discuss the many ways in which government can fail. But solving common problems is the object of public life. In the end, liberals and moderates, Democrats and the many Republicans and Independents who have not bought into a radical free market agenda must resist the war against public life that has dominated our politics for so many years.

Less government, lower taxes, freedom for the entrepreneur, rewards for success, self-reliance. Compared to these apparently concrete goals, the alternatives seem abstract: *Common good, equality of opportunity, community, compassion, a clean environment, corporate responsibility, justice, fairness.* And the specific goals of programmatic liberalism seem hard to reach: *Health care and child care for all, safe and family-friendly workplaces, better education, access to college, better pay for low-wage workers, prescription drugs for seniors, rights for HMO patients, stopping global warming, ending gun violence.*

But by flipping the above paragraph around, it's possible to see how both the abstract and the concrete goals of liberalism might become attractive. All of the ambitions on programmatic liberalism's list are popular—and nothing on the conservative list would achieve them. Every abstraction listed above as a progressive goal commands broad support. George W. Bush has worked hard not to be seen as an enemy of any one of them. Doesn't that say something?

And progressives lose as much as they gain when they narrow their focus to bite-sized programs because narrow goals are easily co-opted. When Democrats said that prescription drugs for the elderly under Medicare was their major theme, they not only left out the large numbers of Americans who had no health care coverage at all. They also made it easy for Republicans to say that they, too, were for prescription drug coverage and allowed Republicans to pass a bill that did not challenge pharmaceutical companies on high drug prices and contained the seeds of the destruction of the entire Medicare program. Similarly, Republicans could declare themselves supportive of the rights of patients, even if they were reluctant to regulate health care provision within the HMOs.

As Bush has shown with some brilliance, absolutely nothing stops conservatives from dressing up a program based largely on tax cuts and deregulation in the rhetoric of compassion and social decency. Vague rhetoric works when it goes unchallenged.

But what if progressives were to become bolder—and more candid—about the philosophy behind their ideas? What if they began linking their programs to larger purposes? "The left-of-center presents a confusing picture of where it wants to go," says John Podesta, Clinton's former chief of staff. The alternative, he says, "is to be coherent, to work from values that make sense to people."

Radical individualism rejects any notion of the common good beyond the individual pursuit of wealth and happiness. Should progressives be so afraid of making the case that individual wealth and happiness are, and always have been, most satisfying—and more *likely*—in a society in which a sense of justice, fairness, and equal opportunity creates social harmony and mutual respect? At the end of the 1990s, when unemployment dropped below 4 percent, did not the poor advance along with the rich? Didn't the previously dependent enjoy unprecedented opportunities to leave the welfare rolls? Was there not a reduction in crime, racial resentment, teen birthrates, and family breakup in a period when prosperity was widely shared?

And yes, where individualism is concerned, government is central to protecting the rights of individuals—including their rights both within and against corporations. Bush's signing of the national "Do-not-call" list legislation was a classic case of acknowledging that the market by itself does not always protect individuals against abuse. Why is it so difficult to apply this lesson more broadly? If conservatives have been so successful at playing against the power of government, why are liberals so afraid to speak candidly—as Theodore and Franklin Roosevelt were not—about the dangers of concentrated economic power? It is, after all, the power of democratic government that checks the potential abuses of private power. Didn't many stockholders wish that government had caught up with Enron's abuses before they lost fortunes small and large in a company that violated their trust? Weren't mutual fund participants grateful that an Attorney General in New York challenged abuses that threatened to plunder their honest investments?

Moderation is a great and honorable American disposition. Moderation entails a balance between public and private ends, between individual goals and desires and social justice and cohesion. Individual liberty is threatened not only by an excessively powerful state but also by social breakdown that can lead to chaos. "We were against revolution," Franklin Roosevelt declared in 1936. "Therefore, we waged war against those conditions which make revolutions—against the inequalities and resentments which breed them." Revolution is not now in the air. But a society that battles against "inequalities and resentments" is far more likely to be successful than a society that ignores them.

The goals of contemporary conservatism are easy to state, easy to fight for, but narrow and incomplete. The goals of contemporary liberalism are difficult to achieve, but widely shared, idealistic but practical, intricate, perhaps, but balanced. It's a fair fight if those who take the liberal view are willing to wage it.

And given the increasing aggressiveness of the conservative agenda, it's obvious that liberals and moderates now need to make common cause. "Moderate" and "centrist" are both relative terms. Moderate compared to what; centrist on whose political spectrum? The success of Bush and the conservatives hangs in part on their ability to push the argument to the right and thereby redefine the political center. If moderation simply means chasing the center to wherever the right succeeds in moving it, the notion of a center loses all substantive meaning. Moderates lose their political purpose and ultimately destroy themselves.

Moderates and centrists, including many Republicans, have ample reason to make common cause with others, including liberals and progressives, who see current policies as decidedly immoderate and irresponsible. Moderates have always argued for fiscal responsibility. They have always worried about excessive tax cuts as well as excessive government spending. They have never given up on the idea of government as a problem solver. They have always seen a government role in protecting the environment, in enhancing social mobility, in looking out for children and the poor. They have always believed in a sensible internationalism in foreign policy.

In the meantime, liberals have never been as sympathetic to capitalism as they are today. They have never spoken as much about markets. They have never been as committed to fiscal responsibility. Not since the days of Truman, Roosevelt, and Kennedy have liberals been as clear in talking tough about a strong American role in the world. This is true even as many of them rejected Bush's unilateralism and as some of them rejected his policy in Iraq.

The first task of politics now is to prevent a sharp turn to the right. That requires an alliance between the center and the left, which means, in turn, giving up on some of the rote disputes between center and left that are no longer relevant. It means understanding the stakes of politics *now.*

There are many reasonable arguments in which center and left might engage. How much should a plan for universal health care rely on the market and how much on government? What are the right pressures and incentives to improve schools and the quality of teaching? What is the role of direct regulation in cleaning up the environment and where can the government use market inducements to encourage companies to do the right thing? Are private school vouchers or new programs in public schools the best way to provide preschool and after-school care? But all these arguments assume that there is a will to use public resources to solve public problems. *Before any of these arguments is even possible, the current push to starve the public realm of funds and devalue government's potentially useful role must be defeated.* Neither the center nor the left can win this fight on its own.

The need for common cause between moderates and liberals is especially urgent in the battle for control of the federal courts. Judges appointed by one president can lock in a worldview for a generation or more. Attacks on "the imperial judiciary" were once the stuff of conservative polemics against a "liberal activist" Supreme Court. That is changing, and not just because of the 5-to-4 decision that made Bush president.

In a shift that is momentous in historical and political terms, liberals are beginning to sound alarms about conservative justices using states' rights and other doctrines to void environmental, economic, social, and civil rights legislation. The liberal fear is that the Supreme Court is marching back to its pre–New Deal days, when justices relied on strict interpretations of property and contract rights—and narrow interpretations of governmental authority—to strike down laws on wages and hours and to invalidate other forms of regulation.

Quietly, conservative judges have been moving in this direction. In 2000, for example, the Supreme Court struck down a law that allowed the victims of rape and domestic violence to sue their attackers in federal court. The court said this was a state issue. It also said state employees couldn't use federal laws to bring age discrimination suits against state governments. "The court has imposed by fiat limitations on the exercise of federal power," says Senator Joseph Biden, the former Judiciary Committee chairman. "The Supreme Court, in case after case, is freely imposing its own view of sound public policy—not constitutional law, but public policy. What is at issue here is a question of power, whether power will be exercised by an insulated judiciary or by the elected representatives of the people." The phrase "judicial activism" has "often been used by conservatives to criticize liberal judges," Biden acknowledged. But "under this Supreme Court, the shoe is plainly on the other foot: It is now conservative judges who are supplanting the judgment of the people's representatives and substituting their own."

Biden's argument is important because he is speaking not just for himself but for an entire school of judges and legal scholars who fear that the courts may be on the road to invalidating many years of regulatory legislation. On the Court itself, Justices David Souter, Stephen Breyer, and John Paul Stevens have all raised alarms. Souter, for example, has warned of "a return to the untenable jurisprudence from which the court extricated itself almost 60 years ago." David Strauss, a law professor at the University of Chicago, argues that what unites many of the recent decisions and arguments is a desire to undermine regulation, whether enacted by Congress, state legislatures, or voter referendums. The trend, he says, involves "aggressive interpretation of federal statutes where they preempt state regulation" and "narrow interpretation" of federal regulatory statutes.

"I don't think they care about the states; they want to get rid of regulation," Strauss says. He argues that many judicial conservatives are more interested in advancing a new and stronger interpretation of property rights than in safeguarding states' rights.

In the battles over judicial appointments, it is routine to look to the abortion issue as the litmus test. But far more is at stake than *Roe* v. *Wade* or even old-fashioned arguments about states' rights. The struggle over judges will be lost unless the larger issues of democratic authority and conservative judicial overreach become central questions in the national debate—and unless liberals and moderates understand their shared stake in a judiciary that is not dominated by extremes. That includes, it should be said, extreme positions of the left as well as the right.

The fight over the courts underscores why liberals and moderates need to join hands. But it is not the only question on which center and left must find common ground. The struggles for reasonable gun regulation, environmental protection, and the preservation of a decent system of social insurance are all areas where center and left might disagree on specific approaches, but share a desire to move forward—and to stop a sharp shift to the right. And as conservatives become more audacious in pushing their agenda forward, moderates in the Republican Party will find themselves in an increasingly awkward position. Progressives who did not follow Jim Jeffords out of the party nonetheless empathized with his sense of isolation. The crisis for moderate Republicans will deepen as they face pressure from conservatives who threaten to run campaigns against them in primaries and from moderate constituents frustrated over the Republican Party's direction.

II

There are many signs that the radicalism of the Bush administration has finally called forth a desire to fight back. The tone of the 2004 Democratic primary campaign was set by Howard Dean's insurgency, despite Dean's failure to win the nomination. Dean created a mass movement not simply because he opposed the Iraq War, but also because he spoke to the impatience of what so many Democrats and liberals saw as a policy of appeasement toward the Bush administration. Many Democratic leaders in Washington would complain that they had, in fact, taken on Bush—and were hit hard by the right for doing so. Congressional leaders also had the responsibility to conciliate colleagues with a wide range of views, and all the problems that obligation created. Dean was unencumbered by such worries, and he sensed the mood in his party more clearly, and earlier, than any of his rivals. In many ways, the Dean movement resembled the Goldwater movement of the 1960s. Conservatives saw Goldwater's campaign as an opportunity to demonstrate the power of their cause and to organize for the future. Dean's supporters saw their candidate's effort as an opportunity to organize, to protest against the dominant political powers, and to demonstrate the political strength of the liberal opposition.

Partly because of Dean but also because of the frustrations that came to the fore after the 2002 election, the spirit of opposition became stronger throughout 2003 and into the 2004 primaries. The administration's questionable claims about the immediacy of the threat posed by Saddam Hussein, the failure to find weapons of mass destruction, and the false assertions made about the state of his nuclear program weakened the administration's case and emboldened its critics. The president himself was eventually forced to admit that Saddam had nothing to do with 9/11—though he did so only after American troops were committed to Iraq. The claim that Saddam had reconstituted his nuclear program was simply untrue. Even more damaging to the administration was the failure of its optimistic predictions that Americans would be treated as liberators in Iraq. The inadequacy of the administration's prewar planning for the occupation was obvious even to friends of the Iraq policy. The administration was simply not prepared for the tasks it would confront once the United States had to run the country. Having been sold on the war and the occupation as an easy thing, many Americans recoiled when it turned out to be hard, dangerous, expensive, and deadly.

Representative Richard Gephardt, who had negotiated with Bush to push through a war resolution, declared him an "absolute failure," to much acclaim in the Democratic Party. Senator John Edwards was especially bold in pushing the economic argument. Edwards, the son of a millworker, played on his autobiography to declare Bush the friend of "wealth over work." Senator John Kerry, who voted for the war resolution and lost support to Dean as a result, voted against Bush's $87 billion request in October 2003 for reconstruction in Iraq. Kerry said the Bush administration's behavior before the war "may be the most arrogant, deceptive moment in our foreign policy in many decades," and he added: "It was bad enough to go it alone into the war. It is inexcusable and incomprehensible to go it alone in the peace." Even Senator Joe Lieberman, the strongest supporter of the war in the Democratic field, criticized Bush's postwar policies. "We didn't send our young people to war unprepared," Lieberman wrote in an op-ed article in *The Washington Post* in July 2003. "We must not ask them to keep a difficult peace without a clear strategy and adequate resources to do the job. As of today, they have neither." Lieberman also offered a stark contrast to Bush's fiscal policies, proposing sharp increases in taxes on the wealthy matched with tax cuts for the middle class and the poor. Wesley Clark made a call for "a new American patriotism" a central theme of his campaign, drawing on earlier efforts in that direction from fellow Vietnam veteran and primary victor John Kerry.

The Democratic primary campaign also saw the rise of new forms of organizing, particularly in Howard Dean's campaign. His success in raising money from small donors on the Internet was a virtual rebuke to Democrats who insisted that a reformed campaign finance system would hurt the party. His message was: Don't whine. Organize. Dean's astonishing success at financing his campaign through record contribution levels online gave Democrats an alternative to their addiction to raising big money from wealthy people and well-financed interest groups.

Joe Trippi, Dean's campaign manager (until he was fired after Dean's decline) and an evangelist for the gospel of online politics, described the alternatives: A candidate can raise $200 million by asking 100,000 wealthy Americans to give $2,000 each, or by asking 2 million Americans of ordinary means to contribute $100 each. Dean's challenge raised an uncomfortable question for the party: if Democrats can't find a few million people willing to part with a couple of bucks a week, they are in more jeopardy than anyone thought.

What Dean has set in motion will long survive his campaign. He will be seen as a political innovator much as John F. Kennedy was in understanding the power of television, and as both Barry Goldwater and George McGovern were in using direct-mail fund-raising. "Whatever hyperbolic language you use about this, it's true," said Simon Rosenberg, president of the centrist New Democrat Network, who argued at the height of the Dean insurgency that the Internet fund-raising revolution will be especially beneficial to Democrats. While Republicans have long cultivated both big and small donors, Democrats let their small money base atrophy from the 1970s on. Rosenberg saw Dean and organizations such as MoveOn.org proving that the Internet could make small money fund-raising cheap and efficient.

And the Internet is not just about fund-raising. Mark Karlin, the editor and publisher of BuzzFlash.com, a liberal Web site, sees it becoming "the progressive or Democratic alternative to right-wing radio," a place where activists can congregate, exchange views, and organize.

Some left-of-center sites are vitriolic in their commentary on Bush, in the style of conservative talk radio. But Karlin, Rosenberg, and Wes Boyd of MoveOn question the assumption that left-wing ideology is the sole motivator on the progressive Internet. Karlin describes his constituency as "energetic" rather than ideological, while Boyd sees the Internet as rewarding "insurgents" willing "to say something different from what's being said inside the Beltway." The Web, says Rosenberg, tends to favor candidates with "the passion, the cause and the commitment." That is a fair description of Senator John McCain's 2000 campaign, which took the first steps in making effective use of Internet fund-raising.

Like conservatives who felt marginalized by the media in the 1960s, liberals began discussing ways to create their own forms of media in the Bush years. Money was raised for a new cable network and a group of liberal talk radio shows, including a direct challenge to the right from the comedian and satirist Al Franken. Liberal and left media criticism became a growth industry, especially in the long period after 9/11 when Bush received almost universally good press. Right-wing books—particularly books attacking the Clintons—had packed the best-seller lists from the late 1990s. Suddenly, such books had competitors from the liberal left, particularly from volumes attacking Bush. During one week in early November, Michael Moore's and Franken's tough books on Bush and the right pushed Fox News's Bill O'Reilly into third place on a *New York Times* list that also included anti-Bush books by Molly Ivins and Lou Dubose, and Paul Krugman. The war of the books was revealing. It was not just further evidence of the polarization of American politics. It showed that liberals and Democrats were in a mood to do battle.

The same spirit was visible in the labor movement. The growing service unions—the Service Employees International Union, the hotel and restaurant workers, and the United Food and Commercial Workers—looked for inspiration in an updated version of the aggressive organizing by the industrial unions in the 1930s and 1940s. The imperative was to organize—or die. Building on the labor movement's political work, Steve Rosenthal, the AFL-CIO's former political director, set up a series of new organizations aimed at registering and mobilizing lower-income and minority voters who might not be members of unions, yet shared labor's interest in a progressive agenda. And in a fine tribute to Newt Gingrich, progressives set up an organization called PROPAC aimed at raising money to recruit and train left-leaning candidates at the grassroots level. It was, said *The Washington Post*'s David Von Drehle, "the first step in a long-range project to fill the pipeline with a fresh supply of future winners." The group was unapologetically modeled after GOPAC, an organization once headed by Gingrich that supported Republican candidates in state legislative races. Quipped Von Drehle: "If you can't beat 'em, copy 'em."

Similar things were happening in the world of ideas. Like Paul Weyrich and Ed Fuelner, the conservative activists who founded the Heritage Foundation in 1973 to create an outlet for conservative ideas, John Podesta opened the well-financed Center for American Progress in the fall of 2003. The aim, he said, was "to build an idea base for the longer term" and bring about "an enduring progressive majority."

Progressives have "invested in single-issue, stovepipe institutions like on the environment," Podesta argued. Conservatives "built up institutions with a lot of influence, a lot of ideas. And they generated a lot of money to get out those ideas. It didn't happen by accident. And I think it's had a substantial effect on why we have a conservative party that controls the White House and the Congress and is making substantial efforts to control the judiciary."

It was not that liberals lacked for brains, research, or proposals. "We ended up creating a lot of analytic capacity," Podesta added, "but very little of that was linked to an overall vision of where progressives wanted to take the country and the world." He cited a conversation with a businessman who dissected the liberal problem in the language of his profession. "All you guys do is show individual products," the businessman said. "You never show a brand."

In late October 2003, the new think tank organized its first big public splash—and it dedicated its session, held in a hall decorated with American flags, to "New American Strategies for Security and Peace." The mission of the session was not only to solve old liberal problems, but also to seize openings created by the new foreign policy problems confronting the Republicans.

It was an odd turn. In the early 1970s, as we've seen, conservatives such as Fuelner, Weyrich, and Richard Viguerie saw themselves imitating the successful organizing of the left, represented in the labor, civil rights, and consumer movements. They saw an intellectual world that leaned left, and created their own scholarly havens. They saw a press that leaned toward a kind of centrist liberalism, and created media outlets of their own. They created Blumenthal's "Counter-Establishment."

During George W. Bush's years, liberals came to understand the need to create a counter-counter-Establishment to battle conservative dominance, which now stretched to all three branches of the federal government. This might be seen as part of the politics of revenge in the showdown that became inevitable during Bush's presidency. But it was also part of a natural cycle. The old liberal establishment had once dominated the intellectual world and influenced civil servants steeped in the traditions of the New Deal and John F. Kennedy's spirit of activism. It had a powerful hold on foreign policy, burnished its moral legitimacy during the battle for civil rights, and was given a lengthy lease on power thanks to the organizing of the industrial unions and the influence of local Democratic organizations. It began losing its grip after Vietnam—and after Nixon and then Reagan challenged its support among working-class and lower-middle-class voters. Its final demise was delayed during the Clinton years, even if Bill Clinton was neither fully part of, nor always accepted by, that establishment. But especially after the 2002 election, it was clear that neither Democrats nor liberals defined the establishment.

No Democrat, no liberal, no moderate could doubt the need for new departures. The establishment was no longer liberal. Government's power was in the hands of the right. The media were no longer progressive, to the extent that it ever was. Financial resources were flowing to the right and to the Republicans.

The burst of liberal and Democratic organizing during the Bush presidency grew from a recognition of these realities. But Democrats and the center-left developed bad habits over three decades and were locked in futile and divisive debates that did little to advance their own agenda. Move to the center or move left? Compromise or fight? Rally the base or reach out to Independents? These arguments are about positioning, not principles.

III

Recriminations can be good or bad. Good recriminations entail an honest, if painful, assessment of something that has gone wrong. Bad recriminations happen when factions use defeat to score the same tired points against their rivals that they were trying to score before the votes were counted. Bad recriminations strengthen factions. Good recriminations build parties and movements. Bad recriminations lead to pointless arguments. Good recriminations lead to creative arguments.

Let's examine ten tired and useless arguments that Democrats—and liberals and moderates—can't seem to stop themselves from having, and ten new arguments they should start making. We'll label them "The Wrong Stuff" and "The Right Stuff."

THE WRONG STUFF

1. **Big Government vs. Small Government.** What is the point of this argument? Progressives and Democrats clearly favor a rather large government when it comes to Social Security, Medicare, Medicaid, education spending, environmental, worker, civil rights, and consumer protection. There is nothing here that requires apologies. Progressives don't have to defend themselves against charges that they favor the government takeover of private business because they are proposing no such thing. And they have always defended individual liberty against government incursions. The big vs. small government argument miscasts what's at stake. There is nothing wrong with favoring a strong and active government that operates within limits. You might even say that this is the American Way.

2. **Pro-Business vs. Anti-Business.** Since when have Democrats or liberals been anti-business? Didn't business flourish in the Clinton years—and in the Kennedy and Johnson years? Democrats want business to prosper, and their actual policies when they held office have favored growth, prosperity, and entrepreneurship. They also want businesses not to cheat. Remember Enron? They have confidence that capitalism can do what it does best, which is to produce goods and services. Supporting capitalism means opposing fraud, guaranteeing investors honest information, opposing monopoly and oligopoly, and resisting measures that throw government's power on

the side of the most powerful economic actors. Believing in the strength of the capitalist system means countering the idea that regulation destroys business. Some forms of regulation—by the Securities and Exchange Commission, for example—keep business running smoothly. And the country is richer than it was thirty years ago even though environmental regulations are now much tougher. Those who favor reasonable regulation are not the enemies of business.

3. **Populist vs. "Mainstream."** Some Democrats think Al Gore went off the rails when he went "populist." What did Gore do? He attacked big oil companies, polluters, HMOs, and big insurance companies. Does anybody think he lost voters by doing this? Gore went up in the polls after his Democratic National Convention speech that made these points. On many issues, the "mainstream" *is* populist. That's why John Edwards's warnings about "two Americas," one for the rich and one for the rest, struck such a chord during the 2004 primaries.

4. **New Middle Class vs. Old Working Class.** Democrats are supposed to face a choice between rallying working-class voters or appealing to voters in the new middle class. Guess what? They won't win elections unless they get votes from both constituencies. Gore did very well in the new middle class. He fell short among working-class voters, especially in rural areas and the South. George Bush appeals to rich business people and lower-middle-class Christian conservatives. Can't Democrats also walk and chew gum at the same time? Democrats need to hold the gains they have made in the professional classes on the issues of social tolerance. They also need to be more respectful toward religious people and more explicit about supporting economic policies that would create opportunities for voters with modest incomes who now vote Republican on cultural issues.

5. **Globalist vs. Protectionist.** Democrats are told they either have to defend the new global economy or fall back on protectionism. It's a no-win choice. The global economy is not going to go away—and it does create injustices. It also poses challenges to regulations in areas such as labor standards and the environment. These standards are

enforced by national governments, yet globalization makes it increasingly difficult for national governments, acting alone, to work the will of their citizens. Isn't the real issue whether it's possible to create a Global New Deal under which the new economy is accepted as inevitable but under rules that make the playing field fair and protect the vulnerable?

And doesn't the sharp decline in manufacturing jobs over the past few years and the flight of both manufacturing and professional jobs overseas suggest a need for new thinking about the impact of free trade and globalization? In an important essay in *The New York Times* in January 2004, two longtime free traders—Senator Charles Schumer of New York, a liberal, and economist Paul Craig Roberts, a conservative—suggested the need for a new approach to trade. "When American companies replace domestic employees with lower-cost foreign workers in order to sell more cheaply in home markets, it seems hard to argue that this is the way free trade is supposed to work," they wrote. "To call this a 'jobless recovery' is inaccurate: lots of new jobs are being created, just not here in the United States." They concluded: "America's trade agreements need to reflect the new reality."

6. **Deficits vs. Balanced Budgets.** This is a real choice. The Bush administration decided to throw balanced budgets overboard and push all the hard choices into the future by saddling the next generation with debt. Why is it so hard for Democrats—and liberals and moderates—to argue both that the Bush approach is dangerous fiscal policy for the long term *and* that it threatens government's ability to solve problems in the short term? Where is the money to establish universal health insurance, to help state governments balance their budgets, or to stop tuition increases at public universities? And where will the money come from to pay for the retirement of the baby boom?

7. **Strong on Defense vs. Weak on Defense.** Who, these days, is for a weak defense? The challenge to the Bush administration is whether

its unilateral approach protects the United States and strengthens our standing in the world. It's tough, not weak, to insist that Americans will be better protected in a world that does not hate the only remaining superpower. It's tough, not weak, to defend a progressive internationalism that tries to create a more democratic world that will be less hostile to the United States. It's tough, not weak, to think through military commitments in advance and to tell the truth about the costs of these enterprises. It's tough, not weak, to think about what can fairly be asked of a volunteer military and to think through the effect of military interventions on the lives of our men and women in uniform in the National Guard and the reserves and on future recruitment and morale. It's tough, not weak, to say that the United States is better off when allies join in its causes.

8. **Interest Group Dependent vs. Independent.** Why does no one talk about Republican special interest groups—the wealthy, big business, and Christian Conservatives? Here again, Democrats are hopelessly defensive. There is nothing wrong with defending your own, especially when your side is supposed to stand up for the poor, the marginalized, and minorities. Democrats need a much stronger argument about the common good in which the interests of the groups they represent are linked to a common interest. The nation as a whole is stronger when the poor have opportunities to rise, minorities feel their rights are protected, and business is allowed to flourish within decent constraints limiting the abuse of the environment, employees, and stockholders. And why are progressives so prone to battles among their own supporters based on race, gender, ethnicity, and interest? *Solidarity,* a word the left has long prized, is now the characteristic of a conservative movement in which gun owners, abortion opponents, and corporate executives manage to sit down together at the table of political brotherhood. Why should progressives be *less* than the sum of their parts?

9. **Traditional vs. Permissive.** Who, pray tell, is really "permissive"? Most social liberals have kids, worry about porn on television and

the Web, and aspire to a world in which children are raised in strong families. They also aspire to a tolerant world that honors religious liberty and opposes discrimination on the grounds of marital status or sexual preference. Most Americans combine a reverence for tradition with a respect for tolerance. Most believe in the equality of men and women and the equality of the races. Indeed, by all measures, the United States is a *more* tolerant and open country than it was ten or twenty or thirty years ago. As the sociologist Alan Wolfe has shown, most Americans prefer cultural peace to culture wars.

10. **Clinton Is the Solution vs. Clinton Is the Problem.** The Clinton obsession is dangerous to Democrats and to the country. Clinton presided over a booming economy and governed effectively. Republicans and conservatives predicted that his 1993 tax increases on the wealthy would ruin the economy. They were wrong. The supply-siders' theories were—or should have been—discredited. Clinton's program actually led to a lower tax burden on the middle class and the poor and was followed by years of economic growth. At the same time, Clinton got himself inveigled in a scandal (and in dubious last-minute pardons) that turned off millions of Americans who were not at all opposed to his politics. Why is it so difficult both to embrace the positive parts of Clinton's record and to criticize his foolishness? If Al Gore had figured out how to do that, he'd be president. Most Americans find this distinction an easy one to make.

But it is not good enough just to abandon bad arguments. Democrats, liberals, and moderates cannot simply be the defenders of old programs and what former Senator Gary Hart once called "old arrangements." Progressives have always been about the future, about improvement, about reform. Contemporary progressives should not be as fearful as they are about embracing the tradition from which they spring. But neither should they forget that the tradition itself is pragmatic, experimental, and open to new approaches. Progressives need to be much more willing to defend their principles and values while remembering that the answer to a rigid ideology is not to embrace another equally rigid ideology. And progressives need to learn what Franklin Roosevelt taught them in the 1930s and what Ronald Reagan taught conservatives in the 1980s: that Americans of all generations respond to appeals rooted in optimism and hope.

THE RIGHT STUFF

1. **Whose Side Is the Government On?** And, while we're at it, does the new economy require no rules or new rules? Conservatives talk as if they hope that government will shrink to near irrelevance. But most know this will not happen. The real question before voters is: Whom will the government serve? Will the government primarily serve corporate executives, or will it also serve employees and shareholders? Drug companies or consumers? What is government's attitude toward labor (as in, for example, what rules should be established on overtime pay)? How is the environment best protected? Should the government throw its power on the side of the already fortunate, or on the side of those in the middle class and those less well off who are trying to advance their interests and those of their children?

There is a large debate to be had over whether the common good is best served by endless rounds of tax cuts for the wealthy, or by efforts to expand access to health care, child care, and college education. As the Bush administration was cutting taxes, state governments were raising taxes, raising college tuition, and cutting spending on education, child care, highways, transit, and health care. Wouldn't Americans as citizens and taxpayers have been better served if the federal government had intervened to help states avoid deficits, cutbacks, and tax increases? Who, at the end of the last four years, is better off, and who has been hurt? Isn't there a better way to create a prosperity that genuinely lifts all boats? In his important recent book, *The Two Americas*, Democratic pollster Stanley B. Greenberg reported strong public support for a vision he labeled "100 percent America," a place "where everyone has a chance for a better life, not just the privileged few." In Greenberg's polling, this approach soundly defeated an alternative vision rooted in the strongest aspects of Reaganism (including the idea of "an America that empowers the individual and gives entrepreneurs the freedom to make our country richer and create employment"). In this contest of visions, even many conservatives—and a large share of swing voters—preferred the idea of solving common problems over an extreme individualism.

2. **Against Right-Wing Judges Making Law.** The old arguments about "liberal judicial activism" are irrelevant to this period. The new requirement is to resist conservative courts that seek to undermine the New Deal legal consensus. That approach gave federal, state, and local governments the freedom to solve public problems. It looked to the courts primarily to protect individual rights and the rights of minorities. In light of the new conservative judicial activism, liberals will need to temper their own tendencies to rely on the courts for political victories. But they also need to defend the New Deal consensus as an approach that worked.

3. **Individuals Should Be Responsible. So Should the Federal Government.** There is little need to elaborate on the argument for fiscal responsibility. Running enormous deficits for years to come is irresponsible. And—this is said too rarely—undemocratic. The current deficits are especially dangerous because they are being locked in just as the baby boomers prepare for retirement. In the case of the Reagan deficits, there was time to repair the federal budget before the retirement wave hit; and Reagan himself was willing to roll back some of his tax cuts to limit the damage. The Clinton surpluses created room to deal with the costs of both Social Security and Medicare. Now there is none.

Running up huge deficits constrains future presidents, future Congresses, and, by extension, future voters. That's the undemocratic part. A president who took office having received fewer votes than his opponent is nonetheless taking radical steps that will force future Congresses and presidents to cut spending sharply, reduce retirement benefits substantially, or raise taxes sharply. Members of the currently dominant political class are spending money that does not belong to them. If individuals should provide for themselves and be responsible for their futures, shouldn't government be held to the same standard?

4. **Government Can Promote Personal Initiative and Self-Sufficiency.** Remember the GI Bill? It was a great act of civic inclusion. It promoted upward mobility and helped create the economic boom after World War II. The idea was simple: Those who served the nation earned the right to "help toward doing without help," as the philosopher John Stuart Mill once put it. The GI Bill made it possible for millions to reach two of the central goals of middle-class life: a college education and home ownership. A time of economic transition and global competition is precisely the moment for government investments—here the word "investment" instead of "spending" is appropriate—in the future of individual Americans. And a time of national security challenge is also the time to emphasize the reciprocal obligations of Americans to serve their country. If ever there was a time for a new GI Bill, this is it.

5. **Why Do We Assume the World Is Moving Against Us?** In fact, the world is moving our way, in the direction of democracy and markets. We can be vigilant against terrorism without being paranoid or pessimistic. If we assume the whole world hates us and act accordingly, we risk calling forth the very reaction we claim to fear. Recall the arguments of John Judis and Michael Tomasky on behalf of a view of the world that combines realism with optimism, toughness with a decent respect for the opinions of other nations. It's possible to be vigilant and still believe that this is more the world of John Locke than Thomas Hobbes, a world that is moving toward democracy and the quest for a just order rather than toward a war of all against all. The choices in foreign policy are not between those who are "soft" and those who are "tough." The issue is what kind of toughness does this historical moment require? Our time, like Harry Truman's, calls for a new era of creativity in forging global alliances and creating new international institutions. It's possible to be tough, smart, and hopeful.

6. **Are We a Community?** The American tradition has always involved a balance between individualism and community responsibility.

George W. Bush acknowledges this when he insists he is a *compassionate* conservative. From the Progressive Era forward, we built institutions that acknowledged the accidents and misfortunes of life. We decided that the lucky should help the unlucky, the fortunate should help the poor, the strong should stand up for the weak, the privileged should help the less privileged rise up—and have the opportunity to become privileged themselves. The need of the moment is to recognize that our national security depends not only on defending ourselves against terrorists and foreign enemies but also on creating a decent society of opportunity, social mobility, and fairness that could be a model for the world.

7. **Reform vs. Big Money.** Democrats will never be the party of big money and they should give up trying. Why did it take a Republican, John McCain, to move the dangers of big money in politics to the center of the political debate? Howard Dean has shown how an insurgent political movement can build a base of financial support from small donors. His is an example for the future. A political system dominated by the need to seek large contributions will be less responsive to consumer, employee, and shareholder interests. Laws on energy, taxation, and regulation will be shaped by the wealthiest interest groups. The goals of campaign finance reform should not be abandoned; they should be fulfilled through the creation of strong incentives to encourage small donors, partial public financing of elections, and free media time. Broadcast outlets should be reimbursed for some of the costs through tax credits. Following the 2004 breakdown of the system of publicly financed presidential campaigns—a system that had worked very well—Congress should update the system so it can work again. Contemporary progressives can look back for guidance to Theodore Roosevelt, one of the first politicians to warn of the dangers of big money in politics.

8. **Taxes: Progressive or Regressive?** Despite the fondest hopes of Grover Norquist and his allies, taxes will not go away. The issue is how the burden will be shared. At the moment, the burden is being increased on the middle class and the poor while it is being cut on the

very wealthy. Taxes on dividends, capital gains, corporations, and in-heritance are reduced. Payroll taxes stay where they are. In our states and localities, regressive property and sales taxes go up. Instead of cowering before the tax issue, progressives need to go on the offen-sive. Comprehensive reform would focus not only on income taxes but also on corporate and payroll taxes—and on the effects of federal policy on the states. It may be possible to have lower rates overall if the obligation to finance the government is spread more fairly. Lieberman's proposals to combine some tax increases on the wealthy with middle-class tax cuts are steps in the right direction. There is no reason to fear a more comprehensive look at the tax system.

9. **Tolerant Traditionalism: Strengthening Families, Accepting Diver-sity.** This is the flip side of no. 9 on The Wrong Stuff list. To repeat: Most Americans combine a reverence for tradition with a respect for tolerance. This is not a difficult case to make. But it requires broad-ening the moral debate to issues that affect the practical well-being of families, including the creation of family-friendly workplaces and reasonable leave laws. And the country should stop turning away from the excruciating struggles of low-wage workers who face great difficulties in balancing their obligations to earn money to support their families while having enough time to care for their children.

10. **A Society of Service.** After 9/11, our heroes were firefighters, police officers, rescue workers, the men and women in uniform. We were reminded that all our individual striving and wealth accumulation can be threatened rather suddenly. In such circumstances, we rely on those whose lives are animated by their sense of duty and service. Have Democrats forgotten that it was John F. Kennedy who asked us all what we could do for our country?

IV

And so we end where we began: with the challenges created by the at-tacks of September 11, 2001. That horrible day called forth a spirit of solidarity among Americans and created an opportunity to break our political cycle of revenge. Political compromise was possible in the months immediataly after the attacks. There was a recognition that government was more than an imposition on our lives. It was the one institution charged with organizing our common defense and securing the common good.

Unfortunately, President Bush missed his chance to be a different kind of leader. After rallying the country, he turned back to his earlier task of securing passage of his ideological agenda and building his political party. The cycle of revenge began again. Even a war against a brutal dictator in Iraq—a war that might have been as unifying as was the struggle against the Taliban in Afghanistan—was turned to partisan purposes. As a result, Bush confronted political resistance at home and abroad at the very moment when he most needed allies to win the peace and rebuild Iraq.

It did not have to be this way. It does not have to remain this way.

Earlier, I quoted David Frum's amusing definition of compassionate conservatism. But Frum used his joke to make a serious point: that some conservatives resented having to put the word "compasionate" in front of their creed. "Conservatives," he wrote, "disliked the 'compassionate conservative' label in the same way that people on the left would dislike it if a Democratic candidate for president called himself a 'patriotic liberal.' "

In fact, forging a patriotic liberalism—or, as I would call it, a progressive patriotism—is precisely what this moment calls for. Bush, as we have seen, was certainly smart to embrace the compassionate conservative idea. He knew perfectly well that a large number of Americans were suspicious—for good reason, I'd argue, but never mind—that conservatives really didn't care much about the poorest in our midst.

Compassionate conservatism was a brilliant slogan that did three things at once. It acknowledged that conservatives had a problem. It insisted that conservatives really did care about the poor. And it tried to change the debate about poverty by claiming that advocates of programs outside government, especially church-based programs, had better approaches to helping the poor.

By the same political logic, it is necessary to proclaim loudly and without apology that there is such a thing as progressive patriotism. But progressive patriotism should *not* simply be a marketing slogan. Liberalism, the philosophy of Franklin D. Roosevelt and Harry Truman, waged and won America's war against Nazi Germany and Imperial Japan and laid the groundwork for the successful battle against Soviet communism. Jimmy Carter's campaign for human rights created the ideological underpinning of Ronald Reagan's successful Cold War policies.

As a political matter, contemporary liberals and Democrats need to acknowledge that they have a problem. They face regular attacks from their enemies for being, as House Majority Leader Tom DeLay once called them, "the appeasement party." The link between liberalism and patriotism is not as automatic in the public mind now as it was in FDR's day. In the wake of 9/11, that's a genuine problem for liberals. The response to these problems should not be defensiveness but an aggressive attempt to define progressive patriotism.

At its best, American liberalism has always insisted on the ties between individual and social responsibility. It has argued that preserving individual freedom is a mutual responsibility of citizens. It is a scandal that the rhetoric of sacrifice has been deployed so often since 9/11 without any serious call for a sharing of the burdens created by a time of trouble and challenge.

And so, a progressive patriotism would begin with a strong emphasis on service to the country. Senators John McCain and Evan Bayh have proposed expanding service opportunities for young Americans so that 250,000 slots would be available for those who chose to give a year to their country. A program of this size would mean that every young American would know someone who had chosen the path of service. Short-term enlistments in the military should also be encouraged, as they are in other nations. Our current system of seeking long-term recruits, especially in the officer corps, has had the unintended effect of discouraging what Charles Moskos has called the "citizen-soldier." Service opportunities can also be expanded for high school students and for senior citizens. The idea of engaging seniors in civic work is especially important in a society that will have a growing cadre of elderly Americans seeking new ways to use their gifts and to offer something back to their country.

Senator John Kerry has proposed a modern version of the GI Bill. His "Service for College" plan would give young people who performed two years of service college scholarships, set at the tuition rate of the public universities in the volunteer's state. This is a powerful way of underscoring reciprocal responsibilities: of individuals to their country, of the country to individuals. Liberalism has never been about dependency or disengagement. Franklin D. Roosevelt established work programs during the Great Depression precisely because he feared the effects of cash payments to individuals untethered from work. Those who give to the community and earn the community's investment in them embody how a free society can simultaneously strengthen social bonds and enhance the opportunities of individuals.

A progressive patriotism would also make a service commitment and serious civics instruction requirements for high school graduation. This is an idea winning broad support across philosophical lines. In 2002, a commission convened by the Center for Information and Research on Civil Learning and Engagement and the Carnegie Corporation called for a reform of civic education that would combine genuine rigor in the teaching of government and history with a new emphasis on extracurricular activities now endangered by budget cuts.

A progressive patriotism would contrast itself to a radical individualism that rejects any idea of a "common good." It would emphasize both rights and responsibilities. It would tell corporations moving offshore to escape taxes that they have obligations to their country at a time of war and domestic threats. It would urge that we spend what's needed to defend ourselves at home against terrorism.

It would argue that the preservation of freedom is a common project requiring a commitment of citizens to one another across the lines of class, race, and gender. "If a free society cannot help the many who are poor," John F. Kennedy declared, "it cannot save the few who are rich." Doesn't the spirit of solidarity require not only joining together to confront common threats and enemies but also working together to create a

more just nation? A progressive patriotism would insist that a free republic will not prosper if too many of its citizens are deprived of opportunities, of health care, of education, of hope. It would seek to make the
United States a beacon not only of freedom but also of justice.

A progressive patriotism would allow us to cast aside the politics of revenge. It would declare that we are all in this together. That's an old-
fashioned idea that would offer a bold alternative to a status quo that is
dividing, and failing, our country.

Notes

I have tried to provide citations for all material drawn from outside my own reporting. As I note in the Acknowledgments, my debts to friends are enormous, but
wherever possible, I have tried to cite their work here. When the quotations or ideas
were drawn from my own interviews, I say so here. In a few cases where I thought it
might be helpful, I have cited my own previous writings. But I have largely avoided
this because footnoting yourself seems a useless enterprise.

Introduction

2   "I miss Ronald Reagan": Harold Meyerson, "The Most Dangerous Ameri-
     can President Ever: How and Why George W. Bush Undermines American
     Security," *The American Prospect* (May 2003), p. 25.

4   Political philosopher William Galston's theory about "tolerant traditional-
     ists": conversation with the author. Galston has used this phrase on many
     occasions.

5   "By the end, Clinton had forged a kind of amoral majority": Richard Lowry,
     Legacy (Washington, D.C.: Regnery Publishing, 2003), p. 56.

6   "Across the country": David Brooks, "Democrats Go Off the Cliff," *The
     Weekly Standard,* June 30, 2003.

7   "By maintaining high levels of domestic federal spending": Peter Berkowitz,
     "Unradical Son George W. Bush Isn't the Fire-Breathing Reactionary Liber-
     als Love to Hate," *Boston Globe,* August 10, 2003, p. H1.

8   "Now it is true that you can find conservatives": Brooks, "Democrats Go
     Off the Cliff."

8   "restore honor and dignity to the White House": George W. Bush, speech to
     122nd National Guard Association of the United States General Confer-
     ence, Atlantic City, N.J., September 14, 2000.

8   Baker, Cheney, and Kissinger all quoted in Ann Devroy, Daniel Williams, et al., "GOP Attacks Clinton, Claims Incompetence in Foreign Relations," *The Washington Post*, July 28, 1994, p. A23.

9   "the president does not have the divine right of a king": DeLay quoted in Juliet Eiperin and Peter Baker, "DeLay Turns Up Heat on Clinton Claims; House Leader Scoffs at Executive Privilege," *The Washington Post*, May 8, 1998, p. A16.

9   "a jerk": Hatch quoted in Mary McGrory, "A Man Above Speculation," *The Washington Post*, August 23, 1998, p. C01.

Chapter 1. Put on a Compassionate Face

22   "good riddance": Quoted in R. H. Melton, "Warner's War Chest Spurs Political Terror and Envy," *The Washington Post*, May 31, 2001, p. T02.

22   "Sen. James Jeffords of Vermont is not a moderate": Editorial in *National Review*, vol. LII, no. 11, June 11, 2001.

23   "I can see more and more instances where I will disagree": James Jeffords, speech delivered May 24, 2001, in Burlington, Vermont.

25   "Bush described himself as a 'compassionate conservative' ": David Frum, *The Right Man* (New York: Random House, 2003), pp. 5–6.

25   "Bush is the kind of candidate and officeholder": Rove quoted in Ceci Connolly, "The Eyes of the Nation Are Upon You, Gov. Bush," *St. Petersburg Times*, May 19, 1997, p. 1A.

26   "Rove was cerebral; Bush never liked going too deeply into the homework": James C. Moore and Wayne Slater, *Bush's Brain* (Hoboken, N.J.: John Wiley & Sons, 2003), p. 106.

27   "To govern on behalf of the corporate right": Lou Dobose, Jan Reid, and Carl Cannon, *Boy Genius* (New York: Public Affairs Reports, 2003), p. 91. This book and the Moore and Slater book are both essential to understanding Rove.

28   "The purpose of saying you gave teachers a record pay increase": Karl Rove, letter to Bill Clements, quoted in Dubose, Reid, and Cannon, *Boy Genius*, p. 146.

28   "government isn't the solution to our problem.": Reagan quoted in William Schneider, "Clinton's Mission: In (Some) Government We Trust," *Los Angeles Times*, January 26, 1997, p. M01.

28   "Government if necessary, but not necessarily government": Bush expressed

this sentiment many times, but it first appeared in his inaugural address as governor of Texas, January 17, 1995, in Houston, Texas.

28   "Too often, my party has confused the need for limited government with a disdain for government itself": Bush at a news conference, October 6, 1999, in Queens, New York.

28   "the destructive mind-set . . . that if government would only get out of the way": Bush, address to the Front Porch Alliance, July 22, 1999, in Indianapolis, Indiana.

29   "He's taken the hard edge off the party": Cobey quoted in Steven Thomma, "Bush's Moderate Steps Bring Change to GOP," *Philadelphia Inquirer,* January 20, 2002, p. A10.

29   "one of the finest men to have ever served as president": Weyrich quoted in Dionne, "Conservatism Recast," *The Washington Post,* January 27, 2002, p. B01.

30   "Conservatism is something more than mere solicitude": Kirk quoted in George H. Nash, *The Conservative Intellectual Movement in America: Since 1945* (New York: Basic Books, 1979), p. 41.

30   "The invisible hand works many miracles, but it cannot touch the human heart": Bush in Front Porch Alliance address, July 22, 1999.

31   "Reducing problems to economics is simply materialism": Bush's inaugural address as governor, January 19, 1999.

31   "Our national resources are not only material supplies and material wealth": Herbert Hoover, radio address on Lincoln's birthday, February 12, 1931.

31   "In the quiet of the American conscience, we know": President Bush, Inaugural Address, January 20, 2002.

32   "excellent schools, quality health care, a secure retirement": Bush in congressional address, February 27, 2001, quoted in " 'Courage in a Time of Blessing'; Bush Tells Congress, 'Government Should Be Active, But Limited; Engaged, But Not Overbearing,' " *The Washington Post,* February 29, 2001, p. A10.

33   "the brain dead politics of both parties": Clinton quoted in Chris Black, "Clinton Recycles Themes of Ex-Foes; Consensus Aim Both Praised and Criticized," *Boston Globe,* June 9, 1992, p. 6.

34   "the tranquilizing drug of gradualism": Martin Luther King, Jr., "I Have a Dream Speech," August 28, 1963, in Washington, D.C.

34   "are, in effect, Mr. Bush's stealth initiative": Donald Lambro, "Spending Orgy . . . in Behemoth Budget," *The Washington Times,* February 6, 2003, p. A20.

36   "It's an opportunity": Kennedy: interview with author.

37   "The law made proven": Kennedy quoted in Jim VandeHei, "Education Law May Hurt Bush; No Child Left Behind's Funding Liability Could Be '04 Liability," *The Washington Post,* October 13, 2003, p. A01.

38   "The federal government": Pollack: interview with author.

39   Survey conducted by Mark Chaves in 1998: See Chaves, "Testing the Assumptions: Who Provides Social Services," in E. J. Dionne, Jr., and Ming Hsu Chen, *Sacred Places, Civic Purposes: Should Government Help Faith-Based Charity?* (Washington, D.C.: Brookings Institution Press, 2001), pp. 287–96.

41   "from the center out": Breaux quoted in Bruce Alper, "Confusion Bodes Ill for Democrats," *Times-Picayune,* July 5, 1995, p. A1.

43   "As George W. Bush marks the midpoint of his first year": Dick Polman, "A Job Not Likely to Get Any Easier," *Philadelphia Inquirer,* July 25, 2001, p. A01.

43   "When Republicans controlled both houses of Congress": Ron Brownstein, "Strategies Dip as Bush Polls Dip; Presidential Slump Has the White House and Senate Rethinking Their Legislative Strategies," *Los Angeles Times,* July 5, 2001, p. A1.

44   "If congressional Republicans seem worried these days": Charlie Cook, "GOP Fears Pick Up, as Economy Doesn't," *National Journal,* September 8, 2001, p. 2774.

44   "With the weak American economy rising to the top": Wayne Washington, "Bush Seeks Cover as Economy Falls," *Boston Globe,* September 10, 2001, p. A3.

44   "A downward spiraling economy is very likely": Gergen quoted in ibid.

45   "It is hard to think of another administration that has done": Morton Abramowitz, "So Quiet at the Top," *The Washington Post,* September 11, 2001, p. A27.

Chapter 2. "He's Ours. He's All We've Got"

50   Comments by Democratic consultant, Democratic leadership aide, Winston, Penn, Molyneux, Cohen, DiVall: interviews with author.

53   "Patriotism is not only a gift to others": Todd Gitlin, "Varieties of Patriotic Experience," in George Packer, ed., *The Fight Is for Democracy: Winning the War of Ideas in America and the World* (New York: Perennial, 2003), p. 109.

Reference to hanging flag on p. 110. Gitlin's essay is a classic, capturing a moment perfectly.

53 "We've lost 5,000 people": Spratt: interview with author.

53 "the bloody attacks have created a unique political moment": "A New Presidency," *Wall Street Journal,* September 19, 2002, p. A20.

54 "To use this crisis": Levin: interview with author.

54 "Mr. President, the only way you are ever going to get": Vandenberg quoted in William O'Neill, "Acheson: The Secretary of State Who Created the American World," 1998 American Labor Conference on International Affairs, *The New Leader,* October 5, 1998, p. 17.

55 "Chemical agents, lethal viruses and shadowy terrorist networks": President Bush's State of the Union address, January 28, 2003.

56 "George Bush prepared all his life to conduct the Cold War": George F. Will, "Peace Is Hell for Presidents," *The Washington Post,* May 30, 1993, p. C3.

58 "We have no choice but to address the policies and decisions": Rush Limbaugh, "Clinton Didn't Do Enough to Stop Terrorists," *Wall Street Journal,* October 4, 2001, p. A22.

59 "The Clinton curbs": Richard Shelby quoted in Michael Kilian, "Breaks Urged for CIA's Spy Recruiters; Screening Policy Draws Critics," *Chicago Tribune,* September 16, 2001, p. 4C.

59 "what-did-the-president-know": Tom Raum, "Terror Warnings Provide Political Fuel," Associated Press Online, May 16, 2002.

60 "Incendiary [commentary] . . . is thoroughly irresponsible": Cheney, speech in New York City, May 16, 2002, quoted in David E. Sanger and Elisabeth Bumiller, "Traces of Terrorism: The Overview," *New York Times,* May 17, 2002, p. A1.

60 "It's precisely because we're in a war": William Kristol and Robert Kagan, "Time for an Investigation," *The Weekly Standard,* May 27, 2002, p. 9.

60 "I think it's the wrong way to go": Cheney speaking on Fox News, May 19, 2002.

60 Brian Montopoli, "Schlep to Judgment," *The Washington Monthly* (September 2003), p. 38. All subsequent references are to this article.

60 "The question we want to pose to the White House": Lieberman at a news conference in Washington, D.C., October 11, 2002, quoted in David Firestone, "Threats and Responses: Toward an Inquiry," *New York Times,* October 12, 2002, p. A06.

NOTES

60 "Every bureaucracy in this town is scared to death": Senator John McCain at a news conference in Washington, D.C., October 11, 2002, quoted in Montopoli.

61 "If you want to get to the bottom of something": Maureen Dowd, "He's Ba-a-a-ack!" *New York Times*, December 1, 2002, section 4, p. 9.

61 "We have not gotten everything": Governor Kean quoted in Michael Isikoff and Mark Hosenball, "Terror Watch: Full Disclosure?" *Newsweek* Web Exclusive, September 24, 2003.

62 "struggling to regain the initiative": Dan Balz, "A Bid to Regain the Initiative," *The Washington Post*, June 7, 2002, p. A01.

62 "encouraging": Daschle quoted in "Plan Gains Support from Dems, GOP in Congress," *The National Journal Congress Daily*, June 6, 2002 (online publication).

62 "bold and courageous": Harman quoted in Joseph Curl, "Bush Prods Hill to Back Plan for Security Agency, Says He'll Fight 'Turf Battle' If Congress Balks," *The Washington Times*, June 8, 2002, p. A01.

62 Senator Phil Gramm (R-Texas) noted: David Firestone, "Threats and Responses: Legislation," *New York Times*, November 20, 2002, p. A1.

62 "not interested in the security of the American people": Bush quoted in "The Nation, the Iraq Factor; At Home, Most Politics Is Local," *New York Times*, September 29, 2002, p. A1.

63 "vital homeland security efforts": David Espo, "With Her Seat Still in Question, LA Senator's Votes Are Politically Risky," Associated Press, November 19, 2002.

63 "I served this country, and I don't have to prove": Cleland quoted in Jim Tharpe, "Candidates Woo Vets: Both Claim Support of 'Heroes,' " *Atlanta Journal-Constitution*, October 15, 2002, p. 1B.

63 Durbin, Landrieu, and Jefferson comments: interviews with author.

65 "outside money and influence tell them how to vote": Cooksey quoted in Scott Dyer and Marsha Shuler, "Landrieu: GOP Strategy Backfired," *The Advocate*, December 9, 2002, p. 1A.

67 "A person would be right to question any suggestion": Cheney addressing Veterans of Foreign Wars, August 26, 2002, quoted in Bill Sammon, "Cheney Makes Case for War Against Iraq," *The Washington Times*, August 27, 2002, p. A01.

67 "It is less important to have unanimity": Rumsfeld addressing Marines at Camp Pendleton, California, August 27, 2002, quoted in Eric Schmitt,

"Rumsfeld Says Allies Will Support U.S. in Iraq," *The Washington Post*, August 28, 2002, p. A8.

68   "the only realistic way": James A. Baker, "The Only Right Way to Change a Regime," *New York Times*, August 25, 2002, section 4, p. 9.

68   "no-notice inspections, anywhere, anytime": Richard C. Holbrooke, "Take It to the Security Council," *The Washington Post*, August 27, 2002, p. A15.

69   Camp, Petri, Collins, and Bereuter comments: based on interviews with author.

69   Pew Research Center survey: "One Year Later, New Yorkers Troubled, Washingtonians More on Edge," released September 5, 2002.

70   ABC News poll: "Support for war against Iraq drops," released September 3, 2002.

70   "this administration will go to the Congress": Bush quoted in "Bush Says He Will Seek Congressional 'Approval' on Iraq, But Balks at Giving Congress a Veto on His Policy," *White House Bulletin*, September 4, 2002, np.

71   " 'I'm going to wait' ": Bush quoted in "Iraq Rejects Unconditional Return of Weapons Inspectors as Bush Says Turnaround By Saddam Highly Unlikely," *White House Bulletin*, September 13, 2002, np.

72   Levin, Durbin, Thompson comments: interviews with author.

74   "They are using whatever argument": Chafee, July 2003, responding to Paul Wolfowitz's report of the status in Iraq, quoted in Michael Dobbs, "Wolfowitz Shifts Rationales on Iraq War; With Weapons Unfound, Talk of Threat Gives Way to Rhetoric on Hussein, Democracy," *The Washington Post*, September 12, 2003, p. A23.

75   Durbin and Hagel comments: interviews with author.

75   "weeks of negotiations carried out by the State Department": William Kristol and Robert Kagan, "The U.N. Trap?" *The Weekly Standard*, November 18, 2002, p. 9.

76   "Democrats are in this position": Heather Hurlburt, "War Torn," *The Washington Monthly* (November 2002), p. 28.

77   "Really exciting": President Bush, news conference aboard the USS *Abraham Lincoln*, May 1, 2003, quoted in Dana Milbank, "For Bush, the Military Is the Message for '04," *The Washington Post*, May 2, 2002, p. A01.

77   "The White House said today that President Bush traveled": Richard W. Stevenson, "Aftereffects: The President; White House Clarifies Bush's Carrier Landing," *New York Times*, May 7, 2003, p. A20.

78   White House spokesman Ari Fleisher: Richard W. Stevenson, "After the War: Intelligence," *New York Times,* July 13, 2002, p. A1.

79   Cheney's appearance on *Meet the Press* with Tim Russert from "Vice President Dick Cheney discusses a possible war with Iraq," *Meet the Press,* NBC, March 16, 2003.

80   "something on the order of several hundred thousand": Shinseki quoted in Eric Schmitt, "Threats and Responses: The Military; Turkey Seems Set to Let 60,000 G.I.s Use Bases for War," *New York Times,* February 26, 2003, p. A1.

80   "way off the mark": Paul Wolfowitz testifying before the House Budget Committee, February 29, 2003, quoted in Vernon Loeb, "Cost of War Remains Unanswered Question," *The Washington Post,* March 1, 2003, p. A13.

80   "Bring 'em on": Bush press conference, July 2, 2003, in Washington, D.C., quoted in Dana Milbank and Vernon Loeb, "Bush Utters Taunt About Militants; 'Bring 'Em On,' " *The Washington Post,* July 3, 2003, p. A01.

81   "if you break it, you own it": Thomas Friedman, "Present at . . . What?" *New York Times,* February 12, 2003, p. A37.

82   "a fraud": Senator Edward Kennedy, interview with the Associated Press, September 18, 2003, quoted in Steve LeBlanc, "U.S. Case for War a Fraud," *Toronto Star,* September 19, 2003, p. A20.

83   "have spewed more hateful rhetoric": DeLay quoted in Juliet Eilperin, "DeLay Blasts Democratic Critics; Dispute Highlights Growing Rift on War," *The Washington Post,* September 20, 2003, p. A11.

83   "Tom DeLay is a bully": Kerry quoted in ibid.

84   "This is the same kind of response": Kennedy quoted in Steve Marantz, "Ted K, GOP Feud Over Bush Bash," *Boston Globe,* September 20, 2003, p. 3.

84   "Kennedy's rant reflects the Democrats' blinding Bush hatred": Charles Krauthammer, "Ted Kennedy, Losing It," *The Washington Post,* September 26, 2003, p. A27.

84   "moral clarity": DeLay speaking at the Heritage Foundation, September 25, 2003, quoted in Clark Hulse, "The Struggle for Iraq: Congress; Democrats Step Up Attacks on War," *New York Times,* September 25, 2003, p. A10.

Chapter 3. What's Wrong with the Democrats?

87   "I don't think you ever kill any political party": Rove quoted in Nicholas Lemann, "The Controller: Karl Rove Is Working to Get George Bush Re-

Elected, But He Has Bigger Plans," *The New Yorker,* May 12, 2003, p. 68. Lemann's is a brilliant and seminal article on Rove.

88   "The Republicans have a clear view": Satterford quoted in Adam Nagourney and Janet Elder, "Bush's Support Strong Despite Tax Cut Doubts," *New York Times,* May 14, 2003, p. A1.

91   "the Democratic problem in 2002": Daniel Casse, "An Emerging Republican Majority?" *Commentary* (January 2003), p. 17.

92   "fierce, relentless, highly effective partisanship": Jeffrey Bell, "Understanding Strong Presidents; A Handy Guide," *The Weekly Standard,* November 12, 2002, p. 13.

94   Wellstone comments: based on reporting by author.

96   "bourgeois bohemian": David Brooks, *Bobos in Paradise* (New York: Touchstone, 2000).

97   "politics without a lodestar": Philip Collins, "A Story of Justice," *Prospect* (UK), May 2000.

99   George Will on the Judis-Teixeira thesis: George Will, "Politics and the 'Ideopolis,' " *Newsweek,* September 16, 2002.

99   a shift noticed early: Dan Balz, "Clinton Broke Republican Grip on Some Suburban County Strongholds," *The Washington Post,* November 10, 1996, p. A24.

100   "Particular elections depend on a host of contingencies": Ruy Teixeira, "Postindustrial Hopes Deferred," *The Brookings Review,* Summer 2003, Vol. 21, No. 3, p. 40.

100   Teixeira on 2002 election: See Ruy Teixeira, "Postindustrial Hopes Deferred: Why the Democratic Majority Is Still Likely to Emerge," *Brookings Review* (Summer 2003), pp. 41–42, 43.

100   "It seems obvious": See Matthew Dowd, "The Continued GOP Majority," *Brookings Review* (Summer 2003), pp. 43–44.

Chapter 4. Talking the Other Guy's Talk

103   "Hell, make 'em cry, or make 'em laugh": Robert Penn Warren, *All the King's Men* (San Diego, Calif.: Harvest Books, 1996).

103   "If thought corrupts language": George Orwell, "Politics and the English Language," *The Orwell Reader* (Orlando Fla.: Harcourt Brace and Company, 1984), p. 364.

104   "You can fall in love with your outrage": Todd Gitlin, *Letters to a Young Activist* (New York: Basic Books, 2003), p. 145.

104   "In the United States at this time": Lionel Trilling, *The Liberal Imagination* (Garden City, N.Y.: Anchor Books, 1954), pp. 5–6.

105   "We used to call for immunizing": Ann Lewis, interview with author.

108   "from the beginning of the administration": Letter from religious leaders to George W. Bush, June 2003.

109   "How can it be when even after this boom": Matthew Miller, "Would You Buy This Idea?" *The Washington Post,* September 28, 2003, p. B2.

110   "the social virtues" behind "the creation of prosperity": Francis Fukuyama, *Trust: The Social Virtues and The Creation of Prosperity* (New York: Free Press, 1995).

111   One of the striking aspects of Bush era conservatism: See William Greider, "The Right's Grand Ambition: Rolling Back the 20th Century," *The Nation,* May 12, 2003, p. 11.

111   "There is no other period in the nation's history": Richard Hofstadter, *The American Political Tradition* (New York: Vintage Books, 1957), p. 164.

112   Dreyer: interview with author.

113   "The Problem with Executive Pay": "Where's the Stick?" *The Economist,* U.S. edition, October 11, 2003.

115   On the idea of privatizing profits and socializing losses: This is a variation on a classic formulation offered in different ways over many years by my friend, the late Michael Harrington. His voice is still missed.

116   no single piece of legislation: Robert Kuttner, "Rules That Liberate," *The American Prospect* (May–June 1997), p. 6.

117   "Americans seem easily to forget that individual rights": Stephen Holmes and Cass Sunstein, *The Cost of Rights: Why Liberty Depends on Taxes* (New York: W. W. Norton, 1999), p. 14. All further references to Holmes and Sunstein are drawn from this excellent book.

120   "Mr. Bush generally supports reducing": Matt Richtel with Richard W. Stephenson, "F.C.C. Chief Will Support Phone Curbs," *New York Times,* September 30, 2003, p. C5.

120   "conclusion of the American people and the legislative branch": Bush quoted in Richtel and Stephenson, ibid.

121   "Carter's paralysis over Iran": Michael Tomasky, "Between Cheney and Chomsky: Making a Domestic Case for a New Liberal Foreign Policy," in George Packer, ed., *The Fight Is for Democracy: Winning the War of Ideas in America and the World* (New York: Perennial, 2003), p. 30.

121   "San Francisco Democrats" . . . who "blame America first": Kirkpatrick

NOTES

quoted in David Hoffman, "Address Slams Democrats; Kirkpatrick Rallies Party," *The Washington Post,* August 21, 1984, p. A1.

122 "Kissinger favored negotiation": John Newhouse, *Imperial America: The Bush Assault on the World Order* (New York: Knopf, 2003), p. 32. This very helpful book on Bush's foreign policy can be usefully read in tandem with another fine book with a somewhat different point of view, Ivo H. Daalder and James M. Lindsay, *America Unbound: The Bush Revolution in Foreign Policy* (Washington, D.C.: Brookings Institution Press, 2003).

124 "an overwhelming preference for smoothing over" and subsequent Reich quotations are from: Robert Reich, *The Resurgent Liberal* (New York: Times Books, 1989), p. 278–83.

125 "end welfare as we know it": Clinton quoted in Gwen Ifill, "The 1992 Campaign: The Democrats; Clinton Presses Welfare Overhaul, Stressing Job Training and Work," *New York Times,* September 10, 1992, p. A1.

125 "rhetoric in defense of freedom": Clinton quoted in E. J. Dionne, Jr., "Clinton Credits Reagan for the Fall of Communism," *The Washington Post,* October 17, 1991, p. A4.

130 "the issue that performs best in a poll": Noam Scheiber, "The People Who Run the Democratic Party," *The New Republic* (February 24, 2003). Subsequent references are from this important article.

131 "Compared with his son, George H. W. Bush": Tomasky, "Between Cheney and Chomsky," in George Packer, ed., *The Fight Is for Democracy,* p. 41.

132 "Bush, influenced by his Pentagon": John Judis, "The Real Foreign Policy Debate," *The American Prospect,* May 6, 2002, p. 10.

Chapter 5. We're All in This Together

137 "We come with a strong point of view": Labash quoted in "No Comment," *The Ledger* (Lakeland, Fla.), May 23, 2003, p. A16. I am grateful to Al Franken for unearthing this passage and quoting part of it in *Lies and the Lying Liars Who Tell Them* (New York: Dutton, 2003), p. 353.

139 "The conservative press": Norquist quoted in Paul Galstris, "Why Democrats Get Tough," *The Washington Monthly* (March 2002), p. 38.

140 conservative crack-up: This phrase has been widely used. It originated with R. Emmett Tyrell, Jr., *The Conservative Crack-Up* (New York: Summit Books, 1992).

NOTES

141 a conservative "counter-establishment": Sidney Blumenthal, *The Rise of the Counter-establishment: From Conservative Ideology to Political Power* (New York: Times Books, 1986).

141 Meyerson and O'Beirne comments: interviews with author.

142 "I think that because I'm so systematically purposeful": Gingrich quoted in Don Balz and Charles R. Babcock, "Gingrich, Allies, Made Waves and Impression; Conservative Rebels Harassed the House," *The Washington Post,* December 20, 1994, p. A1 and quote box.

142 "one of the great problems in the Republican Party": Gingrich quoted in Bob Herbert, "In America: The Mean Strategy Backfires," *New York Times,* May 28, 2001, p. A11.

143 "You're fighting a war": Gingrich quoted in John M. Barry, *The Ambition and The Power* (New York: Penguin, 1990), p. 162.

146 "You can only beat one idea with another idea": Irving Kristol, quoted in Blumenthal, *The Rise of the Counter-establishment.*

148 "The conservative elite has been built": Blumenthal, *The Rise of the Counter-establishment.*

149 "an extensive communications and marketing capacity": Karen Paget, "Lessons of the Right Wing Philanthropy," *The American Prospect* (September 1998). All further references to Paget are drawn from this article.

149 "12 conservative foundations provided": Stephan Salisbury, "Liberal Think Tanks Study Conservative Foundations to Learn Why They Have Been so Successful in Establishing Policy," *Philadelphia Inquirer,* August 20, 1997.

150 "seem intent on discouraging engagement": Beth Shulman, "A Wake-up Call to Liberal Foundations," *In These Times,* September 22, 1997, p. 12. All further references to Shulman are drawn from this article.

150 "institution builders": Cohen quoted in Shawn Zeller, "Conservative Crusaders," *National Journal,* April 26, 2003, p. 1286. All further references to Cohen are drawn from this article.

151 "into the trenches": Clint Bollick quoted in ibid.

151 "At the same time that conservative foundations": David Callahan, "Liberal Policy's Weak Foundations," *The Nation,* November 13, 1995, p. 568.

154 When Walter Isaacson . . . held a widely publicized meeting: David Bauder, "New CNN Chairman Isaacson Travels to Capitol to Meet with Republican Leaders," Associated Press, August 6, 2001; see also Jim Rutenberg, "A Nation at War: The News Media," *New York Times,* April 16, 2003, p. 9.

154 "the liberals have NPR all day": Gingrich quoted in Lars-Erik Nelson, "Gingrich Tunes Out Public," *Newsday*, February 21, 1995, p. A07.

155 "Whatever audiences Fox and Rush": Zev Chafets, "The Right Needs a Public Voice, Too," New York *Daily News*, June 6, 2003.

155 "Most influential papers happily drifted": Jack Shaffer, "The Varieties of Media Bias, Part I," *Slate* magazine, February 5, 2003. All further references to Shaffer are drawn from this article.

157 "Like Richard Nixon, the grassroots Right": Michael Kazin, *The Populist Persuasion* (New York: Basic Books, 1995), p. 259. All further references to Kazin are drawn from chapter 6 of this excellent and essential book.

159 "The people who chafed at the intrusion": Alan Brinkley, *Voices of Protest: Huey Long, Father Coughlin and the Great Depression* (New York: Knopf, 1982), p. 159. This is a superb and engaging history. For the purposes of this argument, see especially pp. 156–68.

160 "the happiest group of people in America": Charles Peters, "Clintons Could Overcome Their Self-pity Problem by Emulating," *Charleston Gazette*, December 17, 1994.

160 "When Rush Limbaugh is out there talking": Mitchell quoted in Clay Chandler, "Flat Tax Proposals Take Center Stage, More Republicans Embrace Idea, Giving New Life to Old Concept," *The Washington Post*, September 3, 1995, p. A1.

161 "Whitewater is about health care": *Rush Limbaugh* (television show), April 25, 1994.

161 "It will relegitimize middle class 'security' ": Kristol memo, December 2, 1993, "Defeating President Clinton's Health Care Proposal," quoted in Stanley Greenberg. *Middle Class Dreams* (New Haven, Conn.: Yale University Press, 1996), pp. 282–83.

162 "Under the Clinton plan": *Rush Limbaugh* (television show), September 30, 1993.

163 "job-killing recession": Gingrich quoted in Jim Luther, "House Approves Clinton Deficit Plan," Associated Press, August 5, 1993.

163 "the brave old world of balanced budget liberalism": Paul Gigot, "As Deficit Retires, Liberalism Bids for a Comeback," *Wall Street Journal*, January 9, 1998.

163 Emanuel comments: interview with author.

165 "the real problem with politics": David Grann, "The Nihilists," *The New Republic*, 8 (February 1999), p. 13.

165 "sodomite" . . . "get AIDS and die": Savage quoted in "MSNBC Yanks Sav-

age After Gay Diatribe," *Broadcasting and Cable*, July 14, 2003.

166 "a little social concern in the NFL": Limbaugh quoted in Leonard Shapiro, "Forward Progress for Minorities is Seen," *The Washington Post*, October 1, 2003, p. D04.

166 "Sports is a world that is relentlessly reality-tested": Thomas Boswell, "Reality Test Results in Failure," *The Washington Post*, October 3, 2003, p. D01.

167 "Good evening once again": *The News With Brian Williams on CNBC*, September 24, 2002.

169 "Ultimately, the presidency of the United States": R. W. Apple, Jr., "Gore Campaign Vows Court Fight Over Vote with Florida's Outcome Still Up in the Air," *New York Times*, November 10, 2000, p. A1.

169 "count the votes and respect the decision": Breaux quoted in ibid.

170 "unquenchable thirst for power": "Rush Limbaugh, Radio Talk Show Host, Discusses the Present Problem with the Presidential Election," *Tim Russert*, CNBC, November 18, 2000.

170 "It's not even a question": Limbaugh quoted in Robin Toner, "Counting the Vote, the Conservatives; From the Anti-Gore Right, A Battle Cry of 'Stop, Thief,' " *New York Times*, November 26, 2000, p. A37.

170 "We know the whole thing has been rigged": *Rush Limbaugh* (radio show), November 22, 2000.

170 "illegitimate if Al Gore becomes president": William Bennett on CNN's *The Capital Gang*, November 18, 2000. Bennett's comments are all from this source.

170 "The Clinton-Gore operatives": Noonan quoted in Toner, "Counting the Vote: the Conservatives," *New York Times*, November 26, 2000, p. A37. All quotes from Noonan are from this source.

171 "I hope that Al Gore will want": Mara Liasson, "Special Report Roundtable," on *Fox Special Report with Brit Hume*, November 10, 2000.

171 ". . . it is worrying that Mr. Gore": "A Fateful Step Towards Court," *New York Times*, November 10, 2000, p. A32.

172 "I don't believe that the people of America": James A. Baker III, Associated Press, November 27, 2000.

172 "We must now show our commitment": Bush quoted in Frank Bruni, "Bush Claims Victory, Urges Gore to Bow Out," *New York Times*, November 27, 2000, p. A16.

173 Price and Kerry comments: interviews with author.

173 "We are witnessing nothing less": DeLay quoted in "DeLay Criticizes

Florida Supreme Court Decision," *PR Newswire,* November 17, 2000.

173   Zimmer: interview with author.

174   "These ballots are not difficult to tabulate": Barnett quoted in Michael Janofsky, "Out West, The G.O.P. Seeks a Hand Recount," *New York Times,* December 3, 2000, p. A40; see also N. M. Portales, "Bush Picks Up Votes in Roosevelt County; Not Enough to Overturn Gore Lead," Associated Press State and Local Wire, November 30, 2000.

174   "Ideally, perfection would be the appropriate": Justice Ruth Bader Ginsburg in *George W. Bush, et al., Petitioners* v. *Albert Gore, Jr., et al.,* December 12, 2000. The quotations from Justices Souter and Breyer are from the same source.

176   "the stupid party": Conservatives have been reflecting on Mill's phrase—he was talking about British Tories—ever since; see, for example, William Kristol, "On the Future of Conservatism: A Symposium," *Commentary,* February 1997.

Chapter 6. A Fair Fight

177   "My fellow Americans": President John F. Kennedy, Inaugural Address, Washington, D.C., January 20, 1961.

177   "No matter how honest and decent we are in our private lives": President Theodore Roosevelt, Speech to Civil War Veterans, Baldwin, Kansas, August 31, 1910.

177   "We have nothing to fear but fear itself": President Franklin Delano Roosevelt, Inaugural Address, Washington, D.C., March 4, 1933.

178   "democracy as a way of life": On Dewey, see two excellent books, Alan Ryan, *John Dewey and the High Tide of American Liberalism* (New York: Norton, 1995), and Robert Westbrook, *John Dewey and American Democracy* (Ithaca, N.Y.: Cornell University Press, 1991).

180   Free and Cantril offered a classic analysis: See Lloyd A. Free and Hadley Cantril, *The Political Beliefs of Americans* (New Brunswick, N.J.: Rutgers University Press, 1967), pp. 137–41.

181   Hillary Clinton told the story: interview with author.

185   "We were against revolution": Frankin Delano Roosevelt quoted in Bruce Miroff, *Icons of Democracy* (Lawrence, Kans.: University Press of Kansas, 2000), p. 258.

187   Biden: interview with author.

NOTES

187   "a return to the untenable jurisprudence": Justice Souter quoted in Linda Greenhouse, "High Court Kills Law Banning Guns in a School Zone," *New York Times,* April 27, 1995, p. A1.

188   "aggressive interpretation of federal statutes": Strauss: interview with author.

190   "absolute failure": Gephardt quoted in Jim Abrams, "Gephardt Calls Economy Biggest Issue," Associated Press, October 22, 2002, np.

190   "wealth over work" : Edwards quoted in Mike Allen, "Bush Hits Road with Economic Sales Pitch," *The Washington Post,* July 20, 2003, p. A5.

190   "may be the most arrogant": Kerry quoted in William Saletan, "Post-Hawk Revisionism," *Slate* magazine, September 30, 2003.

190   "We didn't send our young people to war unprepared": Senator Joseph Lieberman, "Getting Back on Track in Post-War Iraq," *The Washington Post,* July 7, 2003, p. A7.

191   Rosenberg, Karlin, and Boyd: interviews with author.

193   "to build an idea base": Podesta quoted in Matt Bai,"Notion Building," *New York Times Magazine,* October 12, 2003. I have also drawn here on my own interviews with Podesta.

197   "When American companies replace": Charles E. Schumer and Paul Craig Roberts, "Second Thoughts on Free Trade," *New York Times,* January 6, 2004, p. A23.

200   "100 percent America": Stanley B. Greenberg, *The Two Americas* (New York: Thomas Dunne Books/St. Martin's Press, 2004), pp. 311–18.

202   "help toward doing without help": Mill, from *Principles of Political Economy* quoted in Steven Holmes, *Passions and Constraint: On the Theory of Liberal Democracy* (Chicago: University of Chicago Press, 1995), p. 23.

205   "Conservatives disliked the 'compassionate conservative' label": Frum, *The Right Man,* p. 6

206   "the appeasement party": DeLay quoted in Chuck Lindell, "Tamer DeLay Quickly Fitting into New Role," *Austin American-Statesman,* April 27, 2003, p. A1.

206   the "citizen-soldier": See Charles Moskos, "Patriotism Lite Meets the Citizen Soldier," in E. J. Dionne, Jr., Kayla Meltzer Drogosz, and Robert E. Litan, *United We Serve: National Service and the Future of Citizenship* (Washington, D.C.: Brookings Institution Press, 2003), pp. 33–42.

207   "If a free society cannot help": President John F. Kennedy, Inaugural Address, January 20, 1961.

Acknowledgments

I have had a singular honor. In September, 1996, *The Economist* magazine, a journal I greatly admire, used my acknowledgments in an earlier book as its prime example of a trend toward excessively long thank-you's. They went right at me. Among other things, I was accused of thanking "a regiment of colleagues at *The Washington Post.*" My reaction was: Why shouldn't I? I owe 'em. Still, I love *The Economist* and could not ignore its critique of "Gratitude That Grates," as its editors harrumphed in their headline. Other friends had already accused me of writing what one called "epic acknowledgments." So, yes, I'm sure this problem is real.

But as I have tried to explain before, someone in my line of work—and, I suppose, someone of my temperament—ends up feeling very grateful to a very large number of people who offer information, give editorial guidance, argue through ideas, and poke holes in theories. I would be lost without these friends, editors, informants, and colleagues—and many of them play more than one of these roles.

Still, one must respond to constructive criticism. So to save space, I ask all who were thanked in the earlier books to consider themselves thanked again. *The Economist* was right about how long those lists were, so I've just saved a lot of space. But I mean it when I say that they all should know how much gratitude I feel toward them.

This list will be long enough. I begin by thanking my friends and colleagues at *The Washington Post.* I won't name the entire "regiment," but I must say a special thanks to the people on the editorial staff, and at the Washington Post Writers' Group and the paper's Outlook section. Many of the ideas presented here and a good deal of the reporting were given a first run in my columns and Outlook pieces. Thanks, first, for permission to use that material, but more importantly for the chance to do the work in the first place. My gratitude to Fred Hiatt, the *Post*'s editorial page editor; to Jackson Diehl and Colby King, the deputy editorial page editors; and to Ken Ikenberry, who oversees the op-ed page day after day with a gift for finding the right words and a generous spirit toward all his writers. The late Peter Milius, who spent years as the editorial page's social conscience and eventually served as its deputy editor, taught so many journalists lessons that I hope we always remember. Our nation's political dialogue still suffers from Peter's absence.

At the Writers' Group, Alan Shearer, a gifted journalist, editor, and entrepreneur, first had the idea of syndicating my column. I owe him a lifelong debt for that, for his friendship, and for our shared love of sports—particularly those involving our children. James Hill edits the column twice a week and is as great an interlocutor, friend, and fraternal corrector as any writer could want. Anna Karavangelos was my first editor at the Writers' Group. She was both inspiring and careful, attentive and committed. She, like Jim Hill, is exactly the kind of editor a writer prays for. Thanks also to Russell James, Chris White, Karen Greene, Richard Aldacushion, and Kerrisue Wyson.

The *Post*'s Outlook section provided a first home for some parts of this book. Steve Luxenberg, who edits the section, has been a friend for more than three decades. He takes friendship and his role as editor seriously. I cannot describe here how loyal, warm, helpful, intelligent, and vigilant Steve has been on my behalf. Please just take my word on it. Some of the words in this book were first edited by Steve, and some of the ideas here first saw light of day because he asked me to write for him. He's not to blame for the conclusions—he lets his writers reach their own conclusions—but he was an inspiration. At Outlook, thanks also to Frances Stead Sellers, Steve Mufson, Nancy Szokan, Kathleen Cahill, and Fred Barbash.

I have worked at the Brookings Institution since 1996, and my debts there are enormous. But the first thing that must be said is that this is not a Brookings book because it is far too polemical to be sponsored by an institution that proudly and fairly describes itself as nonpartisan. My own experience tells the tale: I was first hired when Michael Armacost was Brookings' president. Mike gained acclaim by performing public service and became well known for his work at high levels in Republican administrations. He could not have been more encouraging and helpful—and, given that he probably didn't agree with everything I was up to, that spoke to his belief that Brookings, like a good university, should be an open place. Now, the institution's president is Strobe Talbot, who gained acclaim as a journalist and writer and also because of his public service in a Democratic administration. Strobe has been exceptionally warm, supportive, and helpful—and he, too, insists that Brookings should remain nonpartisan and independent.

I say all this because in the course of this book, I make the point that progressives need to be more conscious of the power of ideas and the way in which conservatives have mobilized ideas and think tanks on behalf of their political agenda. Having said that, I am still glad to be working at a place that resolutely does *not* have a party line. Brookings is welcoming to many points of view and has a wonderfully old-fashioned sense of the importance of independent public policy research. My hope is that we can fight our way through our current divisions and partisanship so we might return to a time when the open and civil spirit that defines Brookings might play a larger role in our politics. At a time of great political division, I have been able to work at Brookings on issues—the role of religious faith in politics, the work of faith-based institutions, the importance of national service, the critical contributions of the voluntary sector—that blessedly do not always break down along partisan lines.

So thanks to Mike Armacost and Strobe Talbott. Particular thanks to Tom Mann, who first brought me to Brookings and is such a dear friend that we actually relish the rare moments when we *disagree* on a political question. And thanks to Carol Graham, Paul Light, Pietro Nivola, Steve Hess, Ron Haskins, Belle Sawhill, Richard Haass, Ivo Daalder, Jim Lindsay, Belle Sawhill, Mike O'Hanlon, Jim Steinberg, Henry Aaron, Peter

ACKNOWLEDGMENTS

Orszag, and William Gale. Thanks also to Brenda Szittya, another great editor who encouraged me to write on many of these themes.

For their inspiration on the role of religion in public life, thanks to Luis Lugo and Jean Bethke Elshtain. I feel particular gratitude to Melissa Rogers and Sandy Stencel, who have been such smart, stalwart, and creative colleagues in this work. My friend John DiIulio puts his money, his body, and his spirit where his mouth is and makes the rest of us realize that we're not doing enough. Msgr. Phil Murnion would have been a brilliant politician had he not devoted his life to the Catholic Church. His death in 2003 was a terrible blow to his friends, to a church that badly needed him, and to those engaged in the work of justice.

At Georgetown University, where I began working as this book was ending, thanks to its president, Jack DeGioia, and to Judy Feder, dean of the Georgetown Public Policy Institute; and also, for reasons that they know, to my colleagues Cynthia Schneider, Bill Gormley, Clyde Wilcox, Kent Weaver, and Kerry Pace.

The hardest part is to give adequate acknowledgment to all the people who have taught me about politics. That's why I again remind readers to refer to the lists in the earlier books. For this book, I am in particular debt to Harold Meyerson, Guy Molyneux, Jo-Ann Mort, Paula Newberg, Tom Donilon and Kathy Russell, Peter and Peggy Steinfels, Linda and Fred Wertheimer, Janet Hook, Mike Tomasky, Ruy Teixeira, John Judis, David Brooks, Sharon Parrott, Bill Kristol, Tom Nides, Tony Corrado, Anna Greenberg, David Cohen, Bill Galston, Bob Borosage, Will Marshall, Bruce Reed, Roger Hickey, Al From, David Winston, Robert Greenstein, Les Lenkowsky, Jamie Galbraith, Jim Wallis, Paul Glastris, Amy Sullivan, Tom O'Donnell, Mike Kazin, Ellen Alberding and Kelly Welsh, Lane Windham, Steve Rosenthal, David Ellwood, Todd Gitlin, and Marshall Whitman. Special thanks to Judis, Tomasky, and Gitlin for their inspiring intellectual clarity in the post-9/11 period. And, yes, there is the problem of how to thank that regiment of *Washington Post* colleagues. I'll concede to *The Economist* by not naming them all, but I would be remiss if I did not mention Dave Broder, Dan Balz, and Tom Edsall.

ACKNOWLEDGMENTS

Nobody has been as lucky as I have in the people who worked with and for me. I'd burden these pages terribly if I explained why. But I hope that Staci Waldvogel, Andrea McDaniel, Ming Hsu Chen, Kayla Drogosz, Christina Counselman, and Katherine Moore know the depth of my admiration and my gratitude toward them.

Missy Daniel, a gifted editor, read through an early version of this manuscript and made so many helpful suggestions. Thanks to Bob Barnett, a wise enthusiast for both books and politics, for representing me in this endeavor. Thanks to Eulynn Shiu, Stephanie Sutton, and Kristin Volz for being exceptionally helpful with the notes.

Of course no one on this list is responsible for the conclusions I draw in this book. Many of them would be frightened by that thought.

At Simon & Schuster, Alice Mayhew and Roger Labrie are justly famous for brilliant editing. Alice pushed and prodded, proposed reorganizations, cuts, and additions. She pays attention simultaneously to large themes (and problems) and to the choice of a particular word in a particular sentence. My friends at *The Economist* took me to task particularly for an earlier acknowledgment to Alice that read: "Only if you know her can you actually believe that God made a person with so much energy, warmth, intelligence, talent and fortitude." Okay, guys, it does seem over the top. But it's true, and that ought to be the measure of these things. And Roger is the best—a smart editor, a gifted wordsmith, and a skilled diplomat.

This book is dedicated to my children, James, Julia, and Margot. I could say the usual things about how tolerant they were when their dad had to disappear to write and report and all that. But I am especially grateful to them for the ways in which they *don't* go along with things. (Well, most of the time; and I do reserve the right to alter this view when they become teenagers.) They are already developing strong views about life and politics, about what's just and unjust. They give as good as they get in arguments and are fiercely loyal to those whom they love and care about. If there is one area in which I really *do* go over the top, it's on the subject of my children. So I'll stop there except to say to each of them: I love you.

ACKNOWLEDGMENTS

My wife, Mary Boyle, usually reaches the intelligent political conclusion long before her husband does. From Mary, our whole family has learned love, loyalty, commitment, perseverance, thoughtfulness, and wisdom. A political candidate once ran under the slogan: "Unique. Irreplaceable." Mary is that, and much more than that. That's why the author and those to whom this book is dedicated love her so much.

Index

abortion rights, 157, 188
Abraham Lincoln, USS, 77–78
Abramowitz, Morton, 44–45
Adams, John Quincy, 12
Afghanistan, war in, 17, 48–49, 55, 69, 73, 205
African Americans, 40, 66, 101, 108, 116
Agnew, Spiro T., 156
Ailes, Roger, 154, 161–62
airport security, 53, 58
Allen, Woody, 123
All the King's Men (Warren), 103
Al Qaeda, 17, 69, 77, 78, 133
Alterman, Eric, 137
American Enterprise Institute, 147, 148, 149
American Political Tradition, The (Hofstadter), 111–12
American Prospect, 2, 148
Ashcroft, John, 115

Baker, James A., III, 8–9, 67, 68, 172, 175
Balz, Dan, 62, 99
Barnes, Fred, 158
Barnett, Mickey, 173–74
Barr, Robert L., Jr., 50, 164
Bayh, Evan, 36, 206
Bell, Jeff, 93
Bennett, William, 145, 170

Bereuter, Doug, 69
Berkowitz, Peter, 7–8, 9
Berlin Wall, fall of, 56, 57
Biden, Joseph R., 47, 129, 187
Bingaman, Jeff, 36
bin Laden, Osama, 55, 57, 63
Blair, Tony, 81*n*, 95, 97
Blumenthal, Sidney, 141, 148, 193
Bogart, Humphrey, 123
Bollick, Clint, 151
Bosnia, 76
Boston Globe, 7, 44
Boswell, Thomas, 166
Bowles, Erskine, 130
Boyd, Wes, 191
Bradley Foundation, 149, 151, 152
Breaux, John, 41, 169
Breyer, Stephen, 175, 187
Brokaw, Tom, 166
Brooks, David, 6–7, 8, 9, 96, 155
Brownstein, Ronald, 43–44
Bryan, William Jennings, 143
Buchanan, Pat, 158
Buckley, William F., Jr., 30, 147
Bush, George H. W., 56, 67, 121, 123, 125–26, 160, 170, 172
conservatism of, 24–25, 29, 125, 168
Gulf War and, 131
Bush, George W.:
approval ratings of, 44, 85

Bush, George W. *(cont.)*
  conservatism of, 2, 6, 9–10, 11, 15,
    16–17, 22, 23, 24–25, 26, 27,
    28–29, 30–33, 35–37, 38–42,
    53–54, 111, 117, 119, 143, 203,
    205
  in election of 2000, *see* election of 2000
  inaugural address of, 31–32
  political anger inspired by, 1–3, 6–8,
    9–10, 13–15, 17, 18, 51, 53–54,
    58–63, 64–65, 71–72, 82–85,
    135–36, 176
  political shrewdness of, 9, 16, 35–37,
    57–58, 119–20, 205
  Rove and, 24, 25–26
  State of the Union address of (2003), 78
  as Texas governor, 31, 35
Bush, Jeb, 25
Bush (George W.) administration:
  agriculture program of, 37
  as anti-government, 9, 28–29, 32,
    34–35, 37, 92, 98, 119, 186, 200,
    201–2
  attempts to silence critics of, 50, 55,
    58–60
  centrist language co-opted by, 14,
    16–17, 21–22, 32–33, 41–42,
    119–20, 183–84
  deficit running of, 9, 33–35, 90, 92,
    197, 201–2
  "do-not-call" list and, 119–20
  energy and environmental policies of,
    30, 37, 42, 43, 44, 56
  and faltering economy, 42, 44
  immediate post-9/11 foreign policy of,
    17, 48–49, 55, 205
  Jeffords's switch and, 17, 22–24, 42,
    43–44
  labor policies of, 30, 37
  Medicaid reform proposed by, 38
  9/11 investigation and, 56, 58, 59,
    60–62

  9/11 used by, 6, 10, 11, 16, 17–18,
    47–85, 91–94, 205
  political floundering of, 11, 16–17,
    21–45, 84–85
  pre-9/11 foreign policy of, 44–45, 48
  Bush's Brain (Moore and Slater), 26

cable networks, conservatism of, 5, 13,
    153–54, 155, 165–67
Callahan, David, 151–52
Call to Renewal, 107–8
Camp, Dave, 69
campaign finance reform, 203
Cantril, Hadley, 180–81
capitalism, 15, 26, 109–14, 181
  in Bush era, 26, 111–12, 143, 180
  government regulation necessary for,
    112, 114, 116, 118, 119, 195–96
Carlson, Tucker, 154
Carnegie Corporation, 207
Carnegie Endowment for International
    Peace, 45
Carter, Jimmy, 44, 89, 158, 206
  Iran hostage crisis and, 121
  presidential campaigns of, 121, 123,
    157
Case, Clifford, 16, 24
Casse, Daniel, 91
Cato Institute, 148, 149
Chafee, Lincoln, 74
Chafets, Zev, 155
Chambliss, Saxby, 63
Chaves, Mark, 39
Cheney, Dick, 9, 42, 56, 60, 72
  Iraq war and, 66, 67, 68, 69, 75,
    79–80, 81, 131
child care, government and, 4, 182, 200
Chirac, Jacques, 83*n*
Chocola, Chris, 72–74
Choice, Not an Echo, A (Schlafly), 156
Christian right, 27, 108, 157, 198
Christopher, Warren, 171

Churchill, Winston, 57–58
civil rights, 156, 182, 194
Clark, Wesley K., 69, 126, 135–36, 190
Clarke, Richard, 61
Clay, Henry, 12
Cleland, Max, 63, 64, 84
Clements, Bill, 28
Clinton, Bill, 32–33, 44
  conservatism of, 125–26, 141–42,
    143–45
  conservative attacks on, 4–6, 8–9, 13,
    102, 126, 137, 141, 144, 145–46,
    192
  in Lewinsky scandal and impeachment
    proceedings, 5–6, 8, 10, 13–14, 15,
    18, 102, 137, 145–46, 163–65, 166,
    176, 199
Clinton, Hillary, 42, 90, 181
Clinton administration, 68, 88, 121–26,
  135, 194
  economic policies of, 90, 98, 162–63,
    195, 199, 201
  foreign policy of, 75–76, 125–26
  health care and, 42, 90–91, 160–62,
    181
  legacy of, 5, 19, 98, 144–45, 146, 184,
    199
  media war and, 5, 160–62, 163–65
  9/11 intelligence issues and, 58–59
  Third Way and, 95–97, 143–45
  welfare reform and, 124–25, 127–28
Club for Growth, 24
CNBC, 164, 166–67
CNN, 154, 158, 166, 170
Cobey, Bill, 29
Cohen, Rick, 150–51
Cohen, William, 51
Cold War, 54–56, 122, 132, 206
  end of, 27, 30, 54, 56, 57
Collins, Philip, 97
Collins, Susan, 69
Commentary, 91

communism, 54, 55, 120, 122
compassionate conservatism, 2, 16, 19,
  24, 25, 26, 27, 28, 29, 30–31, 119,
  203, 205
Congress, U.S., 3, 119–20
  Bush's address to joint session of
    (2001), 32–33
  and Iraq war resolution, 70–71, 72, 75
  and 9/11 commission, 56, 58, 60–62
  post-9/11 bipartisanship and, 6, 9, 17,
    18, 47–54, 58–85, 91
conservatives, conservatism, 1, 5–9,
  15–16, 84, 105, 128, 138, 181–82
  in Bush era, 26–27, 111, 143, 180
  Clinton impeachment and, 5, 8, 10,
    102, 137, 145–46, 163–65, 176
  compromise and, 35, 176, 179
  foundations funded by, *see* founda-
    tions, conservative
  government as viewed by, 32, 115,
    119, 161, 163, 178, 179, 180, 181,
    186, 200
  heroes of, 177–78
  institutional offensive of, 137–76,
    193
  libertarianism vs. traditionalism in,
    29–30
  marginalization of, 104–5, 176, 191
  means of, 5–6, 7, 9, 10, 13, 14, 137,
    138–39, 145–46, 168–76, 180
  movement building of, 139–40,
    146–48, 150, 152, 176
  Nixon's fall and, 157
  objectives of, 147, 178, 179, 180, 183,
    185
  underlying contradictions of, 178
Cook, Charlie, 44
Cooksey, John, 65
Coolidge, Calvin, 147
corporations, 113–15
  financial scandals of, 15, 66, 112–13,
    119, 184–85

corporations *(cont.)*
  government regulation of, 114, 116,
    184–85, 195–96
*Cost of Rights, The: Why Liberty Depends
  on Taxes* (Holmes and Sunstein), 118
Coughlin, Charles, 159
Coulter, Ann, 8
courts, federal, 186–88, 201
crime, Democrats and, 121, 123, 126–27
Crossfire, 154

Daschle, Tom, 33, 41, 47, 55, 62, 83
  in election of 2002, 73, 74
Davis, Gray, 6
Davis, Tom, 49
Dean, Howard, primary campaign of
    (2003–2004), 41, 69, 83, 89,
    188–91, 203
  Bush challenged in, 11–12, 66,
    188–89
  Iraq and, 71, 126
Death of Outrage, The (Bennett), 145
death penalty, 121, 123, 124, 127
defense:
  Democrats as "soft" on, 75–76, 126
  unilateral vs. multilateral approach to,
    131–34, 186, 197–98, 202
deficits, 33–35, 90, 197, 201–2
DeLay, Tom, 9, 42, 82–84, 137, 142,
    173, 206
Democrats, Democratic Party, 16
  as alienated and angered by Bush, 1–3,
    6–8, 9–10, 13–15, 17, 18, 51,
    53–54, 63, 64–65, 71–72, 82–85,
    135–36, 176
  attack on patriotism of, 8, 63, 65,
    71–72, 74, 83, 84, 206
  attempts to stifle anti-Bush criticism of,
    8, 50, 55, 58–60, 82–85
  Bush economic policies and, 41–42,
    53, 71, 72, 90, 92, 135, 197, 203–4

Clinton impeachment and, 13–14, 15,
    102, 146, 164, 165, 168–69, 199
Clinton legacy and, 15, 144, 145, 146,
    165, 168–69, 199
conservative institution-building and,
    137–76, 193, 194
deficit issue and, 33–35, 90, 197,
    201–2
education reform bill and, 35–37
in fight against Republican tactics, 9,
    11–12, 63–66, 82–85, 135–36,
    188–90
health plans and, 90–91
homeland security issue and, 17,
    61–63, 64, 65, 72, 74, 84, 92, 93,
    100, 129, 135
identity crisis of, 1, 2, 11, 16, 18,
    87–102, 104, 138, 140
moral argument ceded to right by, 18,
    107–9, 138, 180
new demographics and, 99–101
opposition rhetoric of, 18, 103–36
post-9/11 Bush support of, 6, 9, 10,
    11, 17, 18, 47–50, 51, 54, 58, 62,
    91, 92
progressive tradition in, 15–16
solidarity issue and, 88–91, 138, 140,
    148, 168, 176, 198
ten tired and useless arguments of,
    195–200
ten useful new arguments of, 200–204
Third Way and, 95–97, 144–45
voter support for, 98–100, 128
see also specific candidates and elections
Depression, Great, 31, 207
Devine, Donald, 30
Dewey, John, 178, 181
direct mail, 157–58, 191
DiVall, Linda, 53, 58
Dole, Elizabeth, 130
"do-not-call" list legislation, 119–20, 184

Dowd, Matthew, 100–101
Dowd, Maureen, 61, 164
Drehle, David Von, 192
Dreyer, David, 113
Dubose, Lou, 192
Dukakis, Michael, 121, 123
Durbin, Richard, 63, 72, 75, 129

Earned Income Tax Credit, 90, 127
Economist, 113–14, 225, 228, 229
education:
    Bush administration and, 35–37
    government help for, 35–37, 118, 181,
        183, 195, 200, 202
Edwards, John, 12, 66, 71, 91, 135
    in primary campaign (2003–2004), 98,
        190, 196
Eisenhower, Dwight D., 16, 49, 85
election of 1968, 156
election of 1976, 123, 157
election of 1980, 121, 141, 147, 157
election of 1988, 56, 121, 123
election of 1992, 56
election of 1994, 160, 162
election of 2000:
    Gore in, 14–15, 18, 23, 36, 38–39,
        73, 101, 102, 146, 165, 168–69,
        170
    other ballot recounts in, 173–74
election of 2000, Florida ballot recount
    in, 22, 73, 137, 146, 168–76
    Bush campaign and, 169, 170,
        172–74, 175
    Democratic and liberal timidity in,
        146, 171
    Gore urged to capitulate in, 169–73
    media war in, 169–71
    Supreme Court and, 6, 14, 98, 102,
        174–75, 186
election of 2002:
    attack ads in, 63, 93–94, 130

Bush electoral machine in, 12, 63–66,
    72, 74, 91–94, 100–101, 128–30,
    135
economics issues in, 64, 65, 66, 72, 73,
    74, 92, 129–30
homeland security and patriotism is-
    sues in, 17, 62–63, 64, 72, 74, 84,
    92, 93, 100, 129, 135
Iraq war and, 66, 71–72, 92, 100, 128,
    129, 135
judicial nominees as issue in, 93
Landrieu's victory in, 64–66
reasons for Democratic losses in,
    91–94, 100
Republican voter mobilization in, 100,
    101
election of 2004, Democratic primary
    campaign in, 11–12, 41, 66, 69, 71,
    83, 89, 98, 126, 135–36, 188–91,
    196
Emanuel, Rahm, 163
Emerging Democratic Majority, The (Judis
    and Teixeira), 99
Engel, Elliott, 119
Enron, 66, 111, 112–13, 184–85, 195
environmental regulations, 37, 181, 186,
    188
equal protection doctrine, 174, 175
ESPN, 166

Face the Nation, 133–34
Fair Deal, 111
faith-based initiative, 29, 38–41, 43
    supporters of, 39–40, 107–8
    in 2000 campaign, 38–39, 40
Falwell, Jerry, 50
Families USA, 38
family leave laws, 181, 204
Fatah, Chakah, 47
Federal Communications Commission
    (FCC), fairness doctrine of, 159

Federal Trade Commission, 119
feminist movement, 156–57
flag, American, post-9/11 flying of, 52, 53
Fleischer, Ari, 78
Florida, in election of 2000, *see* election of 2000, Florida ballot recount in
Ford, Gerald, 122–23, 157
Ford Foundation, 148
Forstmann, Ted, 152
Foster, Vince, 8, 146
foundations, conservative, 149–53
  partisanship of, 147–48, 150–51
  started or expanded in 1970s, 148–49, 193
foundations, liberal, 150–53
  conservative attacks on, 139, 148
  liberal civil war and, 148
  new, 193
Fox News Channel, 60, 162, 165, 171
  conservatism of, 13, 153–54, 155
France, Iraq war and, 75, 82*n*, 83*n*
Franken, Al, 137, 167, 192
Free, Lloyd, 180–81
Free Congress Foundation, 29
free trade, 196–97
Friedman, Thomas, 81
Frum, David, 16, 25, 205
Fuelner, Ed, 193
Fukuyama, Francis, 110–11
fusionism, 30

Galston, William, 4
Gephardt, Richard, 49, 55, 59–60, 71, 73–74, 91, 135, 190
Gergen, David, 44
Germany, Iraq war and, 75, 82*n*, 83*n*
GI Bill, 202, 207
Gigot, Paul, 163
Gilded Age, 111–12, 143
Gingrich, Newt, 7, 9, 24, 28, 34, 99, 119, 135, 192

and conservative Republican ascendancy, 141–43
  federal budget balance and, 162–63
  public radio and television funding challenged by, 155
  tactics of, 142–43
Ginsburg, Ruth Bader, 174–75
Gitlin, Todd, 52–53, 55, 104, 140
Giuliani, Rudy, 127
globalization, 196–97
Goldberg, Jonah, 166
Goldwater, Barry, 23, 147, 156, 189
GOPAC, 192
Gore, Al, 32, 78, 115, 167
  Clinton legacy and, 15, 146, 165, 168–69, 199
  in election of 2000, 14–15, 18, 23, 36, 38–39, 73, 101, 102, 146, 165, 196
government:
  Bush reduction of, 9, 28–29, 32, 34–35, 37, 92, 98, 119, 186, 200, 201–2
  as favored by Democrats, 115–20, 181–83, 195, 200–202
  moderates' view of, 185–86
  redistribution by, 116, 118–19
  regulations of, *see* regulations, government
  rights enforced and enhanced through, 116, 117, 118, 184–85
  right-wing conservatives and, 32, 115, 119, 161, 163, 178, 179, 180, 181, 186, 200
  in shifting language of politics, 114–20, 181
  U.S. personal and collective prosperity dependent on, 117–18
Graham, Bob, 69, 70–71
Gramm, Phil, 23, 62, 163
Grann, David, 165
grass-roots projects, 151, 152, 153

Great Britain, 78, 82n
Great Society, 32
Greenstein, Robert, 38
Greider, William, 111
Grenier, John, 23
Gulf War, 69, 82n, 131
gun regulations, 188

Hagel, Chuck, 75, 129
Hanna, Mark, 143
Hannity, Sean, 153
Hardball, 164
Harman, Jane, 62
Hart, Gary, 89, 199
Hastert, Dennis, 49, 55
Hatch, Orrin, 9
health insurance, 109, 110, 135, 182,
    183, 186
Heritage Foundation, 84, 141, 142, 148,
    149, 160, 193
Hiss, Alger, 56
HMOs, 14, 183, 196
Hobbes, Thomas, 133, 202
Hofstadter, Richard, 111–12, 113
Holbrooke, Richard C., 68, 76
Holt, Rush, 173
homeland security, in election of 2002,
    17, 62–63, 64, 65, 72, 74, 84, 92,
    93, 100, 129, 135
Homeland Security, Department of,
    61–63, 70
    civil service protections in, 62, 63, 93
Hoover, Herbert, 31
Horton, William, 121
Hughes, Karen, 65
Hume, Brit, 153, 154
Humphrey, Hubert, 89, 131
Hussein, Saddam, 7, 10, 12, 55, 57, 63,
    67, 68, 69, 70, 73, 74–75, 78, 80,
    81n, 82n, 83, 89, 117, 131, 179,
    189

ideopolises, 99
individualism, community and, 202–3
inheritance tax, 29, 118
Internet, 168, 190–92
Iran, hostage crisis in, 121
Iraq:
    first war in, *see* Gulf War
    weapons inspections in, 67, 68, 69, 70,
        71, 72, 74, 75, 76, 81n
Iraqi National Congress, 80
Iraq war, 6, 7, 63, 66–85, 205
    ambivalence about, 68–70, 73, 84,
        189–90
    anti-Al Qaeda fight vs., 69
    Bush credibility eroded by, 77–82,
        189, 205
    congressional resolution on, 70–71,
        72, 75
    costs of, 10, 81, 82n, 84, 117, 190
    Democrats and, 10, 17, 41, 63, 70–71,
        72, 75–76, 81–85, 89–90, 128–29,
        130–34, 135, 189–90
    election of 2002 and, 66, 71–72, 100,
        128, 129, 135
    major administration miscalculations
        about, 79–82, 189
    opposition to, 12, 17, 41, 71, 72,
        74, 83n, 126, 129, 166–67, 186,
        189
    politics of terrorism and, 55, 57–58,
        132
    postwar period of, 12, 15, 72, 77–85,
        189–90
    rationales offered for, 10, 12, 33,
        78–79, 179, 189
Isaacson, Walter, 154
Ivins, Molly, 167, 192

Jackson, Henry "Scoop," 122
Javits, Jacob, 16, 24
Jefferson, William, 64

Jeffords, Jim, Republican party defection of, 17, 22–24, 42, 188
Johnson, Lyndon B., 178, 195
    Vietnam War and, 122, 148
judges, conservative, activism of, 10, 186–88, 201
Judis, John, 99–100, 132–34, 202

Kagan, Robert, 66, 75
Karlin, Mark, 191
Kay, David, 12
Kean, Tom, 61
Kelly, Michael, 164
Kennedy, Edward M., 36–37, 89
    on Bush Iraq policy, 82–84, 129
Kennedy, John F., 84, 147, 177, 178, 191, 194, 195, 204, 207
    liberal media and, 155–56
    Vietnam War and, 122
Kennedy, Robert, 89
Kerry, John, 12, 36, 55, 66, 83–84, 136, 173, 207
    Iraq war support and, 71, 190
    in primary campaign (2003–2004), 126, 136, 190
King, Martin Luther, Jr., 34
Kirk, Russell, 30
Kirkpatrick, Jeanne, 121
Kissinger, Henry, 9, 61
Krauthammer, Charles, 84
Kristol, Irving, 146, 147
Kristol, William, 66, 75, 161
Krugman, Paul, 192
Kuchel, Thomas, 24
Kurtz, Howard, 160
Kuttner, Robert, 105

Labash, Matt, 137, 139, 146
Labor Party, British, old vs. new, 97
Lambro, Donald, 34
Landrieu, Mary, 63–66
Latinos, 99, 100, 101

Leach, Jim, 49–50, 69
Legacy (Lowry), 5
Letterman, David, 21
Levin, Carl, 72, 129
Levin, Sandy, 54
Lewis, Ann, 105
Lewis, Anthony, 156
Liasson, Mara, 171
Liberal Imagination, The (Trilling), 104
liberals, liberalism:
    balkanization of, 140, 148
    boldness needed by, 177–208
    compassionate conservatism vs., 30–31
    conservative program of attack against, 137–76
    as fearful of appearing to support government, 115–20, 181–83
    former dominance of, 104–5, 140, 151, 194
    goals and objectives of, 181–84, 198, 207
    moral argument ceded to right by, 18, 107–9, 180, 181
    in New Deal era, 123–24
    as pragmatic, 178, 180–82, 199–200
    weaknesses of, 180–81
    see also Democrats, Democratic Party; moderates; progressives, progressivism; *specific issues*
libertarians, 29, 30, 31, 140
Lieberman, Joe, 36, 61, 91
    in call for commission on 9/11, 60
    in election of 2000, 38
    Iraq war support of, 71, 129, 190
    tax cut program of, 135, 204
Limbaugh, Rush, 59, 154, 155, 159–64, 166, 167, 170
Locke, John, 133, 202
Long, Huey, 159
Long Thompson, Jill, 72–74, 129
Los Angeles Times, 43–44
Louisiana, 63–66

Lugar, Richard, 129

McCain, John, 6, 94, 191, 206
  in call for commission on 9/11, 60–61
  campaign finance reform and, 203
McCarthy, Eugene, 89
McCarthy era, 12, 13, 19, 102, 122
McCaughey, Elizabeth, 162
McGovern, George, 89, 131, 191
McKinley, William, 26–27, 111, 143
McLaughlin Group, The, 158
McNabb, Donovan, 166
Maher, Bill, 50
Matthews, Chris, 164
media, conservative, 156–58
  Clinton administration and, 160–62,
    163–65
  on election of 2000, 169–71
  partisanship of, 139–40, 154, 158,
    159–62, 165–67, 169–71
  rise of, 156–59, 167, 191, 193
media, establishment, 58–59, 167–68
  Clinton-Lewinsky scandal and,
    163–64
  conservative bias in, 155, 165–68, 176
  election of 2000 and, 170–71
media, liberal:
  in 1960s, 155–56, 157, 167, 192
  start of conservative campaign against,
    156–58
  Web and, 168
media war, 153–71
  cable networks in, 165–67
  Clinton administration and, 5, 13,
    160–62, 163–65
  conservative tactics in, 137, 139–40,
    141, 153–55, 156, 157–59, 160–62,
    165–67
  roots of, 155–58
  talk radio in, 159–61
Medicaid, 38
Medicare, 179, 181, 195

Medicare prescription drug bill (2003),
  12, 183
Meet the Press, 79, 80, 81, 164
Meyer, Frank, 30
Meyerson, Adam, 141
Meyerson, Harold, 2
Michel, Robert, 142
middle class, 196
  conservatives and, 179–80, 197
  taxes and, 118, 135, 180, 203–4
Mill, John Stuart, 176, 202
Miller, George, 36
Miller, Matthew, 109
Mitchell, Daniel J., 160
moderates, 3, 4, 5, 14, 15, 19–20, 23,
  204
  common cause needed between liberals
    and, 185–88
Molyneux, Guy, 50–51
Mondale, Walter, 89, 92
Montopoli, Brian, 60
Moore, Michael, 192
Moskos, Charles, 206
MoveOn, 191
MSNBC, 165–66
Murdoch, Rupert, 154
Muslims, U.S., 48

Nader, Ralph, 169
Nation, 151
National Interest, 148
National Journal, 44, 150, 164
National Public Radio (NPR), 154–55,
  171
National Review, 5, 22–23, 147, 166
Nelson, Lars-Erik, 155
neoconservatives, 66, 67, 146–48
New Deal, 12, 16, 32, 104, 105, 111,
  194, 201
New Democrat Network, 191
Newhouse, John, 122–23
New Jersey, 173

INDEX

New Mexico, 173–74
New Republic, 129, 162, 165
New York Daily News, 155
New Yorker, 87
New York Herald Tribune, 156
New York Times, 61, 68, 77–78, 81, 88,
    120, 156, 158, 164, 171, 173, 192,
    197
New York Times/CBS News polls, 88
Nixon, Richard M., 1, 13, 89, 121, 147,
    156, 157, 158, 194
"No Child Left Behind Act," 35–37
Noonan, Peggy, 170
Norquist, Grover, 34, 139–40, 203
Novak, Robert, 154, 158

O'Beirne, Kate Walsh, 142
O'Reilly, Bill, 153, 154, 192

Paget, Karen, 148–49
patient's bill of rights, 14, 32, 42, 183
Patriot Act, 50, 115
patriotism:
    9/11 and, 17–18, 52–53
    progressive, 205–8
Pelosi, Nancy, 83
Penn, Mark, 50
Pentagon, terrorist attacks on, *see* September 11, 2001, terrorist attacks on
Peters, Charles, 160
Petri, Thomas, 69
Philadelphia Inquirer, 29, 43, 149
Podesta, John, 184, 193
political language, rightward shift in, 102,
    103–36, 138, 181, 185
Politically Incorrect, 50
"Politics and the English Language" (Orwell), 103
politics of revenge, 4–5, 11, 12, 13–15,
    59, 164, 169–76, 206
Pollack, Ron, 38

Polman, Dick, 43
poor, 38, 39, 107–8
    Democrat and liberal support of programs for, 182, 198
    taxes and, 118, 203–4
populism, 14–15, 98, 196
Populist Persuasion, The (Kazin), 157–58
Powell, Colin, 48, 67, 75, 131
Powers, William, 164
prescription drug benefit, 14, 32, 42, 183
Presidential Power (Neustadt), 21
Price, David, 173
Progressive Era, 111, 112, 203
progressives, progressivism, 15–16, 24,
    107–9, 185
PROPAC, 192
protectionism, 196–97
Public Interest, 148
Pure Food and Drug Act, 112

Quinlan, Al, 65, 66

Racicot, Marc, 173
radio:
    right wing use of, 159
    see also talk radio
Ramos, Steven and Josefina, 33
Reagan, Ronald, 2, 158, 200
    in election of 1980, 121, 141, 147, 157
    foreign policy of, 49, 125–26
Reagan administration, 27, 28, 29, 30,
    34, 49, 77, 99, 168, 170, 194, 200,
    201, 206
Reaganism, 27, 28–29, 30, 95, 201
Rector, Ricky Ray, 124
Redford, Robert, 123
regulations, government, 187–88
    capitalism and, 112, 114, 116, 118,
    119, 184–85, 195–96
    environment and, 37, 181, 186, 188
Reich, Robert, 124

religion, 107–9, 167

Republicans, Republican Party:
  anti-Clinton campaign of, 4–6, 8–9, 13, 102, 137, 141, 144, 145–46, 192
  attempted silencing of Democratic critics by, 8–9, 50, 55, 58–60, 73–74, 82–85
  Clinton health care plan opposed by, 160–62
  conservative takeover of, 15–16, 138, 139, 141–43, 147, 157, 178
  and education issue, 35–37
  heroes of, 177–78
  Jeffords's defection from, 17, 22–24, 42
  moderate, 22–24, 142, 188
  and new demographics, 101
  political base of, 2, 6, 9–10, 15, 16, 27, 29, 39, 40–41, 42, 58, 92, 196, 198
  and post-9/11 congressional bipartisanship, 48–50, 51, 54
  progressive tradition and, 15–16, 24, 185
  Rove's vision for, 26–28
  southernization of, 23, 99, 142
  split over Iraq war in, 66–72, 74–75
  see also conservatives, conservatism; specific candidates and elections

Resurgent Liberal, The (Reich), 124

Rice, Condoleezza, 61, 78

Richtel, Matt, 120

Right Man, The (Frum), 21

Rise of the Counter-Establishment, The (Blumenthal), 148

Roberts, Cokie, 164

Roberts, Paul Craig, 197

Rockefeller, Nelson, 157

Rockefeller Foundation, 148

Roemer, Tim, 60

Roe v. Wade, 157, 188

Roosevelt, Franklin D., 49, 57, 84, 120, 123, 144, 177, 178, 181, 184, 185, 200, 206, 207

Roosevelt, Theodore, 15, 16, 177, 181, 184, 203

Rosenberg, Ethel and Julius, 56

Rosenberg, Simon, 191

Rosenthal, Steve, 192

Rove, Karl, 4, 11, 24–28, 34, 35, 65, 85, 87, 91, 94, 101, 129, 134, 135

Rowley, Colleen, 61

Rumsfeld, Donald, 122
  Iraq war and, 66, 67–68, 69, 75, 77, 131

Russert, Tim, 79, 81, 164

Safire, William, 156, 158

Salisbury, Stephan, 149–50

Salvation Army, 40

Satterford, Wendy, 88

Savage, Michael, 8, 165

Scalia, Antonin, 174

Scaroborough, Joe, 166

Scheiber, Noam, 129–30

Schlafly, Phyllis, 156

Schneider, William, 171

school vouchers, 35, 36, 37, 152, 179

Schroeder, Gerhard, 83n

Schumer, Charles, 197

Schwarzenegger, Arnold, 52, 101

Scowcroft, Brent, 67

Securities and Exchange Commission (SEC), 196

Senate, U.S., 22, 23, 98

September 11, 2001, terrorist attacks on, 19, 21, 132–34
  Bush administration's uses of, 6, 10, 11, 16, 17–18, 42, 47–85, 91–94, 131–32
  commission for investigation of, 56, 58, 60–62

September 11, terrorist attacks on *(cont.)*
  dissent and discourse after, 8, 50
  heroes of, 204
  national solidarity in wake of, 6, 10,
    15, 17, 18, 42, 47–54, 58, 192,
    204–5
  patriotism and, 17–19, 52–53,
    205–8
  pro-government sentiment after, 51
Service for College plan, 207
Shaffer, Jack, 155–56
Sharon, Ariel, 83*n*
Shelby, Richard, 23, 59
Shinseki, Eric K., 80
Shulman, Beth, 150
Slate, 155
Snow, Tony, 153–54
Social Market Foundation, 97
Social Security, 29, 34, 130, 179, 180,
  195
Souter, David, 175, 187
Soviet Union:
  arms control agreements with, 122–23
  in Cold War, 54, 55, 122–23, 132, 206
  collapse of, 30, 54
Spanish-American War (1898), 143
Spitzer, Eliot, 114, 185
Spratt, John, 53
Starr, Kenneth, 14, 164, 165
Stephanopoulos, George, 164
Stevens, John Paul, 187
Stevenson, Richard W., 120
Strauss, David, 187–88
Sulzberger, Arthur, 156
supply-side economics, 147, 160, 199
Supreme Court, U.S., 13, 187–88
  election of 2000 and, 6, 14, 98, 102,
    174–75, 186

Taliban, 17, 48–49, 55, 205
talk radio, 159–61

Clinton presidency as fuel for, 5, 13,
    160–61, 164
  political power of, 160, 162
tax cuts, Bush, 6, 14, 16, 17, 18, 22, 30,
    32, 37, 39, 42, 43, 44, 54, 57, 138,
    180, 200, 203–4
  on capital gains, 37, 53, 204
  Democrats and, 41–42, 53, 64, 90, 92,
    135, 197, 203–4
  rationale for, 118
  ultimate aim of, 9, 33–35, 98
taxes:
  Clinton and, 4, 5, 199, 201
  flat, 160
  on poor and middle class, 118, 135,
    180, 203–4
Teixeira, Ruy, 99–100
telemarketers, 119–20, 184
Tenet, George, 78
Terrell, Suzanne Haik, 65
terrorism, politics of, 54–58
  Cold War politics and, 54–56
  Republican issues favored by,
    54–58
Texas, midterm district redrawing in
    (2003), 6, 10
*They Only Look Dead: Why Progressives
    Will Dominate the Next Political Era*
    (Dionne), 4
Third Way, 95–97, 144–45
This Week, 164
Thomas, Clarence, 13, 174
Thomma, Steven, 29
Thurmond, Strom, 23
Tiananmen Square massacre, 126
Time, 82, 154
Tomasky, Michael, 121, 131–32
Toricelli, Robert, 169
toughness wars, 106
  Clinton and, 124–26, 127
  crime issue in, 121, 123, 126–27

INDEX

Democratic primary and
(2003–2004), 126
Democrats and liberals labeled as "soft"
in, 120–34
Republicans and conservatives on attack in, 120–34
short history of, 120–23
welfare issue and, 127–28
traditionalism, 4, 198–99, 204
traditionalist conservatives, 29–30, 140,
147
Trilling, Lionel, 104
Tripp, Linda, 166
Trippi, Joe, 190–91
Truman, Harry S., 178
Truman administration, 49, 90, 120, 181
Cold War and, 54, 57, 122, 132, 202,
206
Twilight of Common Dreams, The (Gitlin),
140
Two Americas, The (Greenberg), 200–201

unions, 116–17, 192
United Nations, 79
Iraq weapons inspections and, 67,
68, 69, 70, 71, 72, 74, 75, 76,
81*n*
uranium, 78, 79

Vandenberg, Arthur, 54, 55, 57
Vietnam War, 17, 63, 79, 120–22, 148
Viguerie, Richard, 157–58, 193
Voices of Protest (Brinkley), 159

Wagner Act (1935), 116–17
Wallace, Chris, 154
Wallace, George, 156

Wallis, Jim, 107–8
Wall Street Journal, 30, 53–54, 59, 163,
170
Washington, Wayne, 44
Washington Monthly, 60, 76, 160
Washington Post, 37, 40, 45, 62, 84, 99,
125, 158, 160, 166, 190, 192
Watergate scandal, 13
Waters, Maxine, 50
weapons of mass destruction, 12, 77, 82,
179, 189
Weekly Standard, 6, 60, 93, 137
welfare reform, 124–25, 127–28
welfare rights, 118
Wellstone, Paul, 89, 92, 94, 129, 130
Weyrich, Paul, 29, 193
Whitewater, 160, 161
Why Americans Hate Politics (Dionne), 3,
4, 104
Wicker, Tom, 156
Will, George, 56, 99, 158
Williams, Brian, 166–67
Wilson, Joseph, 79
Wilson, Valerie Plame, 79
Wilson, Woodrow, 15, 26
Winston, David, 37, 50, 51, 52
Wolfowitz, Paul, 66, 133
workers, low-wage, 182, 204
World Trade Center, terrorist attacks on,
see September 11, 2001, terrorist at-
tacks on
World War II, 120, 206

Young Americans for Freedom, 147

Zeller, Shawn, 150
Zimmer, Dick, 173